Modern Endgame Practice

Alexander Beliavsky,
Adrian Mikhalchishin

B.T. Batsford Ltd.

First published in 2003
© Alexander Beliavsky, Adrian Mikhalchishin 2003

ISBN 0 7134 8740 2

British Library Cataloguing-in-Publication Data.
A catalogue record for this book is
available from the British Library.

Printed in Great Britain by
Creative Print and Design (Wales), Ebbw Vale
for the publishers,
B.T. Batsford Ltd,
64 Brewery Road,
London N7 9NT

A BATSFORD CHESS BOOK

A member of **Chrysalis** Books plc

Contents

Introduction

With the present work we complete our series of books on the endgame – *Winning Endgame Technique* and *Winning Endgame Strategy*. In the first of these we wanted to show how to correctly solve technical problems with particular material alignments. In the second book we paid great attention to methods of play. In the final part of our work we identify definite mistakes made both by grandmasters as well as young players in the concluding stages of the game. Of course this is not the last word and moreover it is not a definitive list of typical mistakes which every chessplayer might in turn rid himself of by specific work. Our task was to show where there are problems so that all chessplayers can identify and eliminate them from their play.

In the endgame, knowing what you need to do is half the battle – and already a partial solution to the problem at hand.

We pay particular attention to endgames with rooks, which make up nearly 60% of all practical endgames. In this department there are enormous problems both with basic knowledge (knowledge of precise theoretical positions which is the principal factor when evaluating positions that arise) and with the possession of technical methods of play. We also look at different alignments of pawns on opposite flanks.

A great part of the book is taken up by analysis of competitive play at a very high level – in the Chess Olympiad, World and European Championships. Of course one might say that with quicker time controls comes an increased knowledge of automatic technique in the endgame. But in all the competitions we have analysed there is a noticeable tendency towards deterioriation in the quality of endgame play and a lack of serious study of technique on behalf of the players.

Indeed, even many years ago the great J.R.Capablanca and V.Smyslov taught that techniques of endgame play should be studied in youth so that they would then become an automatic habit.

Of course it is not too late to do this also in one's more mature years but a great deal of systematic work is required.

The authors will consider their work a success if chessplayers are able to put to good use the advice given in this book in their own games.

1 When Grandmasters Overlook Certain Manoeuvres

Grandmasters are not gods and also make mistakes – which, however, may not be noticed by many amateurs.

We start with a position from the game

1 Fridstein – Lutikov
USSR 1954

There followed:
1...c3,
and White resigned – he sees only 2 ♖xb3? c2 3 ♖b4+ and the king gets out of check on c7, but he did not notice the intermediate **2 ♖b4+!**.

But an even more fantastic case occurred in the next game.

2 A.Petrosian – Tseshkovsky
Minsk 1976

The game was adjourned, and in the evening Petrosian showed Tseshkovsky Averbakh's endgame book where it said in black and white – Draw! (but with White on the move and not Black), and the rivals came to a peaceful settlement. On the following day, however, Tseshkovsky found on the next page this position with *Black* to move and there it said 'Win' – but it was too late.

And victory is achieved like this
1...b3! 2 ♖d8+ ♔c5!
Not 2...♔c4? 3 ♔e4=.
3 ♖c8+
Or 3 ♔e4 b2 4 ♖c8+ ♔d6! winning.
3...♔d4 4 ♖d8+ ♔e3 4 ♖b8 b2 5 ♔e5 ♔f3!

A very important winning manoeuvre.

6 ♔f5 ♔e2 7 ♔e4 ♔d1 8 ♔d3 c2, and White had to resign.

This had already been pointed out by the great Tarrasch a century ago!

3 **Gligorić – Popović**
Belgrade 1998

Winning at once is 1...b3 2 ♖xa4 b2 3 ♖a5+ ♔c6 4 ♖a6+ ♔b7, but Popović played

1...a3? 2 ♔f6 ♔c4 3 ♔e6 b3

Already no help is 3...♔b3 4 ♔xd6 ♔a2 (or 4...a2 5 ♔c5) 5 ♔c5 b3 6 ♔b4, and a draw.

4 ♖a4+!? – draw. In contrast to Fridstein, Gligorić knew this manoeuvre.

4 **Slobodian – Beliavsky**
Germany 2000

1...♔c4?

Why? Correct is 1...♔a2! 2 h5 b3 3 h6 b2 4 h7 b1=♕ 5 h8=♕ ♕b2+ and draws.

2 h5 b3 3 ♖a4+!

Again this fateful check – Black resigned, **1-0**.

5 **Topalov – Beliavsky**
Linares 1995

One of the co-authors had a similar endgame in his own practice. Bad here is 1 b6? because of the same 1...♖a5+!. Therefore Topalov played **1 ♔b6! ♔d2 2 ♔a7**, and Black resigned, since there is no defence against the march of the b-pawn. Yes, indeed, memory is an important thing!

2 Rook against Pawns

This is a very simple type of endgame but as the reader will be convinced from the first chapter, despite this simplicity, grandmasters very often lose orientation in what seem to be very straightforward cases.

These endgames arise from rook endgames with passed pawns. One of the sides gives up a rook for the opponent's passed pawn, and then tries to support his own passed pawn with his king. There are a minimum number of precise theoretical positions which everyone should know.

Cutting off the king on the rank

6 Instructive Position

1 ♖a5! h3 2 ♖a3 h2 3 ♖h3, 1-0

7 **Reti** 1928

1 ♖d2! d4 2 ♖d1 ♚e4 3 ♚d6 and wins.

8 **Eisenstadt** 1950

1 ♖g6! ♚f4 2 ♚g7! g4 3 ♚h6 g3 4 ♚h5 ♚f3 5 ♚h4 winning.

9 **Korolkov**
1950

1 ♔g8! (the only move) **1...f2 2 ♖e7+ ♔f3 3 ♖f7+ ♔g2 4 ♖g7+ ♔f1 5 ♖h7!**, and White stands his ground.

10 **Instructive Position**

1 g8=♘+ ♔e6 2 ♘h6 with a **draw**.

Very often an important element of play in these endgames is the shouldering away of the opponent's king.

11 **Urmancheev – Podolsky**
USSR 1972

a) 1 ♔b6? (game) **1...♔c4 2 a6 ♖h6+ 3 ♔b7 ♔b5 4 a7 ♖h7+, 0-1;**

b) **1 ♔b4!**, not allowing the approach of the opponent's king, with an immediate draw.

And how the great make mistakes:

12 **Alekhine – Bogoljubow**
World Championship match 1929

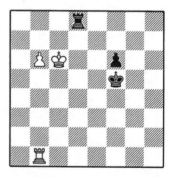

a) 1...♔g4? **2 b7 f5 3 b8=♕ ♖xb8 4 ♖xb8 f4 5 ♔d5 f3 6 ♔e4 f2 7 ♖f8 ♔g3 8 ♔e3, 1-0;**

b) **1...♔e4!**, again not allowing the opponent's king access to his pawn and securing a draw.

As we have already pointed out, the main means of struggle in these endgames is the participation of the king – let us see how a young player makes an incorrect choice.

13 Kukovec – Podlesnik
Bled 2001

a) 1 ♖xh3? ♚e4 2 ♚c4 f3 3 ♖h8 f2, ½-½ (game), again a passion for automatic captures, when correct was to 'mark' the enemy king as in hockey.

b) 1 ♚c4! ♚e4 2 ♚c3 ♚e3 3 ♚c2 f3 (3...♚f3 4 ♖xh3+ ♚e2 5 ♖h8!) 4 ♚d1 ♚f2 5 ♖xh3 ♚g2 6 ♖h8 f2 7 ♖g8+ ♚f3 8 ♖f8+, winning.

14 Leko – Markowski
Polanica Zdroj 1998

Here again quite a few other experienced players have forgot the right method of play.

a) 1...♚d3? 2 ♚f3 h2 3 ♖d8+ ♚c2 4 ♖h8 ♚d3 5 ♚f2 ♚d2?
If 5...c3? 6 ♖h3+!.
6 ♖xh2 c3 7 ♚f1+ ♚d1 8 ♖h8 c2 9 ♖d8+ ♚c1 10 ♚e2, 1-0 (the game continuation);

b) 1...h2! 2 ♖h8 c3 3 ♖xh2+ ♚d3=

The other main motive of these endgames is the struggle of rook against the enemy king.

15 Lerner – Dorfman
Tashkent 1980

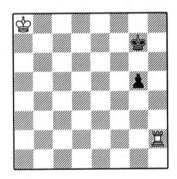

1 ♖f2!!
Not giving the black king any chance of preventing its counterpart from drawing closer.

1...♚h6 2 ♚b7 g4 3 ♚c6 ♚h5 4 ♚d5 g3 5 ♖f8 ♚h4 6 ♚e4, 1-0

16 **Smirnov – Korneev**
Russia 1997

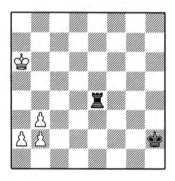

1 a4?
The only losing continuation.
1...♖b4!
Now the king is cut off and the pawns are of no interest.
2 a5 ♔g3 3 ♔a7 ♔f4 4 a6 ♔e5 5 ♔a8 ♔d6 6 a7 ♖b5 7 b4 ♔c7 8 b4 ♖h5, and **White resigned.**

But correct was **1 ♔a5 ♖e2 2 b4 ♖xb2 3 a4 ♔g3 4 b5 ♔f4 5 ♔b6** and **6 a5**, and White has no chances of losing.

17 **Manor – Macieja**
Curacao 2001

1 f4 ♔e6 2 h6 ♔f5 3 ♔h2??

This is quite pointless – going into the corner – after 3 ♔f2 arises a well known drawn position, once again analysed in the 19th century.
3...♔g4!
Not 4 g6 now because of 4...♖h3+.
4 ♔g2
Or 4 ♔g1 ♖h3! 5 ♔g2 ♖h5! with a win.
4...♖b2+ 5 ♔g1 ♔f5! 6 ♔h1
Or 6 ♔f1 ♖b4.
6...♖b4 7 ♔g2 ♖xf4, White resigned, **0-1**.

18 **Wells – Hector**
Oxford 1998

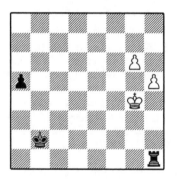

White made the 'logical' forward move
a) **1 ♔g5?** a4 2 h6 a3 3 g7 a2 4 h7 a1=♕ 5 g8=♕ ♕c1+, 0-1, (the game continuation); but it was better to go to the side:
b) **1 ♔f4! ♖g1 2 ♔f5=**.

19 Mortensen – Hillarp Persson
Rode 1997

Here Black forgot what was the main task in such positions.

a) 1...f4? 2 ♔c5 ♔e4 3 ♔c4 ♔e3 4 ♔c3 g5 5 ♖e8+ ♔f2 6 ♔d2 g4 7 ♖e4! g3 8 ♖xf4+ ♔g1 9 ♔e2, 1-0, (game);

b) **1...♔d4! 2 ♖d8+ ♔e3=.**

20 Nurbenoglu – Pichka
Germany 1994

The question is how to hold up the black pawns. There are two ways of positioning the rook – from behind and in front. And in the game Black made the wrong choice:

a) 1...♖f2? 2 f6 ♖f5 3 ♔f7 ♖xg5 4 ♔e7, ½-½, (game);

b) **1...♖a7!! 2 f6 ♔e6** winning.

21 Holuba – Boiselle
Wurzburg 1996

Here it was necessary to activate the king – without fearing the g3 pawn which has no significance.

a) 1 ♖g8? a4 2 ♖xg3 ♔b4, ½-½, (game);

b) **1 ♔d5! ♔b4 2 ♔d4 g2 3 ♖c1! ♔b3 4 ♔d3 a4 5 ♖b1+ ♔a2 6 ♖g1** and wins.

22 Seirawan – Van Wely
Elista 1998

An easy way to draw is by 1...♘d3!. However Black calculated poorly the transfer to a rook versus pawns endgame. **1...♘xh3? 2 ♔xh3 ♔e5 3 ♔g2 ♔d4 4 ♔f2 ♔c3 5 ♔e1 b3 6 ♔d1 ♔b2 7 ♖c8 ♔a1 8 ♖xc5 b2 9 ♖a5+!**, and he had to resign, **1-0**.

23 **Filipov – Krasenkov**
China 2000

1...♔f5!

A very important transfer of the king to an active position.

2 ♔c4 ♔e4!

The opposition is a principal method of play. It is clear even without analysis that 2...♔g4 is wrong.

3 ♔c3 ♔e3 4 ♖e6+ ♔f2 5 ♔d3 h4 6 ♖e2+ ♔f3!

Bad is 6...♔g1? 7 ♔e4! winning.

7 ♔d2 h3, and a draw, ½-½

24 **Aloni**

1 ♔f7!!

As can easily be proved, capturing either pawn leads to a draw.

1...♔g4 2 ♔e6 h5 3 ♔e5! h4 4 ♔d4 h3

After 4...f4 5 ♔e4 ♔g3 6 ♖g7+ ♔f2 7 ♔xf4 h3 8 ♖a7! h2 9 ♖a2+ ♔g1 10 ♔g3 arises a theoretically winning position for White.

5 ♔e3 h2 6 ♖g7+ ♔h3 7 ♔f2 h1=♘+ 8 ♔f3 ♔h2 9 ♖g2+ ♔h3 10 ♖g5 ♔h2 11 ♖f5 ♔g1 12 ♖g5+ ♔f1 13 ♖g2, and White wins.

25 **Socko – Zilberman**
Moscow 2002

Correct here was to go for the rook ending by 1...♖h7! 2 c7 ♖g7!, with an immediate draw, but Black decided to win the rook.

1...h2? 2 ♖g8+ ♔f3 3 ♖h8 ♔g2 4 ♔c5 ♖e8 5 ♖h6 h1=♕ 6 ♖xh1 ♔xh1 7 ♔d6! ♔g2 8 ♔d7 ♖h8 9 ♔xe6 ♔g3

Or 9...♖h1 10 c7 ♖c1 11 ♔d7 ♖d1+ 12 ♔c8 ♔g3 13 e6 ♖e1 14 ♔d7 ♖d1+ 15 ♔e7 ♖e1 16 ♔d6 ♖d1+ 17 ♔e5 with a win.

10 ♔d7 ♖h7+ 11 ♔d6 ♔f4 12 e6 ♔f5 13 e7 ♖h8 17 ♔d7 ♔e5 18 c7!, Black resigned, **1-0**

26 **Bareev – Burmakin**
Tomsk 2001

Here Black still has a pawn left, but White not only manages to exchange it but also brings the game to a drawn haven.

1 ♔g5 ♔c2 2 g4 ♔d3 3 h4
Threatening to exchange.

3...♔xe3
Also no help is 3...♔e4.

4 h5 gxh5 5 gxh5 ♖a5+! 6 ♔g4!
Effectively keeping away the enemy king – draw.

27 **Bartel – Sulypa**
Lviv 2001

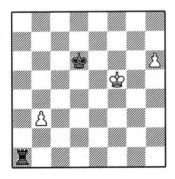

The position looks very simple, but it is not so easy to play. In the game came

1...♔e7? 2 h7 ♖h1 3 ♔g6 ♖g1+ 4 ♔f5 ♖h1 5 ♔g6 ♔f8,

and now if there were no pawn on b3 Black wins, while after **6 b4** – draw.

But winning is **1...♖h1 2 ♔g6 ♔e6 3 h7 ♖g1+ 4 ♔h6 ♔f7 5 h8=♘+ ♔f6**, and the rest is routine.

Exercises

(1) **Fries-Nielsen – Plachetka**
Slovakia 1991

Find the right solution

(2) **Kishnev – Nikolac**
Germany 1991

Find the right continuation

(3) Skembris – Iotti
Italy 2000

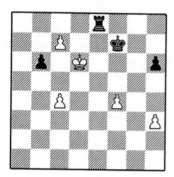

Find the right way for White

(5) Leal – Filguth
Mexico 1978

Black wins

(4) Dias – Dominguez
Cuba 1981

What is the correct way for White?

(6) Dückstein – Keller
Germany 1963

White draws

(7) **Lovegrove – Lasker**
USA 1902

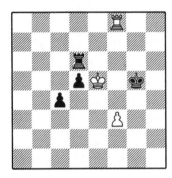

Would you play 1...d4?

(8) **Lein – Benko**
Novi Sad 1972

Black wins

(9) **Marshall – Duras**
San Sebastian 1911

The correct way for White

(10) **Adams – Kramnik**
Moscow 1994

Can White realise his material advantage?

3 Grandmasters' Mistakes in the Endgame

Unceasingly playing for the win in an objectively drawn position (going too far)

Even at the very highest level, in technical positions leading grandmasters lose their sense of reality and cannot get focused in time to search for a win.

28 Epishin – Zhao Zhu
Lausanne 2001

1 ♔c4!?

The plan of approaching with the king is poor but it is doubtful whether 1 e5 or 1 d5 gave real chances of a win.

1...♔f6 2 ♔d5?

But this is already a serious mistake – the check on the fifth is very dangerous. Correct is 2 e5 with some chances of victory.

2...♔g6 3 ♖h8 ♖g5+ 4 ♔e6 ♖h5 5 ♖g8+ ♔h7 6 ♔f7 ♖h3, and White had to resign, **0-1**

29 Short – Beliavsky
Linares 1992

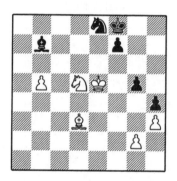

Black is a little worse and he continued

1...f6+

White can play 2 ♔d6 but 2...♔f7 seemed unpleasant to him, while in case of 2 ♘xf6 ♗xg2 3 ♗f5 ♔e7 any chances of a win are insignificant. Therefore he replied

2 ♔e6??

and after

2...♗c8 he was **mated!**

30 Ivkov – Petrosian
Rio de Janeiro 1979

Black has defended stubbornly, but you get the impression that White still has the advantage because of the weaknesses on f7 and g5. Therefore play continued.

1 ♔b1? ♘d5+ 2 ♔c1 ♘f4 3 g3 ♘e6 4 ♗c4? ♘d4!

It seems that 5 ♖xg6+ ♔f8 6 ♖xg5 ♖c8 leads to the loss of a piece.

5 ♖c7 ♖f8

and the pawn cannot be defended.

6 f4 exf4 7 gxf4 gxf4 8 ♔d1 ♘f3 9 ♔e2 ♘e5 10 ♖c5 ♖e8 11 ♗b5 ♖e7, and White resigned, **0-1**

31 Ye Li Chuan – Braga
Mexico 1980

White gets nowhere with 1 ♔d6 ♖d2+ and the king cannot escape the checks, therefore he tried to run with the king to the other side.

1 ♔f5??,

and after

1...♔f7

the threat of mate by 2...♖f2 forces White to surrender, **0-1**

32 Shirov – Kramnik
Dortmund 1998

White has some advantage in view of his better kingside pawn structure and the possibility of creating a weakness on b6. In addition Black's queenside pawns stand on the same colour as his bishop. The defence seems difficult but it is not easy for White to win this endgame. Black tries to create counterplay.

1...a6!? 2 bxa6 ♖a7 3 ♔d3 ♖xa6 4 ♔e4 ♖a7

After 4...♔e8 5 ♔d5 ♔d7 6 ♖f4! and Black has no serious problems.

5 ♔d5 ♖d7+ 6 ♔c6 ♖d6+ 7 ♔c7?

This is risky. Rather better is 7 ♔b5, though chances of victory there are clearly less.

7...♖e6 8 e4 ♔e8 9 e5?!

He should prefer 9 f4!?.

9...♗d8+ 10 ♔c8?

Why not 10 ♔b7, which maintains the balance.

10...♖e7!

Now the white king is cut off.
11 f4 ♖c7+ 12 ♔b8 ♔d7 13 e6+
13...♔c6 was threatened.
13...♔xe6 14 ♖e4+ ♔d7 15 ♗e5 ♖c6 16 ♔a7?
Correct was 16 ♖e1!, activating the rook.
16...♖e6
A deadly pin.
17 ♖e1 ♔c6 18 ♖d1 ♗c7 19 ♔a6 ♖e8, and White resigned, **0-1**

Mate in queen endings

The queen is the strongest piece and even with a material advantage in queen endings it is necessary to play very carefully with one's king in order not to land in a mating net. It sounds strange but frequently the stronger side is the one who gets mated.

33 **Benjamin – Gufeld**
Honolulu 1998

1...♕g2+ 2 ♔f5 ♕h3+ 3 ♔e5??
♕e6 mate.

34 **Avrukh – Timoshenko**
Leon 2001

Black wants to avoid perpetual check after 1...♔d2 and automatically played **1...♔f2??** and was mated after **2 ♕g1 !**

The old masters also made serious blunders.

35 **Borisenko – Simagin**
Moscow 1955

1 ♔g4?? f5+!!
White didn't reckon on this.
2 gxf6 ♕f5+ 3 ♔h4 ♕h5 mate.

36 **Larsen – Keres**
San Antonio 1972

Not wanting to reconcile himself to a draw Larsen 'got out of it' by
1 ♔f4? ♕h2+ 2 ♔g5 ♕g3!
And it became clear that on 3 ♕c6 there is 3...♕e5 – mate! So he had to play
3 ♕e3 hxg4 4 ♕f4 ♕xf3 5 ♕xg4 ♕e3+ 6 ♕f4 ♕e2!
Again mate is threatened.
7 ♕g3 ♕b5+ 8 ♔f4 ♕f5+ 9 ♔e3 ♕xf6, and White is already a pawn down and with no play.

37 **Amateur – Hajeker**
Jena 1936

As always in such situations, White sees that after 1 ♔f4 ♕d4+ draws by perpetual check, and he automatically changed the direction

of his king advance: **1 ♔h4??** and after **1...♕e1+ 2 ♕g3 ♕e7+ 3 ♔g4 ♕g5** was mated.

The late grandmaster Simagin was a 'specialist' in mating in lost positions. Here is another example.

38 **Batuyev – Simagin**
Riga 1954

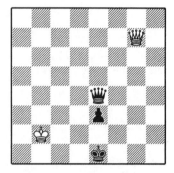

1...e2?? 2 ♕g1+ ♔d2 3 ♕c1+ ♔d3 4 ♕c3 – mate!

39 **Yashtylov – Gagarin**
Moscow 1998

Instead of going back, the international master played **1...♔g4?? 2 ♕h3+ ♔f4 3 ♕f3+** and lost his queen.

40 **Rivas – Mednis**
Rome 1984

Here a simple blunder allows mate in one. **1 ♔g4?? ♕f5**.

42 **Nicevski – Vaganian**
Skopje 1976

Vaganian played **1...♕d1??** and was shocked by the mate by **2 ♕h3!!**

41 **Konshina – Stomikova**
USSR 1967

Here comes the circus.
1 ♕f6??
Correct is 1 g6.
1...♕h3+ 2 ♔g6 ♕h7 mate.

43 **Beliavsky – Johansen**
Linares 2002

Instead of the preliminary exchange on g6 White played **1 ♔f4** and...was mated by **1...♕b8!**.

44 Ehrenfencht – Grabarczyk
Poland 1998

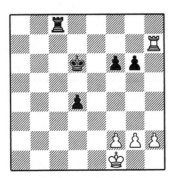

Quite a difficult question arises – how, generally speaking, can White lose this position? Let's see – meanwhile a simple draw was to be had by 1 ♔e2 ♖c2+ 2 ♔f3 or 1 h4 and 2 g4.

1 ♖h6? d3 2 ♔e1 ♖c2 3 ♖xg6 ♖e2+ 4 ♔f1?

Now greed as well – after 4 ♔d1 ♖xf2 5 h4 it's an elementary draw.

4...♔c5 5 ♖g8

He cannot make another capture: 5 ♖xf6 ♖e5 and 6...d2 winning.

5...♔c4 6 f3

But why this? Correct is 6 h4 and 7 g4.

6...♔c3 7 ♖c8+?

Why drive the king where it is going anyway? Correct is 7 h4, creating a passed pawn.

7...♔d2 8 ♖c6? f5 9 ♖c5 f4 10 ♖c4 ♖e1+ 11 ♔f2 ♖c1 12 ♖xf4 ♔c3

Now he has to give up the rook, but he does not construct the drawn position: pawns h6-g5-f4. White loses, **0-1**

Every strong player has some particular problem in the endgame. Here, for example, Nigel Short underestimated the threats to his king.

45 Short – Smirin
Tilburg 1992

It seems logical to advance the king but here the reverse is correct. **1 ♔f3? ♘g4!**, and after **2 ♖xd5 ♖f2+ 3 ♔e4 ♘f6+ 4 ♔e3 ♖xf4** he can resign. Meanwhile the simple **1 ♔g1 ♖c5 2 ♔g2** gives an easy draw – the black king cannot abandon the defence of the g6 pawn.

Why give the opponent a passed pawn?

46 Shirov – Ivanchuk
Kramatorsk 1986

Here 1...♘c4 gives an immediate draw, while a good idea was 1...f6. But Ivanchuk played

1...f5? 2 exf5 exf5 3 g5! ♔e7?

The last chance was 3...f4! 4 h5 ♘f5! 5 ♘f3 ♔e7 6 ♔e4 ♔e6, and Black still holds on.

4 h5 ♔e6 5 h6 gxh6 6 gxh6 ♖a8

After 6...♘f7 7 ♘xf7 ♔xf7 8 ♖xb5 ♖xa3+ 9 ♔c4 White has good chances of victory.

7 h7 ♔f6

Or 7...♖h8 8 ♘g6 ♖xh7 9 ♘f8+.

8 ♖c3! ♘f7 9 ♘xf7 ♔xf7 10 ♖c7+ ♔g6 11 ♔e2! ♖h8 12 ♖xb7 ♖xh7 13 ♖xh7 ♔xh7 14 ♔f3 ♔g6 15 ♔f4 ♔f6 16 d5, and Black resigned, **1-0**

47 Anand – Hübner
Dortmund 1997

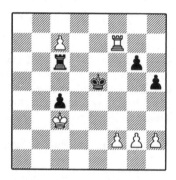

1...h4?

He should assign the following roles – king on f6 or on f5, while the rook waits on c6-c5, since on ♔c3-b4 follows c3!, and Black queens. Again the maxim applies – do not play on the 'weak' flank.

2 ♖g7! ♔f5 3 ♖d7!

With the idea of ♖d4, attacking all the black pawns.

3...h3 4 g3 ♔e6 5 ♖h7 ♔e5 6 f3 ♔e6 7 ♖xh3?

More cunning was 7 ♖h6 ♔f5 8 ♖xh3 ♖xc7 9 ♖h4, creating the possibility of a check on f4.

7...♖xc7 8 ♖h4 g5

The best defence.

9 ♖xc4 ♖f7 10 ♖e4+ ♔d5 11 ♖e3 ♖a7!

The rook moves over to the other side, and White should now

'cleverly' give up one pawn in return for activity: 12 ♔d3! ♖a3+ 13 ♔e2 ♖a2+ 14 ♔f1 ♖xh2 15 ♖e2 ♖h8 16 ♖e7 ♖g8, trying later to go with the king to g4. However there followed:

12 ♔d2? ♖a2+ 13 ♔e1 ♖xh2 14 ♔f1 ♖a2 15 ♖e2 ♖a4 16 ♔g2 g4! 17 fxg4 ♖xg4 18 ♖e8 ♖g7, and a draw, ½-½

Passivity and planless play in a somewhat worse position

48 Chiburdanidze – Brustman
Erevan 1996

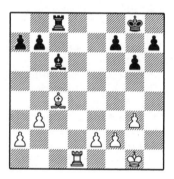

1...♔g7

Better to bring the king to e7 by 1...♔f8.

2 f4 ♖e8 3 ♔f2 a6

Why not fight from the other side with ...h6-g5 ?

4 ♖d6 a5 5 ♗d3 h5?! 6 a3 ♔f8 7 ♖d4 ♔e7 8 ♖c4 ♔f6?

But now not on this side – going to d6 was correct.

9 ♖c5! a4?!

Better really is the more passive 9...♖a8.

10 b4 ♖c8 11 ♗b5 ♔e7 12 ♗xa4 with a winning position. **1-0**

This was typical defence (play) without a plan.

49 Doda – Sliwa
Poland 1967

The question immediately arises, how, generally speaking, is it possible to lose this position? It seems, without particular difficulty.
1 ☖g4+! ☗f5 2 ☖g8 ☖a7 3 ☗g1?
This is a decisive mistake – after the correct 3 ☖f8+ ☗g4 4 ☖g8+ ☗f5 5 ☖f8+ ☗g4 6 ☖g8+ ☗g7 7 ☖c8, then a check and there is no question of a loss.
3...☗d4+ 4 ☗f1 ☗e4 5 ☖e8+ ☗d3

and there is no defence against the manoeuvre ☖a7-h7-h1. His own pawns stop him preventing this along the 3rd rank. White resigned, **0-1**.

Poor calculation of endgame positions

50 Almasi – Van Wely
Tilburg 1996

Here we calculate the simple 1 ☖dxe5 ☗d6 2 ☗b2 ☖xe5 3 ☖xe5 ☗xe5 4 ☗xb3 ☗f5 5 h4 with a straightforward draw.
But in the game there followed:
1 ☗b2? ☖e2+ 2 ☗xb3 e4, and White resigned, **0-1**

51 Van Wely – Leko
Tilburg 1996

Which pawn should he take? – without analysis it is clear that it is necessary to capture the further advanced one: 1 ☖xa3 e4 2 g5 e3 3 ☖a2! ☖h4 4 ☗g7 e2 5 ☖xe2 ☗xe2 6 h8=☖, and the rest is simple. But in the game came
1 ☖xe5? ☖xh7!! 2 ☗xh7

If he goes in for this then such variations should be calculated to the end.

2...♔xc3 3 ♖a5 ♔b2 4 g5 a2 5 g6 a1=♕ 6 ♖xa1 ♔xa1 7 g7 c3 8 g8=♕ c2, and it's a classical draw, ½-½

52 NN

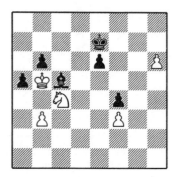

Not taking into account all the factors when transposing to a pawn ending is a minefield.

1...♔f7?

The only move was 1...♔f8! with a draw.

2 ♘xb6 ♗xb6 3 ♔xb6 e5 4 ♔c5 e4 5 fxe4 f3 6 e5 f2 7 e6+! and wins.

'Automatic captures' are a characteristic not only of beginners but also of grandmasters.

53 Rosito – Sorin
Buenos Aires 2000

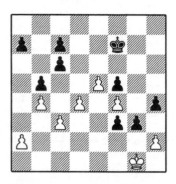

1 hxg3? h3!

Automatic calculation was not appropriate, and now Black wins. Correct was 1 h3!, and on the approach of the king to d5 the white king goes to e1 with a draw.

A lack of attention to the opponent's plans is typical even for grandmasters, particularly at that moment when it seems that any move will lead to the goal.

54 Kir.Georgiev – Ivanisević
Belgrade 2000

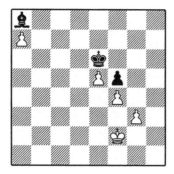

A draw is assured by 1...♗b7 2 ♔e3 ♔d5, and the rest is easy – the king does not allow its counterpart past. In the game followed

1...♔f7?? 2 g4! fxg4 3 ♔g3 ♗f3 4 f5 ♔e7 5 e6 ♔f6 6 ♔f4 ♔e7 7 ♔e5 g3 8 f6+ ♔e8 9 ♔f4!,

and Black resigned, **1-0**

55 Drazić – Lupu
Corsica 2000

1...g5?

Correct was the activation of the rook by 1...♖g5! 2 ♖d7 ♖f5, and then the march of the h5 pawn.

2 ♗e4 g4 3 f4 ♖g3+ 4 ♔c4, and the black king finds itself in a mating net. **1-0**

4 Problems of Realising the Advantage in the Endgame

Even with the greatest players problems arise in realising an advantage.

Here it is quite rare to encounter ignorance of precise theoretical positions, but much more frequently seen are inaccurate methods of play in complex positions and, undoubtedly the most widespread, underestimation of the opponent's counterchances.

56 **Kramnik – Short**
Novgorod 1997

Simplest here was 1 f3! g5 2 ♗b4 ♖d1+ 3 ♔f2, after which the a7 pawn falls. But there followed:

1 ♗c8? ♗b5 2 ♖xa7 g5 3 ♗b7 ♔g7 4 ♗c7 ♖d1+ 5 ♔g2 ♘c5 6 ♗xe5 ♔g6!

And it transpires that it is not easy to queen the pawn while there are threats and the only chance was 7 h3! ♖d7 8 ♖a8 ♘xb7 9 ♖g8+ ♔f5 10 e4+ ♔xe4 11 a7 ♗c6 12 a8=♕ with a win.

7 ♗f3? ♗xa6 8 ♖c7 ♘e6 9 ♖c6 ♗b5 10 ♖b6 ♗c4 11 h4 gxh4 12 gxh4 ♖d2 13 e4 ♗e2 14 ♗xe2 ♖xe2 15 ♔f3 ♖e1 16 ♖b8 f5 17 exf5+ ♔xf5 18 ♗c3 ♔g6 19 ♔g3 ♖g1+ 20 ♔h2 ♖d1, and Black held the draw.

Overlooking tactics (a lack of prophylactic thinking)

57 **Van Wely – Krasenkov**

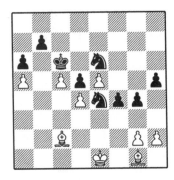

Black should, by means of 1...♘6g5 followed by ...h5-h4, and g4-g3, bury the bishop on g1 for ever and the win is not difficult. However there followed the more natural...

1...♔b5? 2 ♗xe4! dxe4 3 d5 ♘c7 4 c6 bxc6 5 d6 ♘e6 6 ♗b6 ♔c4 7 d7 ♔d5 8 d8=♕+ ♘xd8 9 ♗xd8 ♔xe5 10 ♗c7+ ♔f5 11 ♔d2 c5?

This is a serious mistake – correct is 11...h4! and 12...g3 with chances of victory.

12 g3!

Now it's the end.

12...f3 13 ♗b6 ♔e5 14 ♗xc5 ♔d5 15 ♗b6, Black resigned, **1-0**

Overlooking an intermediate move on the way to a theoretical position

58 Krasenkov – Sveshnikov
Norilsk 1987

The right way is 1...♔f3! 2 ♖f1+ ♔g2 3 ♖f4 ♔xh2 4 ♔xg4 ♖a8!, setting up a frontal attack. The game went:

1...♔f5? 2 ♖f1+ ♔e6 3 ♔xg4 ♖xh2 4 ♔g5 ♖h8 5 ♖f6+

Black overlooked this – after 5 g4? ♖g8 it's a draw.

5...♔e7 6 g4 ♖g8+ 7 ♔g6 ♖a8 8 ♖g7+! ♔f8 9 ♔h6 ♖a6+ 10 ♔h7 ♖a4 11 g5, and Black resigned, **1-0**

A lack of prophylactic thinking and striving to solve technical problems by force (by means of calculation)

59 Shirov – Anand
Wijk aan Zee 2001

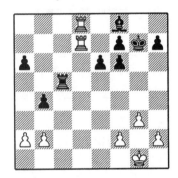

1 ♖b7?

Striving for a direct attack, though after the prophylactic defence 1 ♖d2!, and a subsequent improvement of the king's position, the resulting position would be hopeless for Black.

1...♖c2 2 ♖dd7 ♗c5 3 ♖xf7+ ♔g6 4 ♖xh7 ♗xf2+ 5 ♔f1 ♖xb2 6 ♖h4 ♗c5 7 ♖c4 ♗f8 8 ♖c8?

Continuing in the same style – correct was 8 h4!?, creating some sort of problems.

8...♗d6 9 ♖c6 ♗e5 10 ♖xa6 ♔f5

The activation of the black pieces assumes threatening proportions.

11 ♖bb6 ♔e4 12 ♖xe6 ♖xh2 13 ♖xf6 and a draw was agreed, **½-½**

Decentralisation

This again is a typical mistake of young players, resulting most often from the fear of parting with material – and seen even in games of the great players of the world.

60 Kramnik – Gelfand
Dos Hermanas 1996

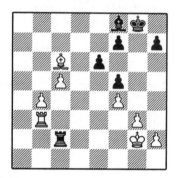

1 ♔g1??

Winning more simply is 1 ♔f3! ♖xh2 2 ♔e3 ♗e7 3 ♗f3, etc., but Kramnik does not want to give up material.

1...♗g7! 2 ♗f3 ♖c3!

He did not reckon on the transfer to an opposite coloured bishop ending.

3 ♖xc3 ♗xc3 4 c6 ♗d4+ 5 ♔f1 ♗b6 6 ♔e2 ♔f8 7 ♔d3 ♔e7 8 ♔c4 ♔d6 9 ♔b5 ♔c7 10 ♔a6 f6! 11 b5 e5 12 ♗g2 exf4 13 gxf4 ♗e3 14

♗d5 h6 15 h3 ♗b6 16 ♗e6 ♗e3 17 ♗d7 ♗b6 18 ♗xf5 ♗e3 19 ♗e4 ♗b6 20 f5 ♗e3 21 ♔a5 ♗d2+ 22 ♔a4 h5! 23 ♔b3 h4, and Black builds a fortress, ½-½

61 Saidy – Popovych
Gausdal 1982

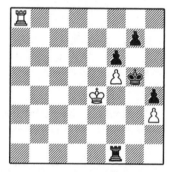

White has a choice of two ways to attack the g7 pawn – having just a small function the rook is stronger on a7, where it defends against ♖e7 as well as attacking g7.

a) 1 ♖g8? ♖e1+ 2 ♔f3 ♖e7 (game), 0-1;

b) 1 ♖a7!=

5 Active and Concrete Play in the Endgame

62 Marić – Kovalevskaya
European Cup, Halle 2000

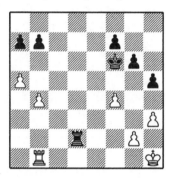

1 Rc1?

Correct was 1 b5! Ra2 2 b6 Rxa5 3 bxa7 Rxa7 4 Rb5! with a draw.

1...Rd4 2 b5 Rd5 3 a6 Rxb5 4 Rc7?!

Better is 4 axb7 Rxb7 5 Rc5 with the idea of 6 Ra5.

4...bxa6 5 Rxa7 a5 6 g4?

Premature activity. Preferable is 6 g3 with the idea of bringing the king into the game by 7 Kh1-g2-f3.

6...hxg4 7 hxg4 Rb4! 8 g5+

No help is 8 Ra6+ Kg7 9 f5 g5! 10 Rxa5 Rxg4 followed by 11...Rf4, and Black wins.

8...Ke6 9 f5+

Or 9 Rxa5 Rxf4 with the idea of Rf4-f5, winning.

9...Kxf5 10 Rxf7+ Kg5 11 Ra7 a4 12 Ra6 Kf5 13 Kg2 g5 White resigned, **0-1**

63 Grosar – Mashinskaya
European Cup, Halle 2000

1 f5??

A decisive mistake. Winning is 1 Kg5! Ke4 2 e6 d4 3 Bd2 Kd5 4 Kf6 Bb5 5 Kf7.

1...Bc8!= 2 e6 Ke4 3 Kg6 d4 4 Kf6 d3 5 Bd2 Ba6 6 Bc3 Bc8 7 e7 Bd7 8 Bd2 Bb5 9 Bb4 Bd7 10 Bc3 Bb5 11 Kg5 Be8 12 Bd2 Bb5 13 f6 Be8 14 Kh6 Kf5 15 Kg7 Ke6 16 Bc3 Bh5 17 Kf8 d2 ½-½

64   Glaser – Ovod
European Cup, Halle 2000

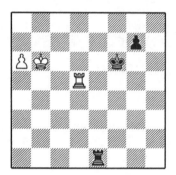

Calculate the sequel of this endgame.

1 a7 ♖e6+ 2 ♔c7 ♖e7+ 3 ♖d7 ♖e8 4 ♔b7?

The only way to win was 4 ♖d8 ♖e7+ 5 ♔b6 ♖xa7 6 ♔xa7 ♔f5 7 ♔b6 g5 8 ♔c5 ♔f4 9 ♔d4.

4...g5 5 a8=♕ ♖xa8 6 ♔xa8 ♔e5!, and the game ended in a draw.

65   Skripchenko-Lautier – Grosar
European Cup, Halle 2000

Calculate the sequel of this endgame with Black to move.

1...♕d1+?

Of course he should activate the king by 1...♔g4! 2 ♕xf7 ♔xg3 3

♕g6+ ♔xh4 4 ♕f6+ ♔h3 5 ♕e6+ (or 5 ♕f2 ♕g4+! 6 ♔f1 ♕d1+ winning) ♕g4+! 6 ♕xg4+ hxg4 7 a4 g3 8 a5 e4, and Black wins.

2 ♔f2 ♕d2+ 3 ♔g1 ♕d1+, and in view of the repetition of position the players agreed a draw, ½-½.

66   Macieja – Gershon
Bermuda 2001

1...♖h5+?

A loss of time, which in an endgame with passed pawns is inadmissible. Best was 1...h5 2 b4 ♖g4 with equal chances.

2 ♔b6 ♖h1 3 b4 ♔g7 4 b5 ♖b1 5 ♖c5 ♖f1 6 ♔c7 ♖f7+ 7 ♔b8 ♖f8+ 8 ♔a7 ♖f7+ 9 ♔a6 ♔g6 10 b6 h5 11 b7, 1-0

67   Bacrot – Short
France 2000

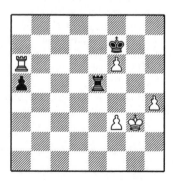

The simplest decision of course was to enter a classical endgame with f and h-pawns after 1...♖f5, but Short did not want to go in for a theoretical position and waited.

1...♖b5 2 ♔g4 a4

Short had already done a great deal of thinking, but his opponent had by now declined to play this endgame.

3 h5! ♖b1?

Correct is 3...a3! 4 f4 a2 5 h6 ♔g6 with a draw.

4 f4 a3?

But this is already too late. Here there is still the chance 4...♖b5!, but now the white king comes into contact with the f6 pawn.

5 ♔g5! ♖b5+ 6 f5 ♖b1 7 ♖a7+ ♔f8 8 ♖xa3 ♖g1+ 9 ♔f4 ♔f7 10 ♖g3 ♖h1 11 ♔g5 ♖h2 12 h6 ♖h1 13 ♖g4 ♖h2 14 ♖h4, and Black resigned, **1-0.**

After 3...♖f2 4 ♖e7+ ♔d6 5 ♖bd7+ ♔c5 6 ♖d3 ♖xh2 7 ♖d5+ everything is clear.

4 ♖e7+ ♔d6 5 ♖bd7+ ♔c5 6 ♖d5+ ♔b6 7 a4!

Threatening mate.

7...a5 8 ♖b5+ ♔a6 9 ♖e8 ♖b6?

The last chance was 9...♔a7 10 ♖xa5+ ♔b6 11 ♖b5+ ♔c7 12 ♖e7+ ♔d6 13 ♖bb7 ♖f2 14 ♖bd7+ ♔c5 15 ♖d3, though even here, in general, the result is predetermined.

10 ♖a8+ ♔b7 11 ♖b8+ ♔xb8 12 ♖xb6+ ♔c7 13 ♖xf6 h5 14 ♖xf4 h4 15 ♔c4 h3 16 ♖h4 ♖h1 17 ♔d5 h2 18 ♔e5!

Here the king hides from the checks.

18...♖f1 19 ♖xh2 ♖xf3 20 ♖c2+ ♔b6 21 ♖c4, and Black resigned, **1-0**

69 Grischuk – Karpov
Linares 2001

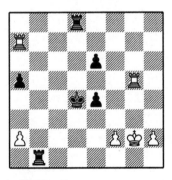

1...♖b2?

It was necessary to coordinate the pieces by 1...e3! 2 fxe3+ ♔xe3 3 ♖axa5 ♔f4!, threatening a rook invasion.

2 ♖axa5 ♖f8?

There were still some chances in 2...♖d5!, again striving to coordinate his forces.

68 Grischuk – Shirov
Linares 2001

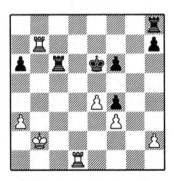

1...♖g8?

A mistake. He should coordinate the rooks by 1...♖hc8!, threatening to go to c2 or c3, which leads to a draw.

2 ♖dd7! ♖g2+ 3 ♔b3 ♖xh2

3 ♖a4+ ♔d3 4 ♖g3+ ♔d2 5 ♖xe4 ♖xa2 6 ♖xe6 ♖a4 7 ♖d6+ ♔c2 8 ♖dd3 ♖af4 9 ♖df3 ♖xf3 10 ♖xf3 ♖h8 11 ♖f4!, and the endgame is lost since the black king is cut off. **1-0**

A lack of understanding of the role of the distant passed pawn in the endgame

70 Seger – Agdestein
Germany 2000

1 c5?
Why? Simpler is 1 bxa5 bxa5 2 h4 a4 3 ♔d2 winning easily.
1...axb4?
But here Black forgets about his distant passed pawn: 1...a4!, after which the only move 2 ♔d2 ♔d5 3 h4 gxh4 4 gxh4 a3 5 ♔c2 e5 6 h5 e4 7 h6 a2 leads to a draw.
2 cxb6 ♔d6 3 h4 b3 4 ♔d3 e5 5 hxg5??
Again forgetting about the passed pawn – winning is 5 ♔c3, capturing the black pawn and realising his own passed pawn.
5...e4+ 6 ♔c3 e3 7 b7 ♔c7 8 b8=♕+ ♔xb8 9 g6 e2, White resigned, **0-1**

A lack of concrete decision making

71 Korchnoi – Topalov
Madrid 1996

One should endeavour to solve all problems concretely and avoid making moves on general considerations. Even the great are not immune...
Black is a pawn down and he should attack the opponent's main strength – the a7 pawn – with the move 1...♖b7 2 ♗e3 ♗xe3 3 fxe3 ♔f8 4 ♖da1 ♖xb2, and the draw is obvious. But he decides to make a move on general considerations.
1...h6?
There follows a typical blow.
2 b4! ♖xb4
After 2...♗xb4 3 ♗e3 c5 4 ♖d7 ♗d2 5 ♔f1 ♗xe3 6 fxe3 the a7 pawn decides the outcome of the battle.
3 ♖xb4 ♗xb4 4 ♗e3 ♔f8
Or 4...c5 5 ♖d7 c4 6 ♗b6! c3 7 ♖d8+ ♖xd8 8 ♗xd8 c2 9 ♗g5!.
5 ♖b1!, and Black resigned, **1-0**

A lack of prophylactic thinking (inattention to the opponent's plans) is particularly typical of young chessplayers, but also grandmasters quite often display this.

72 Gabriel – Oral
Batumi 1999

Prophylactically correct was 1...♕b6!, ready to meet a check by ...♕f6, and only then advance the a7 pawn, but Black plays impulsively.

1...a5? 2 ♕e5+ ♔h7 3 ♕d5! and after 3...♔g8 4 ♕xa5 ♕xd4 5 ♕a8+ it's a draw, ½-½

73 Donner – Velimirović
Havana 1971

Black has an extra pawn, but his position is in no way better in view of the queenside blockade and so Black should play for a draw by 1...♗b5 and 2...♘d7, constructing a fortress. But in the game followed:

1...♗f5? 2 ♔e3 ♗e4 3 ♔d4! ♗xg2 4 ♔e5

White gives up one more pawn, but for instant activation.

4...♔g7 5 ♔d6 ♔f8 6 ♗b3 g5 7 ♗g3 ♔e8 8 ♗e5 ♘d7 9 ♗a4 ♗h3 10 ♗f6 h6 11 ♔c7 ♗f5 12 ♔xb7 ♔f8?

After 12...♗d3 the win for White would not be quite so simple.

13 ♗xd7 ♗xd7 14 ♔xa6, Black resigned, **1-0**

74 Kramnik – Lutz
Germany 1993

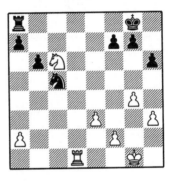

1...g6?
Here too he breaks one of the principles – it is better to bring the king to the centre by 1... ♔f8.

2 ♔g2 ♔g7 3 ♖d2 a6?!
Yet another weakening.

4 ♖d6 ♖c8 5 ♘d4 b5 6 h4!
White plans to create a weakness for the opponent on g6.

6...b4 7 ♖b6 a5 8 ♖b5!
The pawn cannot be defended.

8...♘d3 9 ♖xa5 ♘e1+ 10 ♔g3 ♘c2 11 ♘b3?!
Kramnik himself considered that best was 11 ♘f3 with the idea of 12 ♘e5.

11...♘a3 12 ♖a4 ♖c4 13 ♘d4 ♘c2 14 ♘f3! ♖c5 15 ♖a7 g5 16 h5!
In such cases it is important to have a permanent weakness on h6.

16...♔g8 17 ♘d2 ♘a3 18 ♘e4 ♖c2 19 ♖b7 ♖xa2 20 ♖xb4 ♖c2 21 ♖b6 ♔h7 22 ♘d6!, and it is time for Black to give up, **1-0**

75 **Piket – Shirov**
Aruba 1995

Black has an extra pawn and he has the choice of two different plans to continue the game: either to activate his king or to advance his passed pawn. Because White also has a dangerous passed pawn he should advance his own without loss of time: 1...g4! 2 ♔f5 g3 3 e6 g2 4 ♗d4 ♔h4 with chances of victory. But Shirov played:

1...♔g4? 2 ♖d7 ♔f4 3 ♖d4+ ♖e4 4 ♖d1 ♗c3

It is worth trying 4...♗e1.

5 ♔d5 ♖e2 6 ♖f1+ ♔e3 7 ♖g1 a4 8 ♖xg5 a3 9 e6 with a draw ½-½.

6 Shameful Mistakes

In the workshop of a chessplayer of a high level there are a few so-called 'taboos'. Players involved often wait a long time before talking about their 'feat'. And these feats include resigning in a drawn position, agreeing a draw in a winning position and likewise drawing a classical endgame which should be won in 30 seconds with one's eyes closed, such as, for example, mating with a bishop and knight against a lone king. This endgame is considered one of the simplest, and the algorithm of mating is very simple – with all the forces the king is driven into the corner of the opposite colour to the bishop and then driven over to the other corner and mated. Everything is straightforward, but... around 10% of these endgames are not won and even grandmasters drive the king into the wrong corner! From legendary games ending in a draw we can cite the games Polyak-Zamikhovsky, Semi-final, USSR Championship 1953 and Gufeld-Klarić from the GM tournament in Murcia 1990. There was an assembled gathering of 120(!) grandmasters so it can be imagined how everyone picked on Gufeld even to the point where it was suggested that he should be stripped of his grandmaster title! I recall that in the Olympiad in Moscow 1994, a grandmaster from

Vietnam, Hoang Trang, could not win against Kitty Grosar. From other serious competitons we mention the games Siebrecht-Howell, Hamburg 1995, Jirovsky-Neidig, Pardubice 1998 and the grandmaster encounter Lengyel-Loginov, Budapest 1993.

But this is what happened in the game **Kempinski-Epishin**, Lubeck 2001. It surpassed everything that had gone before. Let us see how Epishin tried to checkmate.

76

20 of the 50 allotted moves had already been used up and here he should play 1...♘d5, driving the king to the black corner. However there followed:

1...♔c5 2 ♔a6! ♗d6 3 ♔b7 ♔b5 4 ♔a7 ♔c6 5 ♔a6 ♗b8 6 ♔a5 ♘d5 Ugh!

7 ♔a6 ♗c7?

How could he allow the king to the white corner, why not 7...♘c3?

8 ♔a7 ♗b6+ 9 ♔b8 ♗c5 10 ♔a8 ♘c7+ 11 ♔b8 ♘b5 12 ♔a8 ♔b6 13 ♔b8 ♘a7 14 ♔a8 ♔a6 15 ♔b8 ♗b6 16 ♔a8 ♘b5 17 ♔b8 ♘d6 18 ♔a8 ♔b5 19 ♔b8 ♔c6 20 ♔a8 ♗a7, and at last Black realised that he would not manage to mate in the white corner, but it was already too late as he had exhausted the move limit and so the game ended in a draw ½-½.

77 Chandler – Z.Polgar
Biel 1987

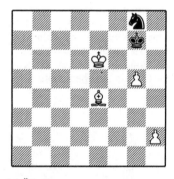

1...♘h6!

Black takes his last chance.

2 gxh6+?? ♔h8! – draw!

It is clear that White reckoned only on 2...♔xh6 3 ♔f7 which is decisive. But winning simply was 2 h4 ♘g4 3 ♔f5 ♘h6+ 4 ♔f4 ♘f7 5 ♗d5 ♘h6 6 h5 ♔h7 7 ♗e6!, cutting off the knight and then proceeding with the king to e8.

Even the author was kicking himself (more precisely he was tearing his hair out!) after the following episode.

78 Miladinović – Beliavsky
Ohrid 2001

1...gxf3??, and there arises a well-known drawn ending. Black wins simply after 1...♖xf3+. The author forgot the theoretical position.

Overlooking a tactical solutions is characteristic when other possibilities, apparently not so favourable, are also present.

79 Ferguson – Adams
Hove 1997

a) **1 ♖xh3? ♖g1!** – a typical covering over of the first rank – White resigned, **0-1**;

b) **1 ♔e1 ♖h5 2 ♔d2**, and White has no problem drawing.

80 **Plaskett – Adams**
Hove 1997

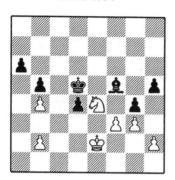

a) **1 ♘f6+?** **♔c4** **2 ♘xh5** **♔b3** **3 fxg4 ♔c2, 0-1**;

b) **1 ♘d2!**, and it is not possible to break through White's position.

81 **Lukov – Dizdar**
Halle 1987

Black has the slightly inferior structure and he needs to think about a draw.

a) **1...♔g7?!** (game) **2 ♔f2 f4? 3 ♕d7+ ♔g6 4 ♕d6+ ♔f5 5 ♕e5+ ♔g4 6 ♕xg5+ ♔xg5 7 e4!**, and Black resigned, **1-0**;

The correct defence is

b) **1...♕h5! 2 ♕g3+ ♔h6 3 ♕d6+ ♔g5** etc.

In the next example White should create a passed pawn himself, while not immobilising his pawn formation.

82 **Short – Kasparov**
London 1993

a) **1 g4? ♗d8 2 ♔c1 ♗e7 3 ♖e3 d5 4 exd5+ ♔xd5**, and a draw;

b) **1 g3** and **2 h4** creates a passed pawn and gives White good chances of victory.

83 **Zaberski – Malaniuk**
Krakow 2001

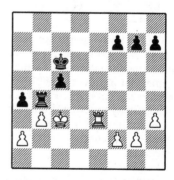

Of course, after the normal 1...axb3 2 axb3 a draw is inevitable, but Malaniuk keeps the a4 pawn and plays **1...♖f4??** but after **2 ♖f3!** the pawn endgame is lost because of White's distant passed pawn. The grandmaster thought that the exchange on f3 badly damaged his structure but the decisive element in the pawn endgame is the passed pawn.

2...♖xf3 3 gxf3 axb3 4 ♔xb3 ♔d5 5 ♔c3 c4 6 f4 f5 7 h4 h5 8 a3 ♔c5 9 a4 ♔d5 10 a5 ♔c5 11 a6 ♔b6 12 ♔xc4 ♔xa6 13 ♔d5 ♔b5 14 ♔e5 ♔c4 15 ♔xf5 ♔d3 16 ♔g5 ♔e4 17 f5! ♔e5 18 f3! Black resigned, **1-0**

84 Rustemov – Bunzman
Germany 2000

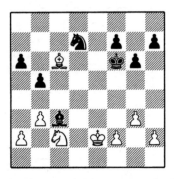

On the board things are perfectly equal and moreover there are no problems for either side in the endgame. But it proves possible to lose even such endings. For this one needs firstly to refrain from prophylaxis and then also from activation, when transposing to a pawn endgame.

1...♔e6?!

Simpler is 1...♔e7, getting out of a future pin, or 1...♘e5 2 ♗b7 a5.

2 ♗b7 a5?

But now better is 2...♘c5 3 ♗c8 ♔d5 4 b4 ♘a4 5 ♗xa6 ♔c4 with maximum activity.

3 ♗c8 ♔d6 4 ♔d3 ♗g7 5 ♗xd7 ♔xd7 6 ♘d4 ♗xd4?

Obligatory was 6...b4 with an inferior but tolerable endgame.

7 ♔xd4 ♔d6 8 a3 f6 9 g4 ♔c6 10 h4 ♔d6 11 g5! fxg5 12 hxg5 ♔e6 13 ♔e4 ♔d6

There is no salvation in 13...b4 14 a4! ♔d6 15 f3 ♔e6 16 f4 ♔d6 17 ♔d4 ♔e6 18 ♔c4 ♔f5 19 ♔b5 ♔xf4 20 ♔xa5 ♔xg5 21 ♔xb4, and White wins.

14 b4! axb4 15 axb4 ♔e6 16 f4 ♔d6 17 ♔d4 ♔e6 18 ♔c5, and White is first to queen **1-0**

Calculating the transfer to a pawn endgame, as before, is considered the Achilles heel of contemporary grandmasters.

85 Fernandez – Glavina
Ferrol 2000

a) **1 ♖xf6! ♖xf6 2 ♕xf6+ ♕xf6 3 ♖xf6 ♔xf6 4 ♔d2 ♔g5 5 ♔xd3 ♔h4 6 ♔e4 ♔xh3 7 ♔f4 ♔h4 8 ♔f5 ♔g3 9 g5!**, and the white king then captures the c5 pawn as is not difficult to calculate;

b) **1 ♖f4? ♕b8! 2 ♕xf6+ ♖xf6 3 ♖fxf6 ♕b1+ 4 ♔d2**, and here 4...♕xa2+ 5 ♔xd3 ♕b3+ 6 ♔e4 ♕xc4+ 7 ♔f5 ♕d5+ 8 ♔f4 ♕g5+ gives a draw.

7 The Difficulties of Defence in Classical Endgames

86 J.Polgar – Kasparov
Dos Hermanas 1996

1 ♔h5?!

Simpler was to exploit the stalemate idea to escape from the edge of the board: 1 ♖f8+! ♘f4 2 ♖g8! ♖h1+ 3 ♔g5.

1...♘g3+ 2 ♔h6

Nevertheless better is 2 ♔g6 ♘e4 3 ♔h6, upsetting the coordination of the black pieces.

2...♘f5+ 3 ♔h7 ♔f4 4 ♖b8 ♖g7+ 5 ♔h8 ♖d7 6 ♖e8 ♔g5 7 ♖e6

White defends against Black's main threat – the transfer of the knight to f6.

7...♘d4 8 ♖e1

No worse was to hold the sixth rank by 8 ♖a6.

8...♔f6 9 ♖d1?!

Stronger is 9 ♖f1+ ♘f5 10 ♔g8.

9...♖d5! 10 ♖a1??

Correct was again to pin down the black pieces by 10 ♖f1+ ♘f5 11 ♖f2 and wait.

10...♘e6! 11 ♖a6 ♔f7 12 ♖a7+ ♔g6 13 ♖a8 ♖d7 14 ♖b8 ♖c7 15 ♔g8 ♖c5 16 ♖a8 ♖b5 17 ♔h8 ♖b7 18 ♖c8 ♘c7!

Another no less effective plan was to secure himself against the checks along the sixth rank by 18...♖b6! 19 ♔g8 ♘g5 and try to transfer the knight to f6.

19 ♖g8+ ♔h6 20 ♖g1 ♖b8+ 21 ♖g8 ♘e8, and White resigned in view of the variation 22 ♖f8 ♔g6 23 ♖g8+ ♔f7 24 ♖g2 ♘f6+.

87 Topalov – Karpov
Monaco 2000

In this classical endgame Black needs to go with his king to h3, and it is very difficult for White to win, if indeed it is possible at all. But Karpov 'walks' to the other side.

1...♔d2? 2 ♔c4 ♔c2?

It is still not too late to return to the kingside by 2...♔e1!.

3 ♘d4+ ♚b2 4 ♚b4 ♚a2 5 ♘df5 ♚b2 6 ♘e3 ♚a2 7 ♘c4 ♚b1 8 ♚c3 ♚c1 9 ♘b2 ♚b1 10 ♘d3 ♚a1 11 ♚b3 ♚b1 12 ♘e2, and mate in three moves! **1-0**

88 Nataf – Short
Delhi 2000

In the following position the rivals had already played 40 moves in this endgame and only 10 more remained to finish the game. As a consequence of this it seemed the English grandmaster was thanking his lucky stars and began to play inaccurately. Now simplest was 1...♖b1. However...

1...♖d7 2 ♖f5 ♖d1??
A decisive mistake – correct was to continue playing for stalemate by 2...♖h7 3 ♖b5 ♖e7+!.
3 ♖b5 ♖e1+ 4 ♗e5, and **Black resigned, 1-0**

It is very interesting that this was not the only time that Short lost an endgame like this.

89 Short – Arnason
Reykjavik 1990

Correct here is 1 ♖h4!, but Short plays to free the rook.
1 ♚a4?? ♚c3 2 ♖h4 ♗c4 3 ♚a5 ♖f6 4 ♖h3+ ♗d3, and White resigned, **0-1**

The author also has something to 'share' with the reader from his practice

90 San Segundo – Beliavsky
Madrid 1997

No one is immune to mistakes, but from time to time immunisation (in the form of endgame study) is necessary.

The opponents reached the main defensive position in this endgame (the rook and king are placed one square vertically or horizontally on squares of opposite colour to the bishop). There followed:

1 ♔e2 ♖h3 2 ♖d8?

Why go away from his post – correct is 2 ♔f2.

2...♖h2+ 3 ♔d1 ♔e3 4 ♖b8??

But this is blindness – after 4 ♔c1 ♖c2+ 5 ♔d1 ♖b2 6 ♖c8 is a well known draw.

4...♖d2+??

And this is blindness from the other side – wasn't it possible to deliver mate by 4...♖h1?

5 ♔c1 ♖c2+ 6 ♔d1 ♖c3 7 ♖b2??

Why shorten the range of the rook – correct is 7 ♖e8!.

7...♗f3+, and White resigned, **0-1**

8 Mistakes of Young Players in the Endgame

Of course, all those mistakes which we come across with grandmasters are characteristic also of young players, only they are expressed even more obviously, or, one might even say, primitively.

How we do not need to play the endgame...

91 **Borisek – Varga**
Bled 2000

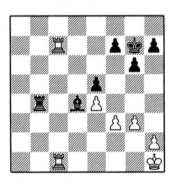

Active play is better than passive. He should play

a) **1 ♔g2 ♖b2+ 2 ♖1c2 ♖b1 3 ♖d7 ♖g1+ 4 ♔h3 ♖f1 5 f4** with a decisive advantage. However White preferred:

b) **1 ♖f1? ♖b6 2 f4 ♖f6 3 ♔g2 ♔f8 4 ♖b7 h6 5 fxe5??** (correct is 5 f5 g5 6 ♖c1 with advantage) **5...♖xf1 6 ♔xf1 ♗xe5 7 ♔e2 ♔g7 8 ♔d3 ♔f6 9 ♔c4 ♔e6 10 ♖b6+ ♔e7**

11 ♔d5 ♗c3 12 ♖b7+ ♔f8 13 g4 ♗f6 14 e5 ♗h4 15 e6 fxe6 16 ♔xe6 h5, and the game ended in a draw.

Passed pawns should be exploited to the maximum, and especially when considering transposition to a pawn endgame...

92 **Areschenko – Borisek**
Marinadior 2000

1...♔c6?
He should boldly go on the offensive **1...c4! 2 ♖c7 ♖c6 3 ♖xc6 ♔xc6 4 ♔f3 h5**, leading the game to a draw.

2 ♖h8 ♔d5 3 ♔f5 c4 4 ♖c8 ♔d4 5 g4 c3 6 g5 hxg5?
Correct is 6...♖d5!, and the king does not have the f4 square.

7 fxg5 ♖d5+ 8 ♔f4! ♔d3 9 g6 ♖d4+ 10 ♔f5 ♖xh4 11 g7, and White won, **1-0**

Mistakes of Young Players in the Endgame 45

93 Ilyushin – Neiman
Erevan 2000

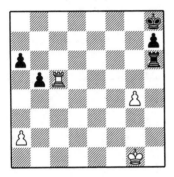

Do not play on the flank where you are weaker (where you have a pawn minority)! White breaks this golden rule.

1 a4?

He should activate the king by 1 ♔g2! with excellent prospects of a draw since wherever the king is in the centre it can count on undermining the queenside pawn mass.

1...♖b6!

The point – now it is bad to exchange pawns on the queenside since the black rook is behind its own passed pawn.

2 a5 ♖g6 3 g5 h6, and he had to resign, **0-1**

94 Kiseleva – Prudnikova
Kraguevac 2000

With a fixed pawn structure the knight is stronger than the bishop. Black has two possibilities of playing for a win, but in one of the variations arises a pawn endgame which Black calculates badly.

1...♘a3+?

He should prefer 1...♘e3+ 2 ♔d3 (or 2 ♔c3 ♔c5 3 ♗f5 ♘f1 4 g4 ♘g3 5 ♗g6 ♘e2+ 6 ♔d2 ♘d4 7 ♔c3 ♘b5+ and then 8...♔b4 winning) 2...♘f1 3 g4 ♔c5 4 ♔e2 ♘h2 5 ♔f2 ♔b4 6 ♔g2 ♔xb3!, and after ...a5-a4 this pawn wins easily.

2 ♔c3 ♔c5 3 ♔b2 ♔b4 4 g4 ♘b5 5 ♗xb5 ♔xb5 6 ♔c3 ♔c5 7 ♔d3 ♔b4 8 ♔c2 a4 9 bxa4 ♔xa4 10 ♔c3!, and later a draw was agreed.

95 Dombrovska – Lisovska
Poland 1987

White's task is simple – to give up his pawns on the squares on which they stand, without deserting the corner, but...

1 ♔g1??

There is an easy draw after 1 ♔h2!.

1...♔h3! 2 ♔h1 ♗c5, and Black wins, **0-1**

Now and then there will be cases when you have to passively await the development of play by the opponent and not become too active.

96 Podrizhnik – Jelen
Ljubljana 1998

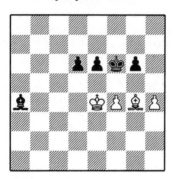

1 h5?
There is no sense in exchanging pawns standing on dark squares. Correct is 1 ♔d4 e5+ 2 fxe5 dxe5+ 3 ♔e3 with a draw.

1...♗c2+ 2 ♔e3 ♗f5 3 ♗f3 g5, and Black wins, **0-1**

One of the rare cases in rook endgames where the weaker side should not activate his king, but try to create weaknesses in the opponent's position.

97 Kaps – Krivec
Maribor 1998

1...♔g7?
It is necessary to quickly break up the opponent's pawn mass by 1...g5! 2 hxg5 hxg5 3 ♔d3 g4 4 f3 gxf3 5

gxf3 (or 5 ♔c3 ♖b8 6 gxf3 ♖f8 with a draw) 5...♖b3+ and draws.

2 ♔d3 ♔f6 3 f3 ♔e5 4 ♔c3, and White won, **1-0**

98 Grosar – Lomineishvili
Croatia 1998

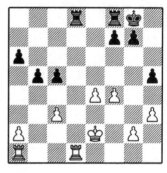

1 ♖d5?
There is no sense in creating a blockaded pawn for himself. Better is 1 a4 with a slight advantage.

1...♖xd5 2 exd5 ♖d8 3 ♖d1 ♖d6 4 ♔e3 ♔f8 5 ♔e4 ♔e7 6 g4
Also here, better is 6 a4! with chances of a draw.

6...hxg4 7 hxg4 ♖h6, and Black has a great advantage.

99 Mista – Gratka
Wisla 2000

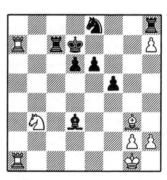

1...♖xh7?

Even in the endgame it is necessary to see tactics – simpler is 1...f4!
2 ♗xf4 ♖xh7, coordinating the
bishop and rook.

2 ♘c5+! dxc5 3 ♗xc7 ♔c6??

Confusion – it is necessary to
fight to the end. 3...♘xc7 4 ♖xc7+
♔xc7 5 ♖a7+ ♔d6 6 ♖xh7 c4 7
♖h8 f4, with a simple drawn
position.

4 ♗e5, and Black soon lost, **1-0**

Lack of a clear plan and particularly ignorance of the opponent's plan

100 Szymanski – Bartel
Swidnica 2000

In the following position there
was an easy draw by **1 ♔f6!**

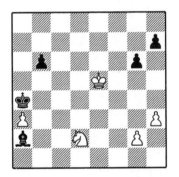

...but White played **1 ♔d6? ♔xa3
2 ♔c6 ♔b4 3 ♔xb6 ♗d5 4 g3 ♔c3
5 ♘b1+ ♔d4! 6 ♔c7 ♗g2 7 ♔d6
♗xh3 8 ♔e7 ♗f5 9 ♘a3 ♔e3 10
♔f6 ♗d3 11 ♔g5 ♔d4! 12 ♔h6
♔c5 13 ♔xh7 ♔b4**, and Black won,
0-1

Breaking the fundamental rule: do not play on that flank where you are weaker

101 Maciol – Bartel
Wisla 2000

a) **1...a5?? 2 b4 axb4 3 ♔xb4
♘c8 4 a5 g5 5 a6?** (better is 5 ♗f1
intending ♗a6 with the advantage)
5...h6 6 h4 ♘a7 7 hxg5 hxg5, and a
draw;

b) correct is **1...g5! 2 b4 h5** with
the idea h4, hxg3, g4, f4, ♘f5 offering chances for both sides.

102 Srebrnić – Novak
Bled 2001

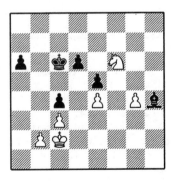

The passed pawn should be exploited to deflect the opponent's forces. Frequently this method of play is not exploited.

1 ②d5 a5 2 ⊉b1 ⊉d8 3 ⊉c2 ⊉h4 4 ⊉d1 ⊉b5 5 ②e3 ⊉g5, and Black held the draw.

But winning is **1 ②h7! ⊉d7 2 g5 ⊉e7 3 g6 ⊉f2 4 g7 ⊉f7 5 ②f6! ⊉xg7 6 ②e8+ ⊉g6 7 ②xd6** followed by ②xc4.

Technical problems of young players are also linked to a deficient knowledge of precise positions and particularly knowledge of methods of play.

103 Matnadze – Zakurdiaeva
Athens 2001

Correct here is **1...⊉f3!** and the approach of the king to g2 is decisive, but there followed:

1...⊉xh2? 2 ⊉h4?

A mistake in reply – correct is to go over to the vanguard method 2 ⊉a3+ ⊉f2 3 ⊉c3! ⊉h1+ 4 ⊉a2 and 5 ⊉c2+.

2...⊉f3 3 ⊉h8 ⊉g3 4 ⊉g8+ ⊉f2 5 ⊉h8 ⊉h1+ 6 ⊉c2 ⊉g2 7 ⊉g8+ ⊉h2 8 ⊉d2 ⊉g1 and a well-known winning position is reached.

104 Gajewski – Macieja
Warsaw 2001

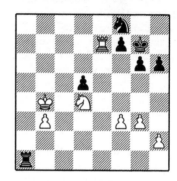

It frequently happens that young players 'have no direction', and each one of their moves is a mistake.

1 ⊉c5?!

Generally stronger is 1 ⊉e5! ⊉h1 2 ⊉xd5 ⊉xh2 3 ⊉c3 with the further march of the b3 pawn.

1...②e6+! 2 ②xe6+ ⊉f6 3 ⊉e8 fxe6 4 b4 ⊉f7 5 ⊉b8?

Stronger was 5 ⊉h8.

5...⊉c1+ 6 ⊉d6?

A decisive mistake – better is 6 ⊉d4.

6...d4! 7 ⊉a8

But now he has to catch up with the opponent's pawn.

7...d3 8 ⊉a2 ⊉c4 9 ⊉d2 ⊉xb4 10 ⊉c5?!

It seems that 10 ⊉e5 was too simple for a young master.

10...⊉a4 11 ⊉b5?

Where is he going? After 11 ⊉xd3 ⊉a2 12 h4 there is an elementary draw.

11...⊉d4, and he had to resign, **0-1**

A lack of prophylactic thinking is strongly pronounced in young players.

105 **Bartel – Kosyrev**
Moscow 2002

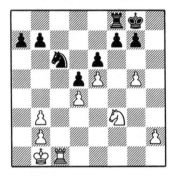

Here Black threatens an approach of the king via g6 and f5 with great chances of victory. Therefore correct was **1 h4!** and after the forced 1...g6 White has slightly the better endgame. Instead of this White played **1 ♔c2?**, when, in place of 1...♔h7, Black played **1...a6?** and offered a draw! ½-½

106 **Svidler – Pelletier**
Biel 2001

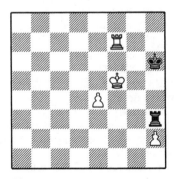

1 e5?

Not missing the win, but simpler is 1 ♖f6+ ♔h7 2 ♖g6 etc.

1...♖xh2 2 ♔f6?

But this already betrays a poor knowledge of the method of playing a precise position – correct is 2 ♖a7!, not giving the black rook more length.

2...♖f2+ 3 ♔e7 ♖a2 4 ♖f1 ♔g6 5 ♖d1 ♖a7+ 6 ♖d7 ♖a8, and a draw ½-½.

107 **Licina – Podkriznik**
Bled 2001

1...♔d6?

A mistake, even if not a decisive one – simpler was 1...♖b8+ 2 ♔a6 ♔d6 3 ♔a7 ♖b1 4 ♖c8 ♔d7 5 ♖b8 ♖a1 6 a6 ♔c7, with a well known draw.

2 a6 ♖b8+?

Correct is 2...♔d7!, reaching a basic theoretical position.

3 ♔a5 ♖b1 4 a7 ♖a1+ 5 ♔b6 ♖b1+ 6 ♔a6 ♖a1+ 7 ♔b7 ♖b1+ 8 ♔c8 ♖a1 9 ♖c7, and Black resigned, **1-0**

108 **Pakleza – Bartel**
Poland 2001

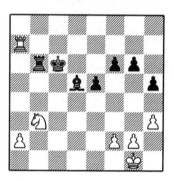

Despite having a passed pawn, White's position is worse – all his pieces are in inferior positions. Here the sides should turn their attention to the fact that in prospect, probably inevitably so, is a rook endgame 4:3 on one flank and it is necessary to be prepared for it. As is well known, in this endgame the side who gets the chances is he who is able to place his pawn on the key square h4. Therefore Black must start with the move 1...h4! with good chances of victory. However he played

1...♔d6 2 h4!?
On 2 ♖a4 strong was 2...g5!.
2...♔e6?
Correct is 2...♖b4! 3 ♖a6+ ♔e7 4 ♖a7+ ♔e6 5 ♖a6+ ♔f5 with chances of victory.
3 ♘c5+ ♔f5 4 a4?!
This pawn is going nowhere – better is 4 ♖d7.
4...♖b4 5 f3?
The black bishop has no support, therefore he should begin to pursue it by 5 ♖d7! ♗a8 6 ♖d8.
5...♖xh4 6 a5 ♖c4 7 ♖c7
This seems strong, but the white a5 pawn cannot go anywhere.
7...♖c1+ 8 ♔h2 ♖c2 9 ♔h3 e4!
Clearing the way for the bishop.
10 g4+ ♔f4

The exchange sacrifice is decisive.
11 ♘e6+ ♗xe6 12 ♖xc2 exf3 13 ♔h4 hxg4 14 ♖c6 f2! 15 ♖xe6 f5,
and White resigned, **0-1**

109 **Gigan – Mikac**
Bled 2001

1...g4
Possible, but the whole plan of defence for Black in such endgames is passive waiting for the critical position: white rook b8 and pawn b7, black king on g7. Then on ♔f5 follows ♖b5+ with a draw.
2 ♖b8 ♔g5 3 b6 ♔g6 4 ♔f1 ♔g7?
Correct is 4...♖b2!=.
5 ♔e2 ♔h7?
Better is 5...♖b2+ 6 ♔e3 ♔h7 with a draw.
6 ♔d2 ♖f3 7 ♔c1! ♔g7?.
But why this? – he should transpose to the Votav position 7...♖f6 with a draw.
8 ♖c8! ♖b3 9 ♖c7+ ♔f6 10 b7 ♔e5 11 ♔c2 ♖b6 12 ♔c3 ♔e4?
The next mistake in the chain – after 12...♖b1 13 ♔c4 ♔d6 a win is impossible – now however follows a typical manoeuvre.
13 ♖c4+ ♔f3 14 ♖b4 ♖xb7 15 ♖xb7 ♔xf2 16 ♔d2 g3 17 ♖f7+,
and White won, **1-0**

110 Sakebsek – Georgin
Atena 2001

1 Ḷc6?

He does not need to give up material – he should capture 1 Ḷg6+ ♔h7 2 Ḷg5 ♔h6 3 f6 with a win.

1...Ḷxc4 2 a4 Ḷxa4 3 Ḷxc5 ♔f6 4 ♔g2 Ḷa2+ 5 ♔h3 Ḷf2 6 Ḷc6+ ♔f7, and Black constructs a fortress, despite White's two extra pawns.

9 Pawn Endgames

Triangulation

The most typical method of playing for a win in pawn endgames is the simplified variation of the method of corresponding squares. Of course the same can be said of zugzwang.

111 Alburt – Kasparov

On the board we have a classical position. Similar ones are met in many other games. The winning method is simple.

1...♔e4 2 ♔f1 ♔e5 3 ♔e1 ♔f5 4 ♔f1 ♔e4 5 ♔e1 ♔e3, and Black wins, **0-1**

It is very interesting that in the game Yudasin-Osnos, Leningrad 1978, White offered a draw, at the same time stating that it was a well known theoretical position – and the experienced international master believed it!

112 Seirawan – Kasparov
Niksić 1984

1...♔c6!

Bad is 1...b3 2 ♔c3 b2 3 ♔xb2 ♔d4 4 ♔b3 ♔xe4 5 ♔c4 ♔xf5 6 ♔b5 ♔g4 7 ♔xa5 f5, and the queen endgame with the h5 pawn is not a win.

2 ♔c4 ♔c7! 3 ♔d3 ♔d7!

Now it's zugzwang!

4 ♔e3 ♔c6! 5 ♔d3

After 5 ♔d4 ♔d6 the black king proceeds to e5.

6...♔c5!

The original position has arisen, but with White to move, therefore he is forced to let the opponent's king go past.

6 ♔e3 b3 7 ♔d3 ♔b4 8 e5 ♔a3!, and Black won, **0-1**

In rook endgames this method is more complicated.

113 **Chernyshov – Petran**
Hungary 1993

1 ♔c3! ♔c8 2 ♔d2 ♔d8

After 2....♖xc4 3 ♖f7 and 4 g7 the king proceeds to h7.

3 ♔d3! ♖g2 4 ♔e4 ♖g1 5 ♖g8+ ♔e7 6 ♔f5 ♖f1+ 7 ♔g5 ♖g1+ 8 ♔h6 ♖h1+ 9 ♔g7 ♖h4 10 ♖h8 ♖xc4 11 ♖h1!, and Black has no defence, **1-0**

114 **Mikhalchishin – Zaid**
Nikolaev 1981

Though White has doubled pawns, his advantage is unquestionable because of the better position of his king.

1 h5 gxh5

After 1...♔d6 2 h6 ♔c6 3 ♔e5 ♔d7 4 ♔f6 ♔e8 5 ♔g7 ♔e7 6

♔xh7 ♔f8 7 ♔h8 f5 8 gxf6 g5 White would need to find the move 9 f7!, and then he wins.

2 gxh5 ♔d6 3 ♔e4 ♔e6

After 3...f6 White would win by 4 g6 hxg6 5 h6.

4 h6! ♔d6 5 ♔f5 ♔e7 6 ♔e5 f6 7 gxf6+ ♔f7 8 ♔f5 ♔f8 9 ♔e6 ♔e8 10 ♔d5 ♔f7 11 ♔c5 ♔g6 12 f7!, and Black resigned, **1-0**

115 **Timmerman – Poulsen**
Correspondence game 2001

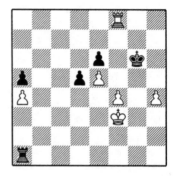

White has an extra pawn but the continuation 1 ♖f6+ ♔h5 2 ♖xe6 ♖a3+ 3 ♔e2 ♔g4! 4 ♖d6 ♔xf4 5 ♖xd5 ♖xa4 6 ♖d3 ♔f5 7 h5 ♖a1 leads only to a draw. Even the computer did not find a win. In the game followed:

1 ♔g3! ♖g1+ 2 ♔f2 ♖a1 3 ♔f3!

This is what White was aiming for. With the help of triangulation he has transferred the turn to move to his opponent, and the black rook is forced to abandon its best position on a1.

1...♖c1 4 ♖f6+ ♔h5 5 ♖xe6 ♖c3+ 6 ♔e2 ♔g4 7 ♖d6 ♖c4 8 ♔d2 ♖xa4 9 e6 ♔xf4 10 h5 and Black resigned, **1-0**

Opposition – the distinctive feature of pawn endgames

It is well known to everyone that the opposition – the most important element of pawn endgames, and the possession of which (signifying that it is the opponent's move, and he is obliged to have it) is the decisive factor. The opposition is in some way a form of zugzwang. But even in elementary cases not everything is so simple.

116 Schmittdiel – Heck
Bad Zwesten 1997

The presence of an extra pawn, and moreover a protected passed pawn, determines a decisive advantage for White. His task, exploiting the factor that the black king cannot enter the square of the passed pawn, is to overcome this opposition and break through into the opponent's camp.

1 ♔f3 ♔d5 2 ♔g3 ♔e5 3 ♔h2 ♔e4

Somewhat more accurate would be to retain the opposition by 3...♔d4, but for the time being everything is in order for Black.

4 ♔h3

Also there is no win by 4 ♔g2 ♔d4 5 ♔f3 ♔d5, etc.

4...♔d5 5 ♔g2 ♔e4 6 ♔h2 ♔d5?

But this is an obvious mistake. Correct was 6...♔d4!, supporting the opposition.

7 ♔h3! ♔d4 8 ♔h4 ♔d5 9 ♔h5 ♔d4 10 ♔g6! ♔e5 11 ♔g5 ♔e6 12 ♔f4! ♔d5 13 ♔f5!

Taking the opposition.

13....♔d4 14 ♔e6! ♔c5 15 ♔e5 ♔c6 16 ♔d4, and Black resigned, **1-0**

117 Staunton – Williams
London 1851

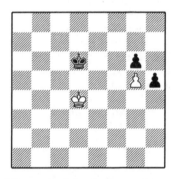

The position is similar to the preceding one, but also here the weaker side makes the same mistake.

1...♔c6 2 ♔e5?

It was necessary to hold the opposition along the diagonal by 2 ♔e4!.

2...♔c5 3 ♔f6 h4 4 ♔xg6 h3 5 ♔f7 h2 6 g6 h1=♕ 7 g7 ♕f3+, and White resigned, **0-1**

It should be mentioned that if on the board were left the f- and g-pawns (or the b- and c- ones), then in the queen endgame it would be a draw.

118 **Barkhagen – Frolov**
Finland 1994

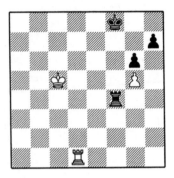

Upon transposing to a pawn endgame it is likewise very important who establishes the opposition. White should hold on to the pawn from behind by 1 ♖g1! ♖f5+ 2 ♔d4, and in all rook endgames after ...h6 there is an easy draw. However he decides to activate his king.

1 ♔d6 ♖f5 2 ♔d5?!

Also here it was still not too late for 2 ♖g1.

2...♖xd5+ 3 ♔xd5 ♔g7 4 ♔e5 h5 5 gxh6+??

Doesn't he know such elementary things?

5...♔xh6 and White resigned, **0-1**

119 **Spielmann – Makarchyk**
Warsaw 1934

Black's task is not to allow in the white king, and it is only possible to achieve this by maintaining the opposition – in the final instance, the distant opposition.

1...♔f6!

Losing is 1...♔g6? 2 ♔e3 ♔f5 3 ♔d4 ♔f6 4 ♔e4 ♔e6 5 ♔f4 or 1...♔e6? 2 ♔e2! (only so!) 2...♔d6 3 ♔d2! ♔e6 (Also losing is 3...♔c6 4 h5) 4 ♔c2 ♔e5 5 ♔c3 (diagonal opposition) 5...♔e4 6 ♔c4 ♔e5 (Or 6...♔f3 7 h5 ♔xg3 8 h6 ♔f2 9 h7 g3 10 h8=♕ g2 11 ♕h2 winning) 7 ♔c5 ♔e4 8 ♔d6 ♔f5 9 ♔d5 ♔f6 10 ♔e4, and White wins.

2 ♔e3 ♔e5 3 ♔d3 ♔d5 4 ♔e3 ♔e5 5 ♔d3 ♔d5 6 ♔c3 ♔e5! 7 ♔b4 ♔d4 8 ♔a4 ♔e4! 9 ♔b5 ♔d5 10 ♔b6 ♔d6 11 ♔a7 ♔e7!, and a draw ½-½.

As we see, Black's plan consisted of not allowing the white king to enter the square d4-d7-h7-h4.

120 **Meyer – Dutschak**
Germany 1998

In this example White simply did not know how to exploit the opposition manoeuvre.

Here the opponents agreed a draw. However after **1 a5! b5 2 ♔e4 ♔d7 3 ♔e3! ♔e7 4 ♔d3 ♔d7 5 ♔e4! ♔d6 6 ♔d4** White wins.

121 Nowak – Witkowski
Poland 1962

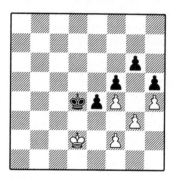

1...♔c5 2 ♔c3?

Correct was the distant opposition by 2 ♔c1!, since White does not have the d3 square to support the near opposition.

2...♔d5! 3 ♔c2 ♔c4 4 ♔d2 ♔b3 5 ♔e3 ♔c3 6 ♔e2 ♔c2 7 ♔e3 ♔d1 8 f3 exf3 9 ♔xf3 ♔e1 10 ♔g2 ♔e2 11 ♔g1 ♔f3 12 ♔h2 ♔f2 13 ♔h3 ♔g1, and Black won, **0-1**

122 Drozd – Bednarski
Poland 1962

Here White offered a draw which was naturally accepted. However it is an easy win:

1 h3 ♔d5 2 ♔e3 ♔c5 3 ♔f3! ♔d5 4 g4! hxg4+ 5 hxg4 fxg4+ 6 ♔xg4 ♔e6 7 ♔g5!

123 Preinfalk – Volchok
Correspondence game 1970

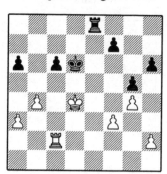

Black's position is worse in view of the weaknesses on both flanks. A very handy way for the white rook to break through is via the fifth rank. Therefore Black provokes White to enter a pawn endgame or to deprive him of the possibility of transposing to a rook endgame.

1...♖e5! 2 ♖xc6+ ♔xc6 3 ♔xe5 ♔b5 4 f4 f6+!! 5 ♔e4 gxf4!

Losing is 5...♔a4 6 f5! ♔xa3 7 ♔d5.

6 ♔xf4 ♔a4 7 ♔f5 ♔xa3 8 ♔xf6 ♔xb4 9 ♔g6 a5 10 ♔xh6 a4 11 g5 a3 12 g6 a2 13 g7, and a draw, ½-½.

124 Najdorf – Kotov
Interzonal 1948

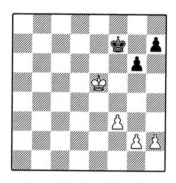

This ending would be simple for an amateur but apparently not for a World Championship Candidate!

1...♔e7 2 g4 ♔f7 3 g5 ♔e7 4 ♔d5?

He should transfer the move by 4 h3! ♔f7 5 ♔d6.

4...♔d7 5 ♔e4? ♔e6 6 ♔f4 ♔d5 7 ♔g4 ♔e5, and he had to concede a draw.

Typical complicated pawn endgames

A very typical pawn endgame is one with a symmetrical pawn structure and a rather more centralised king of one of the sides.

The most widespread elements in these positions are the 'extra' pawn tempo and zugzwang.

We begin with a simple case on one flank.

125 **Humbrich – Kubicek**
Berlin 1949

There followed:

1...♔e6?

Why not 1...h5 2 g3 ♔e6 3 ♔c5! ♔e7!! – a typical diagonal opposition and a draw.

2 ♔c5 h6 3 g3

Also not bad is 3 h5 gxh5 4 g3.

3...h5?

Stronger is 3...♔e7!? 4 h5 ♔d7! 5 hxg6 ♔e6 6 g7 ♔f7 7 ♔d6 ♔xg7 8 ♔e7! ♔g6 9 ♔f8!! ♔f6 10 ♔g8 ♔g6 11 ♔h8!! ♔h5 12 ♔g7 ♔g4 13 ♔xh6 ♔xg3 14 ♔g5 with a win.

4 ♔c6,

And Black resigned – the king proceeds to g8, **1-0**

126 **Rotstein – Marchenko**
Minsk 1985

Black is the first to advance.

1...h5 2 ♔d3?!

White cannot do without h2-h3, and so he should make this move at once.

2...♔f5 3 ♔e3?

One can never allow the opponent's king to travel so far.

3...♔g4 4 ♔f2 ♔h3 5 ♔g1 b5 6 ♔h1 a5 7 ♔g1 a4 8 ♔h1

White simply awaits his execution, but by now nothing can be put right – Black advances his queenside pawns to the maximum, followed by ...h5-h4, and the king heads for e4, then ...g6, and White is in zugzwang.

8...b4 9 ♔g1 h4! 10 gxh4 ♔xh4 11 ♔g2 ♔g4 12 ♔f2 ♔f4 13 ♔e2 ♔e4 14 h3 ♔f4 15 ♔f2 b3, and White resigned, as the black king proceeds to one of the pawns – on b2 or h3. **0-1**

127 **Aseev – Vokarev**
Elista 1996

1...h5!?
Black intends a plan to win on the kingside, though more technical is 1...♔e5, placing the kings in 'symmetry' and then starting play on the flank.
2 ♔d4 f6 3 a4?
Correct is 3 ♔e3 g5 4 hxg5 fxg5 5 ♔e2 h4 6 gxh4 gxh4 7 ♔f2 ♔f4 8 ♔g2, with a draw.
3...g5 4 ♔c5?
It is incomprehensible where the king is going. After 4 hxg5! fxg5 5 ♔e3 arises a position from the preceding variation.
4...g4 5 f4
After 5 fxg4+ ♔xg4 6 ♔b5 ♔xg3 7 ♔a6 f5 everything is clear.
5...♔e4 6 ♔d6
Or 6 ♔b5 ♔f3 7 ♔a6 ♔xg3 8 ♔xa7 ♔xh4 9 a5 g3 winning for Black.

6...♔f3 7 f5 ♔xg3 8 ♔e6 ♔xh4, White resigned, **0-1**

128 **Chuplov – Varlamov**
Russia 1994

1 a4 b6 2 f3 h5?
It is necessary to play on the other flank by 2...a5! 3 g4 f4 4 h3 ♔e6 5 ♔e4 ♔d6 6 ♔f5 ♔d5 7 ♔g6 ♔d4 8 ♔xh6 ♔e3 9 ♔xg5 ♔xf3 with a draw.
3 h3 a6
Now no help is 3...a5 4 g4!, and the g5 pawn will support the attack in all variations.
4 g4 hxg4 5 hxg4 ♔e6
Or 5...fxg4 6 fxg4 a5 7 b3 ♔c6 8 ♔e5 ♔c5 9 ♔f5, winning.
6 b3 f4 7 b4 ♔d6 8 ♔c4 ♔e5 9 a5 ♔d6 10 axb6 ♔c6 11 b7 ♔xb7 12 b5! a5 13 ♔c5 ♔c7 14 b6+ ♔b7 15 ♔b5 a4 16 ♔xa4 ♔xb6 17 ♔b4, and Black resigned, **1-0**

129 Short – Vaganian
Hastings 1982/83

1 b3?

It is necessary first to get going on the other flank: 1 h4! h5 2 f4 f5 3 g3 g6 4 b3 &d5 (4...b6 5 b4!) 5 &d3 b6 6 &c3 &c5 7 &d3, and the black king gets nowhere by proceeding to a3.

1...h5 2 g3 g5 3 g4 h4 4 f3 &d5 5 b4

Or 5 &d3 &e5 6 &e3 f5 7 &e2 fxg4 8 fxg4 &e4 9 &f2 &d3 10 &f3 b6 11 &f2 &c3 winning for Black.

5...&e5! 6 bxa5 &f4 7 &d4 &xf3 8 &c5 &g3 9 &b6 &xh3 10 &xb7 &xg4 11 a6 h3 12 a7 h2 13 a8=♕ h1=♕+ 14 &b8 ♕xa8+ 15 &xa8 f5 White resigned, **0-1**

130 Gligorić – Padevsky
Moscow 1956

1 h4 &d6

After 1...h6 2 h5 f5+ winning is 3 &e5!.

2 f5 gxf5+ 3 &xf5 &e7 4 a4 &f7?

Already an indifferent move – correct was an immediate 4...a5.

5 b4 a5??

But now this loses. Leading to a draw is 5...&e7 6 g5 fxg5 7 &xg5 &f7 8 &h6 &g8 9 h5 &h8 10 &g5 &g7 11 h6+ &f7 12 &f5 &e7 13 &e5 &d7 14 &f6 &d6 15 &g7 &e7!.

6 b5 &e7 7 g5 fxg5 8 &xg5 &f7 9 &f5 &e7 10 &e5, Black resigned, **1-0**

A return to the theme of 'Guru Grigoriev'

Pawn endgames occupied a sufficiently big place in the first of the two volumes, but this theme is inexhaustible – the number of mistakes has in no way diminished, and the impression is such that chessplayers, amongst whom also are included grandmasters, do not work on this aspect of the endgame.

131 Topalov – Morozevich
Frankfurt 1999

1 g4 f6 2 f5 h5??

Correct is 2...g6 3 fxg6 hxg6 4 h4 ♔d5 5 h5 gxh5 6 gxh5 ♔e6 with a draw.

3 gxh5 ♔d5 4 ♔b4 ♔e5 5 ♔xa4 ♔xf5 6 ♔b4 ♔g4 7 ♔c3! f5 8 ♔d2 f4 9 ♔e2, and White won, **1-0**

132 **Seirawan – Benjamin**
USA championship 1999

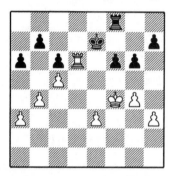

Black should not transpose to a pawn endgame. 1...♖c8!? with the idea of 2...a5=. However Black hurried with **1...♖d8?? 2 ♖xd8 ♔xd8 3 e4 ♔e7 4 e5! h6 5 h4 ♔e6 6 exf6 ♔xf6 7 g5+ hxg5 8 hxg5+ ♔e6 9 ♔e4 ♔d7 10 ♔e5 ♔e7 11 a4** and he lost.

133 **Burmakin – Zviagintsev**
Elista 1997

White could save the game by 1 g4! e4+ 2 ♔e3 exf3 3 gxf5 ♔e5 4 ♔xf3 ♔xf5 5 a3! ♔e5 6 ♔e3!=. But in the game followed:

1 gxh4? gxh4 2 ♔e3

Or 2 a4 f4+ 3 ♔e4 ♔e6 4 ♔d3 ♔f5 with the idea of ...e5-e4.

2...a4! 3 bxa4 ♔c6 4 ♔d3 ♔b6 5 ♔c3 ♔a5 6 ♔b3 e4 7 fxe4 fxe4 8 ♔c3 ♔xa4 9 ♔d2 ♔a3 10 ♔e3 ♔xa2 11 ♔xe4 ♔b3, and Black won, **0-1**

134 **Bets – Golubev**
Alushta 1999

Here White calculated two variations which at first glance were of perfectly equal value:

a) 1...h5 2 b5 (or 2 a6 2 c6) 2...b6, and White must resign;

b) 1...b6, and White loses.

Unfortunately in the game followed

1...b6??

White did not resign, but played

2 cxd6 cxd6 3 axb6 axb6 4 ♔f4 h5 5 ♔f5 h4 6 ♔e6 ♔g4 7 ♔xd6 h3 8 ♔c7 h2 9 d6 h1=♕ 10 d7, and Black could not win, since the c5 square is under control.

135 Pezerović – Lobron
Germany 1999

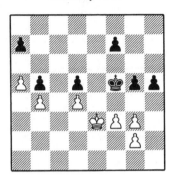

1...g4?

A mistake which leads the game to a draw. He should play 1...a6! winning. A typical continuation on the theme of saving a tempo in pawn endgames. Then White would lose in every variation, for example:

a) 2 ♔e2 h4 3 ♔f2 f6 4 gxh4 (4 ♔e2!? hxg3 5 ♔e3 ♔g6 6 ♔e2 ♔h5 7 ♔e1 f5 8 ♔e2 f4 9 ♔e1 ♔h4 10 ♔f1 g4 11 ♔g1 and now not 11...gxf3 12 gxf3 ♔h3 13 ♔h1 g2+ 14 ♔g1 with a draw, but the triangulation 11...♔g5 12 ♔h1 ♔h5! 13 ♔g1 ♔h4 14 ♔h1 gxf3 15 gxf3 ♔h3 16 ♔g1 g2 17 ♔f2 ♔h2 winning) 4...gxh4 5 g3 ♔g5 6 ♔g2 hxg3 7 ♔xg3 ♔f5! 8 ♔g2 ♔f4 9 ♔f2 f5!, the tempo in reserve – and White is in zugzwang.

b) 2 ♔f2 h4 3 gxh4 gxh4 4 g3 (4 ♔e3 ♔g5 5 ♔e2 ♔f4 6 ♔f2 f6/f5) 4...hxg3+ 5 ♔xg3 ♔g5 6 f4+ ♔f5 7 ♔f3 f6 with a win.

However in the game there followed:

2 f4 a6 3 ♔d3 ♔e6 4 ♔e2 ♔f6 5 ♔f2 ♔f5, and a draw, ½-½

136 Fucak – Kozamernik
1995

1...d4 2 ♔f3 ♔c5?

Obviously better was 2...♔d5 3 g5 d3, and now after

a) 4 ♔e3 d2 5 ♔xd2 ♔e4 6 g6= (6 gxh6=);

b) 4 f5 hxg5 5 f6 gxf6 6 h6 g4+!, and White has problems.

3 g5 ♔xb5 4 f5 hxg5 5 f6, 1-0

137 Dreev – Stohl
Brno 1994

1...b4?

1...♔e5 2 g3 ♔d5 3 g4 winning. Correct was 1...f4! 2 g3 fxg3 3 hxg3 h5 4 f4 b4! 5 f5 ♔e5 6 f6 ♔xf6 7 ♔xd4 ♔f5 and White has to be careful in making a draw.

2 g4! fxg4 3 fxg4 h6 4 h4 ♔e5 5 h5!, and White wins, **1-0**

138 **Kramnik – Kasparov**
New York 1995

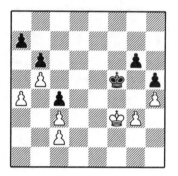

1...♔e5?

Worth considering is 1...g5! 2 hxg5 ♔xg5 3 ♔f2 ♔g4 4 ♔g2 ♔f5 5 ♔f3 ♔g5, and Black draws.

2 g4! ♔e6

Bad is 2...hxg4+ 3 ♔xg4 ♔f6 4 ♔f4 ♔g7 5 ♔e5, and White wins.

3 gxh5 gxh5 4 ♔f4?!

Better is 4 ♔e4! ♔d6 5 ♔d4 ♔e6 6 ♔xc4 ♔f5 7 ♔d3 ♔g4 8 c4 ♔xh4 9 c5, and White wins.

4...♔f6 5 ♔e4 ♔e6 6 a5?

White makes a decisive mistake. Winning is 6 ♔d4 ♔f5 7 ♔xc4 ♔g4 8 ♔b3 ♔xh4 9 c4 ♔g5 10 c5!.

6...bxa5, draw ½-½.

139 **Ye – Xie**
Kuala Lumpur 1994

1 e4?

Correct is 1 g4 g5 (or 1...h5 2 gxh5 gxh5 3 f4 ♔d5 4 f5 ♔e5 5 e4 h4 6 ♔c4 ♔f4 7 f6, and White wins) 2 f4 gxf4 3 exf4 ♔d5 4 ♔b4, and White realises his advantage.

1...h5 2 ♔c3 b5 3 f4?

The last chance was 3 f3 b4+ 4 ♔d3 ♔b5 5 ♔d4 ♔a4 6 e5 winning.

3...♔c6! 4 ♔d4 ♔d6 5 e5+ ♔e6 6 ♔e3 ♔d5 7 ♔d3 b4 8 ♔d2 ♔c6 9 ♔e2 ♔c5 10 ♔e3 ♔d5 11 ♔d3 ♔c5 12 ♔c2 ♔c6 13 ♔b3 ♔b5 14 g4 hxg4 15 g3 ♔c5 16 ♔a4 ♔d4 17 ♔b3 g5!, a clear-cut move establishing the draw, ½-½

140 **Kakhiani – Marić**
Kishinev 1995

1...f5

Losing at once is 1...g6 2 ♔c3 ♔e4 3 ♔c4 ♔xf4 4 ♔d5.

2 a4?

Better is 2 f3 g6 3 ♔c3 h6 4 h4 h5 5 ♔d3 ♔d6 6 ♔c4 ♔e6 7 d5+ ♔e7 8 ♔d4 ♔d6 9 a4 with a decisive advantage.

2...♔d6 3 ♔c4 ♔e6 4 d5+ ♔d7 5 ♔d4 ♔d6 6 f3 g6 7 h3 h6, draw, ½-½

141 Fedorowicz – Chandler
London 1987

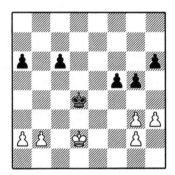

The activity of the king is one of the basic factors in pawn endgames.

1...♔e4 2 ♔e2 a5 3 ♔d2 f4 4 gxf4 ♔xf4 5 ♔e2 ♔g3 6 ♔f1 a4 7 ♔g1 h5 8 b3 axb3 9 axb3 c5 10 ♔f1 ♔h2, and Black won, **0-1**

142 Von Bardeleben – Mieses
Germany 1902

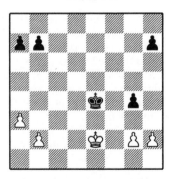

Black's pawn is further advanced, and the position of his king is obviously more active. All this defines Black's advantage. His task is to cramp the opponent's forces and exploit the extra tempo to break through behind enemy lines.

1...b5! 2 ♔d2 ♔d4 3 ♔e2 ♔c4 4 ♔d2 ♔b3 5 ♔c1 ♔a2 6 ♔c2 a5 7 ♔c3 h6 8 h4 h5 9 g3 b4+ 10 axb4 axb4+ 11 ♔c2 ♔a1 12 ♔b3 ♔b1 13 ♔xb4 ♔xb2, 0-1

143 Hort – Petursson
Brocco 1989

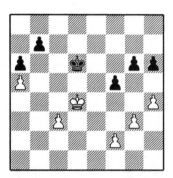

On which flank should White start to advance his pawn mass? As usual White does not begin from the side.

a) **1 f3? h5! 2 f4 ♔c6 3 c4 ♔d6 4 c5+ ♔c6 5 ♔c4 ♔c7 6 ♔d5 ♔d7 7 ♔e5 ♔e7**, (game), ½-½;

b) **1 c4! ♔c6 2 ♔e5 ♔c5 3 h5! gxh5 4 ♔xf5 b6 5 axb6 ♔xb6 6 ♔e4** winning.

144 Ree – Van der Wiel
Eindhoven 1993

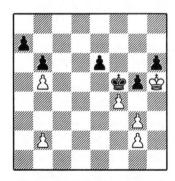

A quite complicated pawn ending to calculate. Nevertheless the presence for White of several tempi on the queenside (the b2 pawn) gives him chances of victory. In the game there followed **1 ♔xh6? gxf4 2 gxf4 ♔xf4 3 ♔h5 e5 4 g4 e4**, and Black at the end of the variation exchanges queens and transposes to an easily won pawn endgame. But correct was **1 b3!! gxf4 2 g4+ ♔f6 3 ♔xh6 ♔f7 4 g5 ♔g8 5 ♔g6!**, winning the black pawns and the game.

145 Tratar – Jelen
Bled 2001

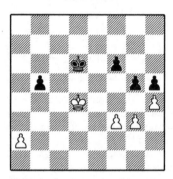

White's more active king position and reserve tempi on the queenside define his advantage. In the game there followed **1 f4? g4 2 ♔e4 ♔e6**, and a draw was agreed at once.

He should play **1 a3! gxh4 2 gxh4 ♔c6 3 ♔e4 ♔c5 4 ♔f5 ♔c4 5 ♔xf6 ♔b3 6 ♔g5 ♔xa3 7 f4**, and White queens wth check, then exchanges queens, and the pawn endgame is once again won for White.

146 Beliavsky – Glek
Germany 2000

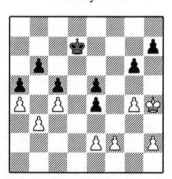

Black has two possibilities:

a) **1...h6? 2 ♔g3 g5 3 e3 ♔e6 4 f4! ♔f6 5 fxg5+ ♔xg5 6 ♔h3**, and there is no defence against the approach of the king to h5; he should prefer:

b) **1...e3! 2 fxe3 h6 3 ♔g3 ♔e6 4 ♔f3 ♔d6 5 ♔e4 ♔e6 6 h3 ♔d6 7 h4 ♔e6 8 h5 g5**, and a draw.

147 Anand – Gulko
Riga 1995

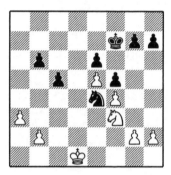

White, exploiting the better position of his king, has the possibility of transposing to a pawn endgame.

1 ♘d2! ♘xd2 2 ♔xd2 g5

Losing at once is **2...♔g6** because of the march of the king to b5.

3 ♔c3 b5 4 b3 gxf4 5 a4, Black resigned, **1-0**

148 Slizevski – Nocikova
Russia 2000

1 ♔e7!

It is interesting that 1 ♔e6? h3 2 ♔f6 f4 3 gxf4 ♔xf4 4 ♔e6 ♔f3 was seen in the game Fedorowicz-Filguth, Lone Pine 1978, when Black wins. Apparently 1 ♔d7 is also sufficient for a draw.

1...♔f3

On 1...♔e5 there is 2 ♔d7=.

2 ♔e6 ♔g4 3 ♔e5 h3 4 ♔e6 f4 5 gxf4 ♔xf4 6 ♔d5, and a draw.

149 **Stone – Gulko**
USA 1986

With a great choice of possibilities, White played 1 ♔d3? ♔b5 2 g4 fxg4 3 fxg4 hxg4 4 hxg4 ♔c6, and there is no defence against the approach of the king to the g4 pawn.

He can make a draw by **1 ♔b2! ♔b5 2 a3! b3 3 ♔c3 b2 4 ♔xb2 ♔c4 5 g4.**

Exercises

(11) **Euwe – Pirc**
Bled 1949

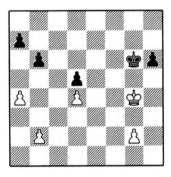

Suggest the right plan for Black

(12) **Hamdouchi – Ibragimov**
Germany 2000

Black continues to play for a win, though he should now be thinking about a draw.

(13) Stangl – Schmittdiel
Germany 2000

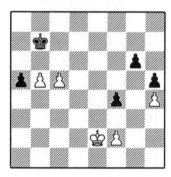

How should White continue?

(15) Janvarev – Scherbakov
Moscow 1995

Which capture is best for Black?

(14) Vavra – Ftacnik
Czech Republic 1995

How should White continue?

(16) Morozevich – Vyzhmanavin
New York 1995

How should White continue?

(17) Kuif – Van der Wiel
Hilversum 1989

*What continuation should
White choose?
Going forward seems natural, but...*

(19) Poldauf – Prohl
Germany 2000

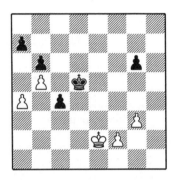

*What continuation should White
choose?*

(18) Kamsky – Tukmakov
Rejkjavik 1990

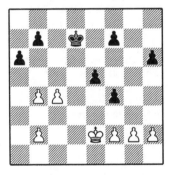

*What continuation should Black
choose?*

(20) Landa – Kozlov
Budapest 1991

*With what move should Black hand
over the move to his opponent?*

10 Rook Endgames

Rook and pawn against rook: Non-edge pawns

This is a very basic endgame and a knowledge of exact positions is absolutely necessary. The greater the strength of play the more the chessplayer knows precise positions and methods of play in rook endgames. These means are applied in the first instance upon the transposition to basic rook endgames.

The fundamental positions here are the Philidor position and the method of 'mate' and the method of defence with the rook on the long side and the king on the short.

150 Philidor

1...♖g6+ draws at once.

151 Liangov – Polovodin
Asenovgrad 1985

The most accurate defence – latching on the rook to the opponent's pawn.

1...♖e4!! 2 ♔e6 ♔f8!
Only on the short side.
3 ♖a8+ ♔g7 4 ♔d6
Or 4 ♖e8 ♖a4!=.
4...♔f7!=.

However, if the reader thinks that grandmasters always possess the technique of play in such endgames – then he is mistaken.

152 Tseshkovsky – Sax
Zagreb 1975

Here Black, to the surprise of his opponent, resigned. But after

1...♔h7 2 f7

Or 2 ♖g7+ ♔h6! (Not 2...♔h8 3 ♖e7 ♖c6+ 4 ♔f5 ♖c5+ 5 ♔g6) 3 ♖g8 ♖c6+ 4 ♔e7 ♖c7+ 5 ♔d6 ♖a7, with a draw.

2...♖c8!

Bad is 2...♖e1+ 3 ♔d7 ♖d1+ 4 ♔e8 ♖e1+ 5 ♔f8 ♖h1 6 ♖e3 and then 7 ♔e7.

3 ♔d7 ♖a8!, and a draw.

153 Poldauf – Pigusov
Panormo 2001

Black makes a decisive mistake.
1...♖a6??, and after **2 ♔f8+** immediately resigned the game. The other move of the rook holds the draw: **1...♖a8!**.

154 Zhu Chen – Taimanov
Roquebrune 1998

The position is hardly a Philidor. It remains only to play 1...♖e1. However...

1...♖h4 2 ♖g3 ♖d4 3 ♖g8+ ♔f7 4 ♖d8 ♖a4 5 ♖c8 ♖d4 6 ♖d8 ♖a4 7 ♖b8 ♖d4 8 ♖c8 ♖d1 9 ♖c2 ♔e8 10 ♔c6 ♔e7

10...♔d8 makes no difference.

11 ♖e2+ ♔d8 12 ♖h2 ♖c1+?

No way is it possible to allow the king to d6. Correct was 12...♔e7 and manoeuvring the rook to the d-file.

13 ♔d6 ♔c8 14 ♖h8+ ♔b7 15 ♔d7 ♖c7+ 16 ♔e6 ♖g7 17 ♖e8?

Winning easily is 17 d6.

17...♖g5?

A crucial mistake. He could save the game by 17...♖g6+ 18 ♔d7 ♖h6.

18 d6 ♖g6+ 19 ♔d7?

Winning is 19 ♔e7! ♖g7+ 20 ♔f6 ♖d7 21 ♔e6 ♖h7 22 d7.

19...♖g1?

A comedy of errors. White again gives his opponent the chance to save the game by 19...♖h6.

20 ♖e7?

Again the move of the rook to the 8th rank wins: 20 ♖f8 or 20 ♖h8.

20...♖g8?

The final and decisive mistake. There is a draw by 20...♖h1.

21 ♖h7 ♖f8 22 ♔e7 ♖f1 23 d7 ♖e1+ 24 ♔d8 ♔c6 25 ♔c8, and White finally wins, **1-0**

155 Pachman – Gligorić
Bled 1961

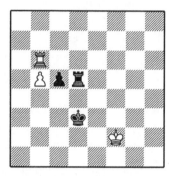

White has three possibilities, but only one of these leads to salvation.

a) 1 ♖c6? c4 2 b6 c3 3 b7 ♖b5, 0-1 (game);

b) 1 ♖b8? c4 2 b6 c3 3 b7 ♖d7 winning;

c) **1 ♔e1! c4 2 ♔d1 ♔c3 3 ♔c1 ♖h5 4 ♖d6 ♖xb5 5 ♖h6 ♖d5 6 ♖h2=**.

156 Arencibia – Vladimirov
Leon 1991

White has several ways to fight for a draw.

a) 1 ♖c5?? ♔b4 2 ♖c1 c5 3 ♖b1+ ♔a3 4 ♖c1 ♖d5, and in this theoretical position he had to resign, 0-1;

b) 1 ♖a6? ♔c3! 2 ♖b6 (or 2 ♔e3 ♖e6+, cutting off once and for all the white king) 2...♖d2+ 3 ♔e1 c5 4 ♖c6 ♖d5 winning;

c) **1 ♔e3!**, preparing to attack the black rook – the only correct strategy in such endgames.

1...♔b4 2 ♖a1 c5 3 ♖b1+ ♔a3 4 ♖c1 ♖d5 5 ♔e4! with a theoretical draw.

157 Mikhalchishin – Losev
Moscow 1976

In analysing this simple endgame the author made a mistake, but also the great analyst M.Dvoretsky did not avoid errors.

1 ♔b2

Dvoretsky criticised this move, suggesting 1 ♔c2 ♔f4 2 ♖e7! ♖h5 3 b6 ♖b5 4 b7 ♔f5 5 ♔c3 ♔f6 6 ♔c4 ♖b1 7 ♖h7 ♔e6 8 ♔c5, but the move in the game is no worse.

1...♔f4 2 ♖c3?

This is a mistake, correct is 2 ♖d3! ♔e4 3 ♔c3 ♖h5 4 ♖d4+ ♔e3 5 b6 with a win.

2...♔e5 3 ♔a3 ♔d6 4 b6 ♔d7 5 ♖c7+ ♔d8!

The only move – after 5...♔d6? 6 ♖c8 White wins.

6 ♖c6 ♔d7, draw.

A very similar position comes from Grigoriev.

158 Grigoriev

1...♖d3!

Bad is 1...♔f6 2 b6 ♖h7 3 ♔c3 ♖b7 4 ♖b1 ♔e6 5 ♔c4 ♔d7 6 ♔b5 ♔c8 7 ♔a6 winning.

2 ♔c2 ♖d5 3 ♖b1 ♖c5+ 4 ♔d3 ♔e5 5 b6 ♖c8 6 b7 ♖b8 7 ♔c4 ♔d6, and a draw.

159 Fischer – Sherwin
Portoroz 1958

1...♔e6?

Where is the king going? Correct is the frontal attack 1...♖a8! 2 ♔h4 ♖h8+ 3 ♔g5 ♖g8+ or 2 g5 ♖f8!, with a typical draw.

2 ♔h4! ♖a8 3 g5 ♖h8+ 4 ♔g4 ♔e7 5 g6 ♖f8 6 ♖f5! Here, because of this manoeuvre, Black loses.

160 Tal – Zaitsev
Riga 1968

White has two possibilities:

a) 1 ♔d3? ♖e1! 2 ♔d2 ♖e6 3 ♖b1 g5 4 ♖e1 ♖xe1 5 ♔xe1 ♔h5 with a win for Black;

b) **1 ♖b1!** The main thing is not to allow the rook to the first rank, where it distracts the white king, which must have the possibility of attacking the rook from the fourth rank. **1...g5 2 ♔d3 ♖e5 3 ♔d4 ♖e8 4 ♖g1** with a draw.

161 Ehlvest – Ljubojević
Rotterdam 1989

After 1 c4 ♖e8! 2 ♖xe8 ♔xe8 3 ♔e4 ♔d8 4 ♔d4 ♔e8 – draw, if there were a pawn on c3 here 5 ♔c4 would win. Therefore White played:

1 c3 ♔f6 2 ♖e3 ♖d8+ 3 ♔c2 ♔f7??

Black plays according to the principle – 'one step forward – one step back'. The correct means of play in these endgames, in fact in all rook endgames, is the method of the 'trailer'. It is necessary to 'latch on' to the pawn: 3...♖c8 4 ♔b3 ♖b8+ 5 ♔c4 ♖c8+ 6 ♔b5 ♖b8+ 7 ♔c6 ♖c8+ 8 ♔d7 ♖c4 9 ♖e6+ ♔f5 10 ♖c6.

4 ♔b3 ♖b8+ 5 ♔c4 ♖c8+ 6 ♔b5 ♖b8+ 7 ♔c6 ♖c8+ 8 ♔d7 ♖c4 9 ♔d6 ♖c8 10 ♖e7+! ♔f6 11 ♖c7!

White establishes a well known winning theoretical position.

11...♖d8+ 12 ♔c6 ♔e6 13 c4 ♔e5 14 c5 ♔d4 15 ♔b7! ♖d5 16 ♔b6 ♔e4 17 ♖h7!, Black resigned, **1-0**

162 **Motylev – Shirov**
Moscow 2001

It is clear that Black only makes a draw by a frontal attack. 1...♖c8 2 ♖e5 ♔d6! 3 ♖e4 ♔d5!, and persistent latching on to the rook. But Shirov played

1...♖c6??,

and after

2 ♖e5 ♖g6+ 3 ♔f5 ♖g8 4 ♖e6!

He needs to hide from the checks from below.

4...♖f8+ 5 ♖f6 ♖g8 6 ♖f7+ ♔e8 7 ♔f6 ♖h8 8 ♖a7 ♖h6+ 9 ♔g7 ♖h5 10 ♖a4 ♖h4 11 ♖e4+ ♔d7 12 ♔g6 ♖g4+ 13 ♔f5 ♖g8 14 ♔f6 ♖g4 15 ♖e7+ ♔d8 16 f5, and Black resigned. **1-0**

163 **Taimanov – Larsen**
Palma de Mallorca 1970

1...♔d4

After 1...♖g8+ 2 ♔f7 ♖g4 3 ♔f6 ♔d4! 4 ♔f5 ♖g8 5 ♖a3 ♖f8+ 6 ♔g6 ♔e4 7 g4 we have a position like the game.

2 ♖a3 ♔e4 3 g4 ♖g8+! 4 ♔h5 ♖h8+ 5 ♔g5 ♖g8+ 6 ♔h4

Here Black has a choice (but this in itself is a problem)

a) 6... ♖h8+ 7 ♔g3 ♔e5! 8 ♖a6 ♖h1=;

b) 6...♔f4 7 ♖a4+ ♔f3 8 ♔h5 ♖h8+ 9 ♔g6 ♖g8+ 10 ♔f5 ♖f8+ 11 ♔e6 ♖g8=;

c) (game) **6...♔e5? 7 ♖a6! ♔f4 8 ♖f6+ ♔e5 9 g5** and Black resigned, **1-0**

A knowledge of precise endgame positions can be utilised not only when these positions arise, but also when calculating a transposition from more complicated endgames into these positions.

164 Geller – Fischer
Palma de Mallorca 1970

1...♔h3? 2 ♖d3 ♔h4

After 2...♔h2 3 ♔g4 g2 4 ♖h3+ ♔g1 5 f5 is a draw.

3 ♖d2?

Correct is 3 ♖d7! and 4 ♖g7 with a draw.

3...♖a1 4 ♔e5?

A decisive mistake – after 4 ♖d8 g2 5 ♖h8+ ♔g3 6 ♖g8+ ♔f3 7 ♔e6! White has a draw.

3...♔g4! 5 f5 ♖a5+, and White had to resign, **0-1**

165 Bareev – Lalić
Lucerne 1997

1...♖g4?

He should immediately transpose to an endgame a pawn down by

1...♖g8 2 ♖f6 ♔b5 3 ♖f5+ ♔c6 4 ♖xh5 ♔d6 with a draw.

2 ♖f6 ♖g5

And now he should hurry back with the king to get a draw.

3 ♖f3 ♔b5 4 ♔h4 ♖e5

After 4...♖g8 5 ♔xh5 ♖h8+ 6 ♔g6 ♖g8+ 7 ♔h7 ♖g4 8 ♔h6 ♔c6 9 ♖f6+ ♔d7 10 ♖g6 White wins.

5 ♖c3! ♔b6 6 ♖c8 ♔b7 7 ♖h8

Also good is 7 ♖g8 and 8 ♖g5.

7...♔c6 8 ♖xh5 ♖e8 9 g4 ♔d6 10 ♖h7! ♔e6 11 ♔h5 ♖f8 12 g5 ♔f5 13 g6 ♔e6 14 ♔g5

Good is 14 g7.

14...♖f1 15 ♖a7 ♖h1 16 g7 ♖g1+ 17 ♔h6 ♔f6 18 ♔h7, and Black resigned, **1-0**

166 Beliavsky – Ree
Kiev 1978

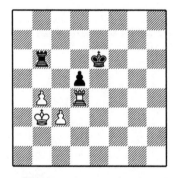

1...♖b8?

Correct is 1...♖c6 2 b5 (bad is 2 c4 dxc4+ 3 ♖xc4 ♔d7 with a draw) ♖c8 3 ♔b4 ♔d6 with excellent drawing chances. Now however follows a typical break.

2 c4! dxc4+ 3 ♔xc4 ♖c8+?

After 3...♔e5! arises a well-known drawn position.

4 ♔b5 ♔e5 5 ♖d7! ♔e6 6 ♖b7 ♔d6 7 ♔a6 ♖c1 8 b5, and Black resigned, **1-0**

167 **Jagupov – Malakhatko**
St.Petersburg 1999

Again the classics show how to practically make a draw:

a) 1 ♖h6? ♖xb3+ 2 ♔f2 ♔d4 3 ♖h4+ ♔c3 4 ♖h3+ ♔c2 5 ♖h4 ♖b4 6 ♖h5 c4 7 ♖h4 ♖a4 8 ♔e2 ♔b3 9 ♖h8 ♖a2+ 10 ♔d1 ♖a1+ 11 ♔e2 ♔c2 (game), 0-1;

b) **1 ♖c6! ♔d5 2 ♖c8 ♖xb3+ 3 ♔f2 ♖d3 4 ♔e2 ♖d4 5 ♖d8+! ♔c4 6 ♖xd4+!=**

168 **Polovodin – Ivanov**
Leningrad 1988

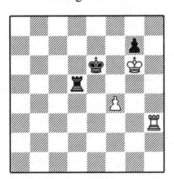

1 ♖e3+ ♔d6 2 ♖e4!!
If 2 ♖xg7 ♖f5 3 ♖e4 ♔d5 4 ♖a4 ♔e6 – draw. Now however Black resigned, **1-0**.

169 **Morovic – Agdestein**
Havana 1998

Black played badly:
1...♔g2? 2 ♖f6 f3 3 g6 ♖a5
No good is 3...f2? 4 ♖xf2+ ♖xf2 5 g7.
4 g7 ♖g5, and a draw, ½-½.

He should go in with the rook **1...♖a1+ 2 ♔d2 ♖g1 3 g6 ♖g3!**, and then ♔g2 and f3.

170 **Bodnar – Sibiriakov**
Correspondence game 2001

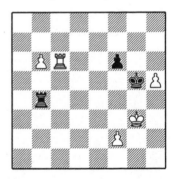

After reaching this, generally speaking, easily winning position (for example, 1 ♔f3! ♔xh5 2 ♖xf6, and the white king goes over to the b6 pawn with a win), White 'improves' the threat.

1 h6? ♚xh6 2 ♖xf6+ ♚g5 3 ♖c6 ♖b3+

Now arises an endgame which has a direct relationship to the present theme. Leading to an immediate draw is 4 f3 ♖b2 and the white king cannot break out of the cage. It only remains to put to the test...

4 ♚g2 ♚f4 5 ♚f1 ♖b2 6 ♚e1

Much time and energy has been devoted to this principal position without for the time being making the final diagnosis that White wins in all variations. White's idea is to go up to the b6 pawn even at the cost of the f2 pawn, but he should give up this pawn in such a way that the black king does not succeed in rejoining forces with the rook. For example, 6... ♚e4 7 ♖h6! ♚d3 8 f4 ♚e3 9 ♚d1 ♚xf4 10 ♚c1 ♖b5 (or 10...♖g2 11 b7 ♖g8 12 ♖b6 ♖b8 13 ♚c2 ♚e5 14 ♚c3 ♚d5 15 ♚b4 – just in time) 10 ♚c2 ♚e4 11 ♚c3, and it is not possible to cross the 5th rank because of the exchange of rooks. In the game followed:

6...♚f5!?

If 6...♚f4 White already has the possibility of leaving his kingside pawns to Black's mercy: 7 ♚d1! ♚g5 (7...♖xf2 8 ♖f6) 8 ♚c1! ♖b5 9 ♖c6.

7 f3! ♚g5!?

The last trap. Now, if 8 ♖c6, then 8...♚f4! 9 ♚d1 ♚xf3 11 ♚c1 ♖b5 12 ♚c2 ♚e4 13 ♚c3 ♚d5 14 ♖h6 ♚c5, with a draw.

8 ♖d6! ♚f4 9 ♚d1 ♚xf3 10 ♚c1 ♖b5

Or 10...♖g2 11 b7 ♖g8 12 ♖b6 ♖b8 13 ♚c2 ♚e4 14 ♚c3 ♚d5 15 ♚b4 with a win.

11 ♚c2 ♚e4 12 ♚c3 ♚e5 13 ♚c4, and White won this long-suffering game.

Rook endgames with connected pawns

Two pawns, if they are not blockaded, usually win easily. However let's look at some cases where grandmasters encountered great difficulties in such endgames.

171 **Acs – Sermek**
Nova Gorica 2001

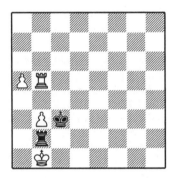

There followed:
1 ♚c1?

Correct is 1 ♚a1 ♖h2 2 ♖b6! and then a5-a6. But not 2 a6? ♖h6! 3 ♖a5 ♚xb3=.

1...♖a2 2 ♚d1 ♚d3 3 ♚e1 ♚e3 4 ♚f1 ♚f3 5 ♖f5+ ♚e4 6 ♖h5 ♚f3 7 ♖h3+ ♚g4 8 ♖c3

Sacrificing a pawn and trying to transpose to a well known endgame, but...

8...♖xa5 9 ♚e2 ♚f4 10 ♚d3 ♚e5 11 b4 ♖a8 12 ♖c5+ ♚d6 13 ♚c4 ♖h8

Not 13...♚d7? 14 b5 ♖c8 15 b6! winning.

14 ♚b5 ♖b8+ 15 ♚a4 ♖a8+ 16 ♚a5 ♖b8 17 ♖a7 ♚c6 18 ♚a5 ♖b5+, draw, ½-½.

172 **Romanishin – Dautov**
Kecskemet 1989

1...♔d4?
Why? – after 1...♖h8! 2 ♔c4 ♖h6
3 ♔d3 ♔f4! Black breaks White's
coordination and makes a draw.
2 ♖e1 ♖b8+ 3 ♔a3?
Correct was 3 ♔a5! with a win.
2...♔e5 4 ♔a4 ♖b7?
A crucial mistake – correct is
4...♖b6! 5 ♔a5 ♖f6! 6 ♔b4 ♔d4 7
♔b5 ♔e5 8 ♔c4 ♖d6 9 ♖e2 ♖a6 10
♔d3 ♖a3+ 11 ♔d2 ♖b3 12 ♖e3
♖b6 13 ♔d3 ♔f4!, and again a
draw.
**5 ♔a5 ♖b8 6 ♔a6 ♖b2 7 ♔a7
♖b5 8 ♖f1 ♔f6 9 ♖c1! ♔e5 10 ♖c4
♖b1 11 ♔a6!**
And now – back!
**11...♖b2 12 ♔a5 ♖b8 13 ♖a4!
♖a8+ 14 ♔b4 ♖b8+ 15 ♔c5 ♖c8+
16 ♔b5 ♖c7 17 ♖c4 ♖d7 18 ♔c6
♖d8 19 ♔c7 ♖d1 20 ♔c8 ♖d6 21
♖a4 ♔f4**
After 21...♖d2 22 ♖a7! ♔xe4 23
f6 White wins.
**22 ♔c7 ♖d1 23 f6 ♔e5 24 ♖a6!
♖d2 25 ♔c8**, and Black resigned

since there is no defence against
f6-f7. **1-0**

173 **Kir.Georgiev – Piket**
Moscow 1994

1 ♖b8
White must transfer the rook to
h5, in order to further advance his
pawns.
**1...♖a5 2 ♖h8 ♔g3 3 ♔e4 ♖b5 4
♖h5 ♖b4+ 5 ♔e5 ♖b5+ 6 ♔d6
♖b6+ 7 ♔c7 ♔g6 8 ♔d7**
Clearly better was 8 g5! ♔f4 9 h4
♔f5 10 ♖h7 etc.
8...♖a6 9 ♖h8?
Again correct is 9 g5.
9...♔f4 10 ♔e7?
He should return to the basic position by 10 ♖h5.
**10...♔g5 11 ♖h5+ ♔g6 12 ♖d5
♖a7+ 13 ♔e6 ♖h7 14 ♖d3 ♔g5 15
♖f3 ♖h6+?**
But here correct is 15...♔g6 16
♔e5 ♔g5 17 ♔e4 ♖e7+, trying to
cut off the king from its pawns.
**16 ♔f7! ♖h7+ 17 ♔g8 ♖h6 18
♔g7 ♖g6+ 19 ♔f7 ♔h4 20 ♖f6!**,
Black resigned, **1-0**

174 Marjanović – Mochalov
Minsk 1982

1...♔g3!

From the theory of such endgames it is well known that the most dangerous pawn for the weaker side is that which is most distant from the king. This means that after the exchange of pawns it is better for Black to retain the g-pawn. Therefore, if 1...g3?, then 2 b7 ♔f3 3 b8=♕ ♖xb8 4 ♖xb8 g2 5 ♖g8 f4 6 ♔d5, draw.

2 ♖g5

If 2 b7, then 2...f4 3 b8=♕ ♖xb8 4 ♖xb8 f3 5 ♔d5 f2 winning.

1...f4 3 ♖b5 ♖h1 4 b7 ♖h8 5 ♔c7

Losing is 5 b8=♕, as already pointed out above.

5...f3! 6 ♖h5 ♖f8 7 ♔f5 ♖g8 8 ♖g5 ♖f8 9 ♖f5 ♖xf5! 10 b8=♕ f2 11 ♔d7+ ♖f4 12 ♕b3+ ♖f3 13 ♕b8+ ♔g2 14 ♕b2 ♔h1 15 ♕h8+ ♔g1 16 ♕d4 g3 17 ♔e7 g2 18 ♔e6

♖h3 19 ♔d5 ♔h1, White resigned,
0-1

175 Anand – Shirov
Teheran 2000

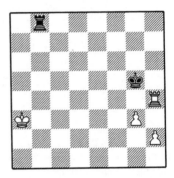

White needs to come to the help of his cut-off king.

1 ♖b4 ♖h8 2 h4+ ♔h5 3 ♖b5+ ♔h6 4 g4 ♖e8 5 ♖b4 ♔g6?

According to an analysis by Shipov, correct is 5...♖e3+ 6 ♔a4 ♖h3 7 g5+ ♔h5 8 ♔b5 ♖e3 9 ♔c5 ♖e8 10 ♖d4 ♖e7 11 ♔d6 ♖e1 12 ♔d5 ♖e8 13 ♖e4 ♖d8+ 14 ♔e5 ♖e8+ 15 ♔f5 ♖f8+ 16 ♔e6 ♖e8+, and the white king cannot get to the critical f7 square.

6 ♖b6+ ♔f7 7 ♖b7+ ♔e6 8 ♖h7 ♖b8?

Chances of a draw are still retained after 8...♔f6.

9 g5 ♔f5 10 ♖h6 ♔e5 11 h5 ♔f5 12 g6 ♔f6 13 ♖h7 ♖g8 14 ♔b3,
Black resigned, **1-0**

176 Sveshnikov – Sermek
Nova Gorica 1998

The position is very simple and winning is 1...♖c4 2 ♖a5 ♔g6 and 3...f5, but there followed **1...♔g6?? 2 ♖g5+!! ♔xg5**, stalemate!

In the majority of cases the main chances of the weaker side lie in the blockade of the further advance of the opponent's pawns.

177 Glek – Leitao
Wijk aan Zee 1999

Black decides to go passive with his rook in order to defend his pawns.

a) 1...♖c1+? 2 ♔g2 ♖c2+ 3 ♔g1 ♖h2 4 ♖b6 ♔f7 5 ♖h6 ♔e7 6 ♖g6 ♔f8 7 ♖f6+ ♔e8 8 ♖e6+ ♔d7 9 ♖h6 h3 10 ♖g6, ½-½ (game); but correct is:

b) **1...h3! 2 ♖g4+ ♖g6 3 ♖a4 h2+ 4 ♔g2 ♖h6 5 ♖g4+ ♔f6 6 ♔h1 ♖g6** winning.

178 Radziewiecz – Vasilevich
Warsaw 2001

1 ♖a3?
Going passive, correct is 1 e5 a3 2 e6+ ♔e7 3 ♖g7+ ♔d6 4 ♖d7+ ♔c5 5 ♖d1, and the black king is cut off.
1...♔f6 2 ♖a1 a3 3 ♖a2 ♖a4, draw, ½-½

With far advanced connected pawns in rook endgames there is a defensive resource – the stalemate position of the king.

179 Kramnik – Speelman
Geneva 1996

1...♖a2+ 2 ♔h1 ♖g2 3 ♖b7+ ♔g6 4 ♖g7+!, and a typical 'raging' rook!

180 Lasker – Janowsky
Manchester 1901

1...♖xh4 2 ♖b3 – draw.
A similar idea was also encountered in the game Mikhalchishin-Karpman.

181 Malakhov – Kveinis
Delhi 2000

It seems like a draw but Black has a terrible trick associated with the transposition to a pawn endgame.
1 ♖f6!! ♖b7 2 ♔f4
He cannot leave the f-file because of the rook check.
2...♖b8 3 ♔f5 ♖b7 4 ♔g6!, and the king gets past the rook from the bottom of the board, Black resigned, **1-0**

In the following position 1 ♔g3! holds the draw, and in this well known blockading position Black

has no chances of a win. But Gufeld calculated the variation badly:

182 Gufeld – Gulko
Volgograd 1985

1 ♔xh5? g3 2 ♖a1 g2 3 ♖g1 ♔f6 4 ♔h4 ♔f5 5 ♔h3 ♔f4
He cannot capture the pawn because of mate, while there is no defence against 6...♔f4-f3 and a rook check from h7. **0-1**

Typical endgames where both sides have passed pawns

Where both sides have passed pawns on different flanks, the primary concern is the further advance of the passed pawn and the coordination of the king and rook to support this passed pawn.

183 Speelman – De Firmian
Moscow 1990

White needs to start advancing his pawns, but how? If e4 and ♔f3-e3, then ...g6-g5 looks somewhat inconvenient, therefore...

1 h4 b5

It seems very logical to take prophylactic measures: 1...h5 2 ♔f3 b5 3 e4 b4 4 ♔e3 b3 5 f3 ♖b1 6 ♔f4 b2 7 e5 ♔f8 8 e6 ♔g8 9 ♔g5 ♖g1 10 ♖xb2 ♖xg3+ 11 ♔f4 ♖h3 12 ♖b7! ♖xh4+ 13 ♔g5 ♖a4 14 f4! and then 15 f5!, utilising the black pawn to defend his own king.

2 g4 b4 3 ♔g3 b3 4 g5 hxg5

Speelman was rather more worried by 4...h5, followed by an attack on the h4 pawn, though even then White ought to win.

5 hxg5 ♔f8

If 5...♖b1, then 6 ♔f4 b2 7 e4 ♔h8 8 ♔e5 ♖g1 9 ♖xb2 ♖xg5+ 10 ♔f6 with a clear victory.

6 f4! ♔e8

After 6...♖b1 7 ♔f3 b2 8 ♔e4! the white king is covered from the checks and breaks through to f6.

7 ♔f3 ♔d8 8 ♔e4 ♔c8 9 ♖b4 ♔c7 10 ♔e5 Black resigned, **1-0**

184 **Romanishin – Polugaevsky**
USSR championship 1974

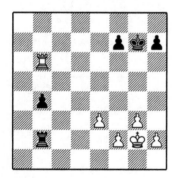

1 e4

White must create a passed pawn.

1...b3 2 ♔f3 ♖b1 3 h4 b2 4 ♔f4 h6 5 ♔f5!

Besides the extra pawn White has an active king which also points to a decisive advantage.

4...♔f8 6 ♔f6 ♔e8 7 e5 h5 8 ♖b7, Black resigned.

But very often it happens that one passed pawn fights on even terms with two passed pawns of the opponent.

One camel runs quicker than two

This Eastern proverb surprisingly applies to rook endgames with pawns on different flanks where one pawn is obviously more important than the two.

185 **Karpov – Miles**
Biel 1990

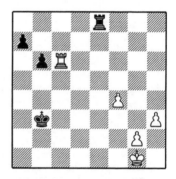

In the game there followed:

a) **1...♖f8?**

Reckoning only on material factors, but Karpov shows that the passed pawn is more important than material.

2 g4! ♖xf4 3 g5 b5 4 g6 ♖f8 5 g7 ♖g8 6 ♖c7 a5 7 h4 a4 8 h5 a3 9 h6 a2 10 ♖a7, and Black resigned, since there is no defence against ♔g1-f2, h6-h7, **1-0**

Correct was the advance of his passed pawn.

b) **1...b5! 2 ♖a6 ♖a8 3 f5 ♔c4 4 f6 b4 5 f7 b3 6 ♖xa7 ♖xa7! 7 f8=♕ ♖a1+ 8 ♔h2 b2,** with a draw – and the variation could be calculated.

186 J.Polgar – Short
Novgorod 1998

1...♔f4 2 ♖xa5 g5 3 ♖a7 g4!

One against three!

4 a5 ♖g8! 5 ♔d2 g3 6 ♖f7+ ♔e4 7 ♖f1 g2 8 ♖g1 ♔f3

It is clear that he should go forward, and not backward – when 8...♔d5? 9 ♔e3 wins.

9 b4 ♔f2 10 ♖xg2+ ♔xg2 11 b5

Inferior is 11 a6? ♖b8 12 c3 ♖b6 or 11 ♔e3 ♖c8 12 a6 ♖xc2 13 b5 ♖a2, with a draw.

11...♔f3 12 ♔d3 ♔f4?

Here Black does not keep his nerve, whereas after 12...♖d8+! 13 ♔c4 ♔e4 14 b6 ♖c8+ 15 ♔b5 ♖xc2 16 b7 (or 16 a6 ♔d5 17 a7 ♖b2+ 18 ♔a6 ♖a2+ 19 ♔b7 ♔c5=) 16...♔d5! 17 ♔b6 ♖b2+ 18 ♔c7 ♖c2+ 19 ♔d7 ♖b2 20 a6 ♖b6 21 ♔c7 ♖c6+ 22 ♔d8 ♖d6+ 23 ♔e8 ♖e6+ 24 ♔f8 ♖f6+ 25 ♔g7 ♖b6!=.

13 ♔d4! ♔f5 14 ♔d5 ♖d8+ 15 ♔c6 ♔e6 16 a6 ♖d6+ 17 ♔b7

♖d7+ 18 ♔b6 ♖d6+ 19 ♔a5 ♖d7 20 c4 ♔e7 21 b6, and Black resigned, **1-0**

187 Pinski – Ilyshyn
Erevan 2000

1...e4?

Simpler and correct in principle in such cases is to go with the king in front of one of the pawns: 1...♔e4!, and then to advance the other pawn and, with checks, drive the white king to the first rank.

2 a6 d4?

Again it was necessary to move the king in front of the pawn, this time by 2...♔e5-d4.

3 ♖f7+ ♔e5 4 ♖e7+ ♔d5?

Now his king had to go round to the kingside.

5 ♖d7+ ♔c5

Again not here – it was still possible to go back.

6 a7 ♖a2+ 7 ♔c1 d3

After 7...♔c4 8 ♔b1 ♖a6 9 ♔c2 e3 10 ♖c7+ ♔d5 11 ♖e7 there is nothing for him.

8 ♔b1 ♖a6 9 ♔c1 ♖a5 10 ♔d2 ♖a2+ 11 ♔e3 ♔c6 12 ♖d8!, and a draw, **½-½**

188 Serper – Shabalov
Philadelphia 1997

1 Rb3!

Bad is 1 Kg3? Rh6! 2 b6 Rh3+ 3 Kf2 Rh2+ 4 Ke3 Re2+ 5 Kd3 g3 6 b7 Re8 7 b8=W Rxb8 8 Rxb8 g2 9 Rg8+ Kf4 winning.

1...Kh4

Now on 1...Rh6 there is 2 b6 Rh2+ 3 Kf1!, holding the position.

2 Rb1 Re6 3 Rh1+

Again bad is 3 b6 Re2+ 4 Kg1 g3 5 b7 Rg2+ 6 Kh1 Rh2+ with a decisive advantage.

3...Kg5 4 Kg3! Re2 5 Rh2! Re6 6 b6 Re1 7 Kf2 Rb1 8 Kg3 Rxb6 9 Rb2! Rf6

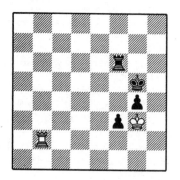

A well known drawn position has arisen, and it was necessary simply to play 10 Rb5+! Rf5 11 Rb1 with an inevitable draw. But White was too lazy to give check.

10 Rb1? Kf5!

This is the point. On 11 Rb5+ the king advances: 11...Ke4 12 Rb4+ Kd3 13 Rb3+ Kc2 14 Ra3 Kb2! 15 Rd3 Kc1! with a win.

11 Ra1 Re6! 12 Ra4 Re4 13 Ra5+ Kf6 14 Ra1 Ke5 15 Ra5+ Kd4 16 Ra4+ Kd3 17 Ra3+ Ke2 18 Ra2+ Kf1 19 Ra1+ Re1 20 Ra2 Kg1 21 Rf2 Re2, and White resigned, **0-1**

189 Fontaine – Fressinet
France 2000

a) 1 Kf6? (game) 1...a5 2 bxa5 bxa5 3 g5 a4 4 g6 a3 5 g7 a2 6 g8=W a1=W 7 Kg6 Wg1+ 8 Rg4 Wb1+ etc., draw, ½-½

b) **1 Kh6!** with a win.

190 Larsen – Portisch
Amsterdam 1977

1...Rc8?

Over-finessing, not allowing the white rook use of the eighth rank. After the simple 1...♔f4 2 Ra8 g4 3 a5 g3 4 a6 Rc1! 5 Rf8+ ♔e4 6 Rg8 Ra1+ 7 ♔b2 Rxa6 8 Rxg3 ♔d5 9 ♔c3 Ra8! the game transposes into the well known Grigoriev position.

2 Rd5 ♔f4 3 a5 g4 4 Rd1 g3 5 b4 g2 6 b5 ♔e5

Going to f2 is senseless.

7 b6 Rd8 8 b7! Rxd1 9 b8=♕+ ♔e4 10 ♕e8+! ♔f3 11 ♕h5+, Black resigned, **1-0**

191 **Portisch – Matanović**
Monte Carlo 1967

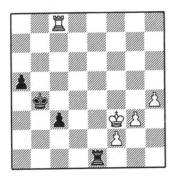

Black played the primitive 1...a4? and after 2 Rb8+ ♔c4 3 Rc8+ ♔b3 4 Rb8+ ♔a2 5 Rc8 ♔b2 6 Rb8+ ♔c1 7 Ra8 a draw was agreed, ½-½

However, despite being a pawn down, Black's position is winning thanks to his more advanced pawns, but the right technique is to use the rook to defend against checks. **1...Re5! 2 g4 a4 3 h5 a3 4 h6 Re7! 5 Rb8+ ♔c4 6 Rc8+ ♔b3 7 Rb8+ ♔a2 8 Rc8 ♔b2 9 Rb8+ ♔c1 10 Ra8 c2 11 Rxa3 ♔b2** and Black wins.

192 **Matanović – Velimirović**
Skopje 1976

1 Rc8!

Incorrect is 1 b7? Rh7 – a typical mistake.

1...Rh7 2 Rc7 Rh8 3 b7 Rb8 4 ♔d2!

The black rook is passive, and so the king goes into the battle against the enemy pawns.

4...♔f3 5 ♔e1 e4 6 Rh7 e3 7 Rh3+ ♔e4 8 Rh7 Rd8 9 Rh4!!

The only correct way – after 9 Rh6? Rg8 10 ♔f1 f3 11 Re6+ ♔d4 12 Rd6+ ♔e5 13 Rb6 Rb8 Black wins.

9...Rg8 10 ♔f1 ♔d3 11 Rh7 ♔e4 12 Rg7 Rh8 13 Rh7 Rb8 14 ♔e1, draw, ½-½

193 **Kramnik – Krasenkov**
Moscow 1991

1 ⌖xh6?

By leaving out the prophylactic ideas, White would have found the right way: 1 g4! ♖a3 2 ♖h1!.

1...♖a3! 2 ♖g1

Bad is 2 h4 ♖g3, and 2 ⌖h5 c4 3 ⌖g4 c3 4 h4 ♖a2 5 g3 c2 6 ♖c1 ⌖d6! 7 ⌖f5 ⌖e7 8 ⌖g6 ♖a4 leads immediately to defeat.

2...⌖d5?

Correct was to advance the pawn: 2...c4! 3 ⌖g5 c3 4 ♖c1 ⌖d5 5 h4 ⌖d4 6 h5 ⌖d3 7 g4 ⌖d2 8 ♖f1 c2 9 ♖f2+ ⌖d3 10 ♖xc2 ⌖xc2 11 h6 ⌖d3 12 h7 ♖a8 13 ⌖f6 ⌖e4 14 g5 ♖a6+!, with a draw.

3 ⌖g5 ⌖e4 4 ♖e1+?

After 4 h4! c4 5 h5 c3 6 g4 and Black is a tempo down on the previous variation.

4...♖e3! 5 ♖c1 ♖g3+ 6 ⌖f6 ♖xg2 7 ♖xc5 ♖h2, and a draw, ½-½

194 Murey – Beliavsky
Graz 1997

1 ⌖d5!

Not hurrying with the advance of the pawn and not allowing the rook to b4.

1...♖h1 2 b5 ♖b1 3 b6 h4 4 b7 h3 5 ⌖c6 ⌖g4 6 ♖h8 g5 7 b8=♕ ♖xb8 8 ♖xb8 h2 9 ♖h8 ⌖g3 10 ⌖d5 g4 11 ⌖e4 ⌖g2 12 ⌖f4, draw, ½-½

195 Urban – Gdanski
Plock 2000

1 ⌖f2?

Correct is 1 ⌖g2 a4 2 h4, trying to get his pawns going, and White has sufficiently good chances of a draw.

1...a4 2 ⌖e3 ⌖c6 3 ⌖d3 b5 4 ♖f4

The pawn endgame is lost but now it is also doubtful whether 4 ♖f3 followed by h2-h4 would be any help.

4...♖xf4 5 gxf4 ⌖d5 6 h4 b4 7 h5 a3 8 ⌖c2 ⌖c4!

Only this!

9 h6 b3+ 10 ⌖b1 ⌖c3 11 h7 a2+ 12 ⌖a1 b2+ 13 ⌖xa2 ⌖c2, White resigned, **0-1**

196 Blehm – Krasenkov
Warsaw 2001

1 ⌖d3?

There is no need for this move – correct is 1 c4 ♔e6 2 ♖d5!, planning 3 ♔c3, ♖a5, when the rook has three(!) functions – defence of a2, attack on a7 and cutting off the king along the rank.

1...♔e6 2 ♖e2+ ♔f6 3 c4 ♖d7+ 4 ♔e3

Now going to c3 makes no particular sense – the f4 pawn in conjunction with the king would be very fast.

4...♖h7 5 b3 ♖e7+ 6 ♔f3 ♖d7 7 c5 ♖d3+ 8 ♔f4 ♖c3 9 ♖e5 ♖c2 10 ♖xf5+ ♔e6 11 ♖e5+ ♔d7 12 a4?

The decisive mistake, correct was 12 a3 ♖c3 13 b4 ♖xa3 14 b5, trying to run with the pawn.

12...♖b2 13 ♖e3 ♔c6 14 ♖c3 a5 15 ♔e3 ♖h2 16 ♔d4 ♖h4+ 17 ♔d3 ♖h3+ 18 ♔c2 ♖xc3+ 19 ♔xc3 ♔xc5, and the pawn ending is drawn.

197 **Smyslov-Rashkovsky**
Moscow 1973

1 f3
Preventing the king from going to e4.

1...♖f1!
Not giving the king the f2 square.
2 ♔f4 ♖e1!
Cutting off the king from the pawn, after which a draw is inevitable.

3 g4 d3 4 ♖d8+ ♔c4 5 g5 ♖g1 6 ♔e4 ♖e1+ 7 ♔f5 ♔c3 8 g6 ♖g1 9 ♖c8+ ♔d4 10 ♔f6 ♔e3 11 ♖d8 ♖f1, draw, ½-½

198 **Svidler – Vyzhmanavin**
St.Petersburg 1991

1...♖g2!
Cutting off the king is half the job.
2 a4 ♔c6 3 ♔c1
If 3 b4, then 3...♖g4 4 ♖b5 ♖c4, followed by the advance of the g pawn.
3...♔d6 4 a5 g4 5 ♖g5 g3 6 b4 ♔c7 7 ♖g6
If 7 b5 then 7...♖a2 and 8...g2.
7...♔b8 8 ♔b1 ♖f2! 9 ♖xg3 ♖f4 10 ♖b3 ♔b7 11 b5 ♖a4 12 a6+ ♔b6, and a drawn blockaded position is reached.

Classical rook endgames with the f and h pawns – Grandmaster practice of recent years

After the classic analysis in this direction made in the 40s by Botvinnik, everything seemed clear. But practice of recent years has shown that these lessons, even at the highest level, have not been learned very well. Grandmasters do not know the most important method of defence in these endgames – which pawn to hold with the king: the more or the less advanced ones. And likewise when to cut off the opponent's king along the rank, and when to push the rook to the first (eighth) rank.

199 **Van der Doel – Dizdarević**
Elista 1998

The plan of defence for Black in these positions runs as follows – the king holds the advanced pawn, while the rook should stand on a1 or b1, in order to retain the possibility of check along the rank or file. The first part the grandmaster has handled well, but the second...

Here he should play: **1...♖b1 2 ♔g5 ♖g1+ 3 ♔f6 ♖f1 4 ♖d8 ♖a1** according to an old analysis by Maiselis; but Black played:

1...♖a5?? 2 ♔g5 ♖a7 3 ♖e6 ♖b7 4 ♖e5! Preparing f5-f6. **4...♔g8 5 f6 ♖b1 6 ♖e8+ ♔h7 7 f7, 1-0**

200 **Timman – Short**
Match, 1993

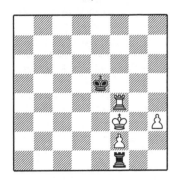

1 ♔g2?

Clever, but bad. Correct is 1 ♖f8 ♖g1 (defending against 2 ♔g4) 2 h4 ♔e6 3 h5! ♖g5 (if 3...♔e7, then 4 ♖f4 ♖g5 5 ♖h4 ♔f7 6 h6 ♖g8 7 h7 ♖h8 8 ♔g4 ♔g6 9 f4 etc) 4 h6 ♖h5 5 ♖a8! ♔f6 (5...♔f7 6 h7!) 6 ♔g4! ♖g5+ 7 ♔h4 ♖g1 8 ♖a3 ♖g8 9 ♔h5 with a theoretically winning position – Averbach.

1...♖a1 2 ♖f8 ♔e6 3 h4 ♔e7 4 ♖f4 ♖a8 5 ♔h3 ♖h8 6 ♔g4 ♖g8+

7 ♔h5

After 7 ♔f5 ♔f7! 8 ♖a4 ♖f8! 10 f4 ♔e7! 11 ♔e5 (or 11 ♔g6 ♖g8+

12 ♔h7 ♖g4! 13 h5 ♔f7, draw)
11...♔f7 12 f5 ♖e8+ 13 ♔f4 ♖e1 14
♔g5 ♖g1+ 15 ♖g4 ♖a1 16 h5 ♔g7,
and this is a well known drawn
position where on each check with a
pawn the king must go "under" this
pawn – this is rule number one.

7...♔e6 8 ♔h6

Yet another try, 8 f3 ♔e5 9 ♖g4
♖f8 10 ♖e4+ ♔d5 11 ♖e1 ♖xf3 12
♔g4 ♖f2 13 h5 ♖h2 14 ♔g5 ♖g2+
15 ♔f6 ♖f2+ 16 ♔g7 ♖g2+ 17 ♔h7
♔d6 18 ♖e8 ♖h2 19 h6 ♔d7 20
♖g8 ♔e7, leads to a well known
theoretical draw.

8...♔e5 9 ♖a4

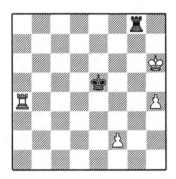

9...♖g2?

A decisive mistake – there is a
draw after 9...♔f6! 10 ♖a6+ (or 10
♖f4+ ♔e5 11 ♖f7 ♔e6 12 ♖f3
♖h8+ 13 ♔g5 ♖g8+, and the king
must go to h3) 10...♔f7 11 ♖a3
♖h8+ 12 ♔g5 ♖g8+ 13 ♔f5 ♖f8!
14 f4 ♔e7+! 15 ♔e5 ♔f7 16 f5
♖e8+ 17 ♔f4 ♖e1!.

10 f3 ♖g3 11 ♖e4+ ♔f5 12 ♖e8!

This is the decisive manoeuvre.

12...♖g6+ 13 ♔h7 ♖f6 14 ♖e7!

Zugzwang – on 14...♖f8 or
14...♔f4 follows 15 ♔g7.

14...♖a6 15 ♖f7+ ♔e6 16 ♔g7
♖a1 17 ♖f6+ with a theoretically
winning position, therefore **Black
resigned.**

As a very rare exception, a higher
standard of technique is shown by a
woman...

201 Zs.Polgar – Ioseliani
Monaco 1993

1...f5 2 ♖g7+ ♔f4 3 ♖a7 ♖d3

Keeping the rook on the g-file
also does not help Black.

4 ♖a4+ ♔g5 5 ♔g2 f4 6 ♖a8 ♖d6

On each check with a pawn the
king will go 'under' this pawn.

7 ♖g8+ ♖g6 8 ♖a8 ♔g4 9 ♖a7
♖e6 10 ♖g7+ ♔f5 11 ♖a7 ♖e3 12
♖a8 ♖g3+ 13 ♔f2 ♖d3 14 ♔g2 h3+

At last Black decides which pawn
to advance.

15 ♔h2 ♔g4 16 ♖g8+ ♔f3 17
♖a8!

After 17...♔xh3 there would still
be some difficulties, but the move in
the game is simplest.

17...♖e2 18 ♖a2+ ♔e1 19 ♖a1+
♖d1 20 ♖a3 ♔e2 21 ♖a2+ ♔f3

On 21...♖d2 there is 22 ♖a1! f3
23 ♔xh3 f2 24 ♔g2, with a draw.

22 ♖a8 ♖e1 23 ♖a7 ♖e3 24 ♖f7
♔e4 25 ♖a7 ♔d3 26 ♖a4 ♖f3 27
♖a3+ ♔e4 28 ♖a4+ ♔f5 29 ♖a8
♖d3 30 ♖a7 ♔g4

and Black achieves nothing, twist-
ing and turning with the king, and
five moves later a draw was agreed
½-½

202 Rychagov – Nielsen
Asker 1997

White is two pawns down but the c7 pawn compensates for the deficit with the simple 1 Rc5 f5 2 a3 Kg5 3 Rc4 making a draw. But in the game followed:

1 Kg3 Kf5 2 a3 Ke6 3 Rc4?
Stronger is 3 Kf4 Kd6 4 Rc4.
3...Kd5 4 Rxa4 Rxc7 5 Ra5+?
Obviously stronger is 5 Rh4!
5...Ke4 6 Rxh5 f5 7 a4?
Better is 7 Rh4+ Ke3 8 Rb4 Rg7+ 9 Kh3 f4 10 Rb3+, trying afterwards to attack the f4 pawn.
7...f4+ 8 Kf2 Rc2+ 9 Kg1 Ke3 10 Re5+ Kf3 11 Rb5 Ra2 12 a5 h6! 13 Rb3+ Kg4 14 Rb6 Kg3 15 Rg6+ Kf3 16 Rxh6 Ra1+ 17 Kh2 Rxa5

18 Rf6?
Why not 18 Rb6 at once?

18...Rg5 19 Ra6 Rg2+ 20 Kh1 Re2 21 Ra1 Re3 22 Kg1
But this transposes to a lost position – after 22 Ra2! Kg3 23 Rg2+ – it's an easy draw.
22...Kg3 23 Kf1 Rb3!
Now the white rook cannot break through to the first rank.
24 Kg1 f3 25 Rc1 Rb2, and White resigned, **0-1**

203 Arlandi – Palac
Pula 1991

There followed 1...f2+? 2 Kf1 h3 3 Ra3+ Kh2 4 Rf3, with a draw, ½-½

Winning is **1...h3! 2 Ra2 Re4 3 Rg2+ Kf4**, and there are no chances of salvation.

204 Jurković – Arhangelsky
Belgorod 1991

There followed:

1 ♔g1?

Cutting off his own king can never be right – correct is 1 ♔h3 with chances of a draw.

1...♔g4 2 ♖f8 f4 3 ♖c8 ♔g3 4 ♖g8+ ♔f3 5 ♖b8 ♖a1+ 6 ♔h2 ♖e1!, and White resigned, since there is no defence against ♔f2 and the advance of the f4 pawn. **0-1**

However, strong chessplayers do not always make mistakes and we should also study their high technique of defence,

205 Karpov – Bareev
Tilburg 1991

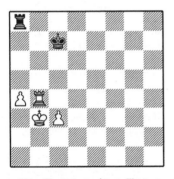

1 ♖f4 ♖a5!? 2 ♔b4 ♖h5 3 a5 ♔b7 4 c4 ♖g5 5 c5 ♖g1!

The correct reaction – with the pawn on the fifth rank the rook must go behind.

6 ♔c4!?

The more typical 6 ♖f7+ ♔a6 7 ♖f6+ ♔b7 we have already seen in the game Polgar-Ioseliani.

There is yet another problem in the defence of such positions.

One should know the last line of defence and not miss the possibility of consolidating it. In our case this means sometimes giving up the obstructing pawn.

206 Kramnik – Beliavsky
Groningen 1993

Correct was the natural 1 ♖b8, activating the rook since the rook endgame with f and h pawns is drawn. But White decides to defend the pawn and, if the opportunity arises, to obtain counetrplay with the help of the a-pawn. But this proves to be a decisive mistake.

1 ♖a1? ♖g3+ 2 ♔f2 ♔g4 3 ♖b1

Here he had to go back as counterplay with 3 a4 did not work because of 3...h3 4 a5 ♖g2+ 5 ♔f1 f4 6 a6 f3 7 a7 h2, and it's time to resign.

3...h3 4 ♖b8 ♖g2+ 5 ♔f1 ♖d2

Quite possible is 5...♖a2, but Black wants to exploit the rook to cover against checks from the side, while he simply pays no attention to the a-pawn.

6 ♔g1 f4 7 ♖g8+ ♔f3 8 ♖h8 ♖d1+! 9 ♔h2 ♔f2

Black wants simply to advance and queen the f-pawn. If now 10 ♖xh3, then 10...f3 11 ♖h8 ♖d3! 13 f4 ♔e2 14 ♖f8 ♖e3! 15 a5 ♖e7! 16 a6 f2 winning.

10 a4 f3 11 a5 ♔f1 12 a6 ♖a1 13 ♖a8

After 13 ♔xh3 f2 14 ♖g8 ♖xa6 15 ♔g3 ♖f6! the win is straightforward.

13...f2 14 a7 ♖a6!

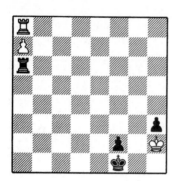

The right idea. Now on 15 ♔xh3 ♔g1 16 ♖g8+ ♔h1 17 ♖f8 ♖a3+ 18 ♔h4 ♔g2! is reached a position from a classic study by Lasker, where Black wins by driving the white king to the seventh rank, while on 15 ♖b8 would follow 15... ♖xa7 16 ♖b1+ ♔e2 17 ♖b2+ ♔e3 18 ♖b8 ♔e4 19 ♖b4+ ♔e5 20 ♖b5+ ♔e6 21 ♖b6+ ♔e7 22 ♖b1 ♖a3! 23 ♖f1 ♖f3 and a king approach.

15 ♔h1 h2!

16 ♖b8

16 ♔xh2 ♖h6+ 17 ♔g3 ♔g1 18 ♖f8 ♖g6+ 19 ♔h4 ♖a6 again goes into Lasker's study.

16...♖xa7 17 ♖b1+ ♔e2 18 ♖b2+ ♔e3 19 ♖b3+ ♔e4 20 ♖b4+ ♔d3 21 ♖b1 ♖f7

Also good is 21...♖e7 with the idea of 22...♖e1.

22 ♖f1 ♔e2 23 ♖xf2+ ♔xf2 White resigned, **0-1**

207 Pedersen – Pelletier
Panormo 2001

White could not imagine that the game would end in a draw just two moves later.

1 h7?? ♖xh7 2 ♖b5 ♖g7+! stalemate.

But winning is **1 f7+ ♔f8 2 h7** with the idea of ♖h5.

Complicated rook endgames - Defence

Defence in rook endgames by exploiting the stalemate idea is a long known motive, but the strongest players in the world handle this method poorly and quite frequently neither see nor exploit it.

208 Bernstein – Smyslov
Groningen 1946

Instead of the simple 1...♖e3+, Smyslov played here **1...b2??** and after **2 ♖xb2! ♖h2+ 3 ♔f3 ♖xb2** – stalemate!

209 **Shirov – Morozevich**
Astana 2001

And here Morozevich simply did not know this familiar theme. To known positions leads 1...♖xh5! 2 ♖a5+ ♔b4 3 ♖xh5 – stalemate. But the number four chessplayer in the world was apparently unaware of the stalemate idea! He played:

1...♔b4?? 2 ♖b6+ ♔c5 3 ♖xh6 ♔b4 4 ♔c2! ♖c3+ 5 ♔d2 ♖h3 6 ♖h8! ♔c5

He cannot take on b3 because of the simple advance of the h4 pawn.

7 ♔c1 ♔b5 8 ♔d2

Incomprehensible manoeuvring. Shirov also does not know how to win. It is unclear why Morozevich did not repeat moves.

8...♔c6 9 h6 ♔b7 10 b4 ♔a7 11 ♔e2 ♖h4 12 ♔f3 ♖xb4 13 ♖g8! ♖h4 14 ♖g6!

Now the king proceeds to g7 with a win.

210 **Shurygin – Malaniuk**
Koszalin 2001

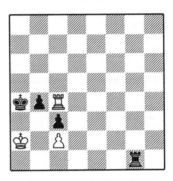

1...♖h1 2 ♖xc3!, with a draw.

211 **Gretarsson – Bjornsson**
Iceland 1992

The right defensive procedure in such positions is to attack the pawn from 'behind' and transfer the king to the short side. But...

1...♖d1+? 2 ♔c6 ♖d8?

It was still necessary to transpose quickly to a theoretical position by 2...♔b8.

3 ♖xf4 ♔b8 4 ♖f6?

And why this? Correct is 4 ♔b6 and 5 c6 with a winning theoretical position.

4...♖g8?

It was necessary to go quickly to the first rank: 4...♖d1.

5 ♖h6?

All the same.

5...♖f8? 6 ♔b6!

At last!

6...♖g8 7 c6 ♔c8 8 ♖h7, Black resigned, **1-0**

As already repeatedly mentioned earlier, when defending a slightly worse position it is important to observe the following elements:

a) to have a plan even if it is a minimal improvement of one's position;

b) to produce a last line of defence;

c) to refrain from a needless weakening of one's position.

212 **Van Wely – Van der Wiel**
Leeuwarden 2001

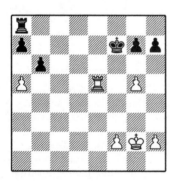

In such situations it is best to take up the last line of defence, but God forbid to play for a win. Despite the passed pawn, a more important argument for Black is the active position of the rook and so the correct move was 1...♖e8!. But in the game there followed:

1...bxa5? 2 ♖xa5 ♔e6 3 h4 a6 4 h5 ♖a7 5 ♔g3 ♔d6?

Why this? He should leave the king near his pawns.

6 f4 g6 7 ♔g4 ♔c6??

A decisive mistake. It was necessary for Black to go back by 7...♔e6. However, instead of this logical assessment, Black decides to count on a variation – which in an endgame is dangerous.

8 f5 gxf5+ 9 ♔xf5 ♔b6 10 ♖e5!

And here is the hole in the calculation – Black reckoned on 10 ♖a1 a5 with a draw.

10...a5 11 g6 hxg6 12 hxg6 a4 13 ♔f6 a3 14 g7 ♖a8 15 ♖h5! ♖c8

Or 15...a2 16 ♖h1 ♔b5 17 ♖a1 ♔b4 18 ♖xa2, and White wins.

16 ♖h3 a2 17 ♖a3 ♖c6+ 18 ♔f5 ♖c5+ 19 ♔g6 ♖a5 20 ♖xa5 ♔xa5 21 g8=♕, Black resigned, **1-0**

213 **S.Garcia – Tseshkovsky**
Cienfuegos 1981

There are numerous positions in which one should part with material to activate one's pieces, in the present case the rook. Bearing in mind the above statement, necessary was 1 ♖b7! ♖xa2 2 ♖b4 ♖a1+ 3 ♔h2 ♖f1 4 ♖b2 e3 5 fxe3+ ♔xe3 6 ♖b3+, and there arises a well-known drawn position. However in the game followed:

1 ♖c2? ♖g8+ 2 ♔f1 ♖b8 3 ♔g1?
And now better was 3 ♖c1 and then to give up the a2 pawn.

3...♖b1+ 4 ♔h2 e3! 5 fxe3+ ♔xe3 6 ♖c3+ ♔e2 7 ♖c2+ ♔d3,
and White lost due to the fact that he has not given up the a2 pawn – when after 8 ♖a2 it would be a draw!

One of the authors was an eye-witness to this game. Black pawns were still standing on g6 and f5, and a white one on g3 – and Garcia could immediately have given up the a2 pawn with a draw, but he fought on with it to the end...

214 Polovodin – Hugoni
Italy 1990

The main task of the white king is to get past the rook to the a pawn.

1 ♔e3 ♖d1 2 ♔e4 ♖d2 3 ♔e5 ♖d1
The black rook cannot abandon the central d-file.

4 ♔e6 ♖d4 5 ♔e7 ♖d1 6 a4!

After White has improved the position of his king to the maximum, the time has come to make a move with the pawn.

6...♖a1 7 ♖g4 ♖d1
The main variation consists of the continuation 7...♔f5(h5) 8 g6!! ♔xg4 9 g7 ♖e1+.

If 10 ♔f7 ♖f1+ 11 ♔g6?! ♔f4!! and in a surprising way Black saves himself – just in time the king gets into the square of the a4 pawn. Let's say, 12 a5 ♔e5! 13 a6 ♖g1+ 14 ♔f7 ♖f1+ 15 ♔e8 ♖g1 with a draw.

However the advance of the king to the other side wins: 10 ♔d7! ♖d1+ 11 ♔c7 ♖c1+ 12 ♔b7 ♖b1+ 13 ♔a7!, and the g7 pawn surprisingly promotes to a queen.

However in the game there followed:

8 ♖b4! ♔xg5 9 a5 ♖a1 10 ♖b5+ ♔g6 11 ♖b6+! ♔f5 12 a6 ♔e5 13 ♔d7 ♔d5 14 ♔c7 ♖h1 15 a7 ♖h7+ 16 ♔b8 ♖h8+ 17 ♔b7 ♔c5 18 ♖c6+ ♔b5 19 ♖c7, and Black stopped the clocks **1-0**

215 Planinc – Polugaevsky
Mar del Plata 1972

Black finds a study-like way to achieve victory.

1...♔c1!

Upon other continuations (1...♔b3 2 ♖d3+ or 1...♔b1 2 ♖d1+) White manages to defend himself.

2 ♖g2

Bad is 2 ♔d3? because of 2...♖b3+!.

2...♖b2!!

The strongest move, after which Black manages to tip the balance in his favour.. Weaker is 2...a3 3 ♔d3! ♖b3 4 ♔c4.

3 ♖g1+ ♔c2 4 ♖g2+ ♔c3 5 ♖g8 ♖b5!

Polugaevsky considered this to be the only reply.

However in the game Tiulin-Polovodin, Jaroslavl 1975, it became clear that also winning is the equally worthy continuation 5...♖b6! after which the covering of the sixth rank is decisive.

6 ♖c8+ ♔b2 7 ♔d2 ♖d5+! 8 ♔e3 a3 9 ♖b8+ ♔c3 10 ♖c8+ ♔b4 with victory.

216 Lputian – Polovodin
Riga 1980

How to neutralise White's advantage? The unpleasant continuation d5-d6 is threatened. However **1...♖f6!** allows him to construct an impregnable fortress. The rook on e5 is trapped in a cage and cannot escape. For example **2 ♖e7+ ♖f7 3 ♖e8 ♖f8 4 ♖e6 ♖f6 5 ♖e5 ♔f7**, with an inevitable draw. The white king cannot move across the f-file, while the g5 and h5 squares are likewise out of bounds.

217 Mikhalchishin – Kozul
Maribor 2000

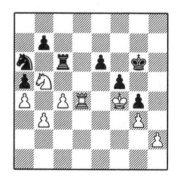

Here there are two possibilities to exchange rooks.

a) 1 ♖d6? ♚f6! 2 ♖xc6 bxc6 3 ♘a7 e5 4 ♚e3 ♘b4, and Black takes over the initiative (game); but he should play

b) 1 ♚e5!, driving back the opponent's king, and centralising his own. 1...♘b4 2 ♖d6 with an excellent game for White.

218 **Serper – Ivanov**
New York 1996

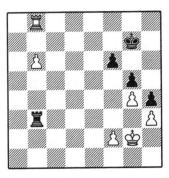

1...♚h7??
Marking time is always dangerous – Black does not see White's threat. Correct is 1...♖b2! 2 ♚f1 ♖b3, with a draw.

2 f3!
But now the king threatens to go to the other flank, while the win of the f3 pawn does not give Black a passed pawn.

2...♚g7 3 ♚f2 ♚h7 4 ♚e2 ♚g7 5 ♚d2! ♖xf3 6 ♚c2! ♖f2+ 7 ♚c3 ♖f1 8 ♖d8! ♖b1 9 ♖d6 ♚f7
After 9...f5 10 gxf5 g4 11 hxg4 h3 12 ♖g6+ ♚h7 13 g5! there is no salvation.

10 ♚c4 ♚e7 11 ♖c6 ♖b2 12 ♚c5! ♖b3 13 ♖d6!
Threatening ♖d6-d4-b4.
13...♖xh3
The pawn endgame after 13...♖c3+ 14 ♚b4 ♚xd6 15 ♚xc3 f5 16 gxf5 g4 17 f6 gxh3 18 b7 ♚c7 19 b8=♕+ wins for White.
14 b7 ♖c3+ 15 ♚b4 ♚xd6 16 b8=♕+, and White won, 1-0

219 **Urban – Macieja**
Poland 2000

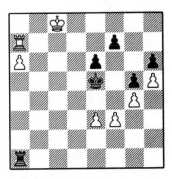

Here White has two ways to realise his material advantage, but one of these gives the opponent dangerous counterplay.

1 ♚d8?
Of course he should prefer 1 ♖xf7! ♖xa6 2 f4+ ♚e4 3 fxg5 hxg5 4 h6 ♚xe3 5 h7 e5 6 ♚d8 ♖h6 7 ♚e7 e4 8 ♚f8 ♚d2 9 ♚g7, winning easily.

1...f5! 2 gxf5 exf5 3 ♖e7+ ♚d5 4 a7 g4 5 fxg4 fxg4 6 ♚c8 g3 7 ♖g7 g2 8 ♚b8 ♖b1+ 9 ♚c8 ♖a1, and the game ended in a draw, ½-½

220 **Short – Topalov**
Novgorod 1997

Again White has a choice – to advance the passed pawn or to activate his king, and again he makes an incorrect decision.

1 c6?

Necessary was 1 ♔c6! e5 2 fxe5 fxe5 3 ♔d5 ♔f6 (bad is 3...e4 4 ♖d4! ♖c2 5 ♖xe4+ ♔d7 6 h4 etc.) 4 c6 e4 5 ♖f2+ ♔e7 6 ♖e2 ♖d1+ 7 ♔xe4 ♔d6 8 ♖c2 ♔c7 9 ♔e5 winning.

1...e5 2 fxe5 fxe5 3 ♔b6 e4 4 ♖d7+!

Inferior is 4 ♖e2 ♔d6, and Black has the preferable position.

4...♔f6!

Bad is 4...♔e6? 5 ♖d8+! winning.

5 ♖d8 e3 6 ♖e8 ♖b1+ 7 ♔c5 ♖e1! 8 c7 e2 9 ♖e3 ♔f5 with a draw, ½-½

221 **Jovicić – Bukić**
Belgrade 1980

1 d7??

Haste. He should build a bridge: 1 ♖e4! ♖h8+ 2 ♖e8 ♖h4 3 d7 ♖h7 4 ♖g8 ♔c6 5 ♔c8 ♖xd7 6 ♖g6+ ♔d6 7 ♖xd6+ ♔xd6 8 ♔b7, and White wins.

Now, however:

1...♖h8+ 2 ♔e7 ♖h7+ 3 ♔e6 ♖h6+ and a draw was agreed, ½-½

222 **Gofstein – Borgo**
Bratto 1998

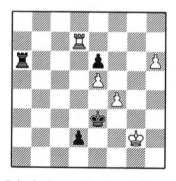

Principal problems appear at critical moments, when required to choose one of several continuations. At times the correct decision is a way of successfully discarding other methods. Despite the extra white pawn, Black plays for a win, since the black king is clearly stronger than its counterpart. Let's see the possible variations to continue the struggle.

a) **1 f5?** exf5 **2 h7** 🖤g6+! **3 🤍f1** 🖤h6 **4 e6** 🖤xh7 **5 e7** 🖤h8 **6** 🖤d6 (if 6 🖤d8 then 6...🖤e8! wins) **6...f4!** (zugzwang) **7 🤍g1** 🖤e8 **8** 🖤e6+ 🤍f3, and White resigned, **0-1**;

b) **1 🤍g3** (an attempt to activate the king) **1...**🖤a1 **2 🤍g4** d1=🖤+ **3** 🖤xd1 🖤xd1 **4 f5** 🖤g1+ **5 🤍h5 🤍f4 6 fxe6 🤍f5**, and Black wins;

c) **1 h7** 🖤a8 **2 f5!** – the only chance, and now Black has two possibilities

c1) **2...**🖤h8 **3 fxe6** 🖤xh7 **4** 🖤d5! 🖤e7 **5 🤍g3** 🖤xe6 **6 🤍h4** (losing is 6 🖤xd2? because of 6...🖤g6+!; nor is there salvation in 6 🤍g4 🖤xe5 7 🖤xe5 🤍d4, and queens with check) **6...🤍e2 7 🤍g5** d1=🖤 **8** 🖤xd1 🤍xd1 **9 🤍f5**, with a draw;

c2) **2...exf5 3 e6 f4 4 e7 f3+** (on 4...🖤e8 there is 5 🖤d8 f3+ 6 🤍g3 f2 7 🤍g2 🤍e2 8 🖤xd2+ 🤍xd2 9 🤍xf2, etc.) **5 🤍g3 f2 6 🤍g2 🤍e2 7** 🖤xd2+ **🤍xd2 8 🤍xf2 🤍d3 9 🤍f3 🤍d4 10 🤍f4 🤍d5 11 🤍f5 🤍d6 12 🤍f6**, with a simple draw.

223 **M.Gurevich – Van Wely**
Germany 2001

The position was analysed in our first book, where we showed the method of struggle for the draw. There followed:

1 🖤f2?

Stronger is the simple 1 🖤c2 with a draw.

1...🖤a5!

The position of the pawn on g6, but not on g5, gives Black this chance of check along the fifth rank.

2 🖤f3+?

Now he should try 2 🖤b2 🖤g5+ 3 🤍h2!.

2...🤍e4 3 🖤f2

After 3 🖤b3 🖤a2+ 4 🤍f1 🖤d2 the white king is out of play.

3...🖤g5+ **4 🤍h2 🤍e3 5** 🖤a2 🖤d5 **6** 🖤a3+

Better really was 6 🤍g2.

6...🖤d3 **7** 🖤a6 g5 **8** 🖤e6+ 🤍f3 **9** 🖤g6 🖤d5 **10** 🖤g8 🖤e5 **11** 🖤g7 🖤e2+ **12 🤍g1** 🖤g2+ **13 🤍h1 g4! 14** 🖤xg4 🖤xg4 **15 hxg4 🤍e2**, and White resigned, **0-1**

And here is an even simpler example.

224 **Rychagov – Klimov**
Russia 1997

A simple draw. Good is 1...🖤b3 or 1...🖤b5. But also the move in the game is not losing.

1...Rc4 2 Ra6+ Kg7 3 Kg5 Rc3
Simpler is 3...Rc7.
4 Ra7+ Kg8 5 g4 Rc6 6 f5 h6+?
But this is a fatal mistake – with the h7 pawn the draw is simple, as in the game Gelfand-Karpov.
7 Kh5 Rb6 8 Re7!, and there is no defence against 9 Re6, **1-0**

Complex rook endgames

225 Gelfand – Ivanchuk
Lviv 2000

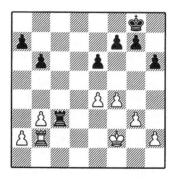

At first glance we see that Black's rook occupies a more active position, but it is not apparent how to improve his game. Ivanchuk demonstrates a plan to activate the king and to create a second weakness in the opponent's camp.
1...g5! 2 Re2 Kg7 3 Re3 Rc1 4 Re1 Rc5 5 Kf3
Or 5 Re2 Kg6 6 Rd2 Rc3 7 Re2 Kh5 8 Kg2 gxf4 9 gxf4 Kg4 10 f5 e5, and White loses material.
5...Kg6 6 Re2 Rc3+ 7 Re3
If 7 Kf2 gxf4 (or 7...Kh5) 8 gxf4 h5 the black king penetrates the opponent's camp.
7...Rc2 8 Rd3
White judged that after 8 Re2 Rxe2 9 Kxe2 gxf4 10 gxf4 Kh5 11 Kf3 Kh4 Black would invade his position. Likewise on 8 fxg5 Rxh2 9 gxh6 Rxa2 Black wins a pawn.

8...Rxh2 9 a4 Rb2 10 Rc3
White has to wait helplessly while his opponent improves his position.
10...h5 11 fxg5 Kxg5 12 Rd3 f6 13 Re3 e5 14 Rc3 a6 15 Rd3 Rc2 16 Re3 b5 17 a5
Losing is 17 axb5 axb5 18 Rd3 b4 19 Re3 Rc3 20 Rxc3 bxc3 21 Ke3 c2 22 Kd2 c1=Q+ 23 Kxc1 Kg4 24 b4 Kxg3 25 b5 h4 26 b6 h3 27 b7 h2 28 b8=Q h1=Q+ 29 Kd2 Qxe4.
17...b4 18 Rd3 Rc5 19 Rd8 Rxa5 20 Rg8+ Kh6 21 Rb8 Rc5 22 Rxb4 Rb5 23 Ra4 Rxb3+ 24 Kf2 Rb6 25 Kf3 Kg5 26 Ra3 Rc6 27 Ra4 Rc3+, and Black wins. **0-1**

226 Timman – Van Wely
Amsterdam 1995

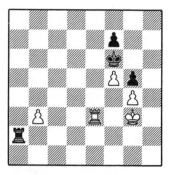

1...Rd2??
After the simple 1...Rb2 White cannot improve his position. If he tries to transfer his king to the queenside, the object of attack becomes his g4 pawn and then also the one on f5.
2 b4
This practically concludes the struggle, since the rook is able to defend both pawns simultaneously and free the king for transfer to the queenside.
2...Rd4 3 Rb3 Ke7 4 b5 Kd8 5 b6 Kc8 6 Rc3+ Kb7 7 Rc7+ Kxb6 8 Rxf7 Rd3+ 9 Kf2 Rd4 10 Kf3

♜d3+ 11 ♔e4 ♜g3 12 f6 ♜xg4+ 13 ♔f5 ♜g1 14 ♜g7, and Black resigned, **1-0**

In complex rook endgames a knowledge of the principles of play in typical positions is necessary.

227 Kozakov – Mikhalchishin
Ptuj 1999

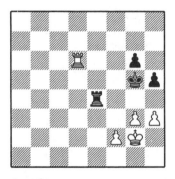

1 f4+ ♔h6!
Bad is 1...♔f5 2 ♔f3, and there is no defence against g3-g4+. Now Black sacrifices a pawn, but activates his pieces.
2 f5 ♔g5! 3 fxg6 ♔h6 4 ♔f3 ♜a4, with a positional draw.

228 Romanishin – Anand
New York 1994

1 ♔e5?

Correct was the activation of the rook by 1 ♜c8 h5 2 ♜h8 ♜g5 3 ♜h6 with an immediate draw.
1...h5 2 ♜h2 ♜h6 3 ♔f4 ♔c5
The black king draws closer to its own pawns.
4 ♔g5 ♜h8 5 ♔f6 ♔d5 6 ♔g7 ♜a8 7 ♜xh5+ e5 8 ♔f6 ♜f8+ 9 ♔g5 e4 10 ♔g4+ ♔d4 11 ♜h7??
But this shows a lack of knowledge of basic principles – attack from the side. 11 ♜a5! leads to a draw.
11...e3, and White resigned, **0-1**

The difficulties in holding a slightly inferior position

229 Alterman – Stefanova
Recklinghausen 1998

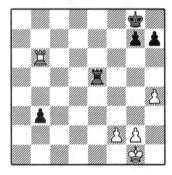

Here it is possible to construct a drawn position at once: 1...h5! 2 ♜xb3 ♔f7, but who would want to give up the pawn right away?
1...♜e1+ 2 ♔h2 ♜b1? 3 ♜b7 h6?!
Better is an immediate 3...h5.
4 h5 b2 5 g4 ♔f8 6 ♔g2 ♔g8 7 ♔f3 ♔f8 8 ♔f4 ♔g8 9 ♔f5 ♔f8 10 ♜b8+ ♔f7 11 ♜b3 ♔e7 12 f3 ♜f1
He must – the threat was ♜b7+ and ♔g6.
13 ♜xb2 ♜xf3+ 14 ♔g6 ♜f4 15 ♜b7+

Black is fighting for a draw and it is clear that he has problems with the direct advance of the king.

15... ♔f8?

Usually it is better to activate: 15...♔e6! 16 ♖xg7 ♖xg4+ 17 ♔xh6 ♖a4 with a draw.

16 g5! ♖g4 17 ♖f7+ ♔e8 18 ♖f5!

Threatening 19 ♔xg7.

18...♖h4 19 ♔xg7 ♖xh5 20 ♖f8+ ♔e7 21 g6 ♖g5 22 ♖f3 h5 23 ♖e3+ ♔d7 24 ♔h6, and Black had to resign, **1-0**

230 Tal – Polugaevsky
Leningrad 1977

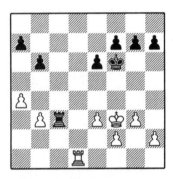

He cannot defend passively, so

1 ♖d7 a5 2 b4! axb4

2...♖c4 3 b5 ♖xa4 4 ♖b7 draws.

3 ♖d6?

3 ♖d4! ♖b3 4 ♖d6 ♖a3 5 ♖xb6 ♖xa4 6 ♖b7 gives drawing chances.

3...b5! 4 a5

After 4 axb5 ♖c5 5 b6 ♖b5 the black pawns move forward.

4...b3 5 ♖d2 ♔e5! 6 ♔e2

On 6 a6 there is 6...♖c6 7 a7 ♖a6 8 ♖b2 ♖xa7 9 ♖xb3 ♖b7, and Black stands to win.

6...♖c4 7 ♔d1

Better is 7 ♔d3 ♔d5 8 ♖b2 ♔c5 9 ♖xb3 ♖a4 and then ♖xa5 with chances of victory.

7...♖a4 8 ♖b2 ♖a3 9 ♔d2 ♔e4 10 ♔c3 ♖xa5 11 ♖d2 ♖a7

Too cautious – simpler is 11...♖a2! 12 ♖d4 ♔f3 13 ♖f4+ ♔g2 14 ♖xf7 ♖xf2 and then b2.

12 ♔xb3 ♔f3 13 ♔b4 ♖b7 14 ♔c5 b4 15 ♔c6 ♖b8 16 ♔c7 ♖b5 17 ♔c6 ♖h5! 18 ♖d7

Or 18 h4 ♖f5 etc.

18...♔xf2! 19 ♖xf7+ ♔xe3 20 ♖b7

After 20 h4 ♔d3 21 ♖xg7 b3 everything is clear.

20...♖xh2 21 ♔d6 ♖g2 22 ♖xg7 b3 23 ♔xe6 b2 24 ♖b7 h5, and White resigned, **0-1**

231 Matulović – Tal
Sarajevo 1966

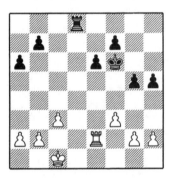

Black has the more active position, and he begins play to create weaknesses.

1...g4! 2 fxg4?!

He should try 2 ♖e3.

2...hxg4 3 ♖f2+ ♔g6 4 ♖d2 ♖h8!

Now White will have a permanent weakness on h2.

5 g3 f5 6 ♖e2 e5!

Black strives in the simplest way to create a passed pawn.

7 ♔d2

After 7 ♖xe5 ♖xh2 and then 8...♖h3 the threat of ...f5-f4 decides.

7...f4! 8 gxf4 exf4 9 ♔e1 ♔f5 10 ♔f1 f3 11 ♖d2 ♔f4

It is interesting to observe how Black activates all his forces.

12 ♔g1 ♔e3 13 ♖d7 f2+ 14 ♔f1 ♖xh2 15 ♖e7+ ♔f3 16 ♖f7+ ♔g3 17 ♔e2 ♖h1! 18 ♖xf2 ♖h2!, and Black resigned. **0-1**

232 Ljubojević – Beliavsky
Tilburg 1986

In the following position all of Black's pieces are more active and in the first instance he should further advance the f4 pawn. Therefore:

1...♖g3 2 g5 ♔d4! 3 ♖g7 f3! 4 ♖xg6 f2 5 ♖f6 ♔e3 6 g6 ♔e2!

It is not worth playing 6...♖xg6? since after 7 ♖xg6 f1=♕ 8 ♖e6+ ♔d4 9 ♖d6+ and ♖d3 the chances of a draw are very great.

7 ♖e6+ ♔f3 8 ♖xa6 f1=♕ 9 ♖f6+ ♔g2 10 ♖xf1 ♔xf1 11 c4 bxc4 12 h5 ♔e2 13 ♔c2 ♔f3! 14 ♔c3 ♔g4 15 ♔xc4 ♔xh5 16 g7 ♔h6!

Black will not be provoked into moving away the rook.

17 g8=♕ ♖xg8 18 a4 ♔g6 19 a5 ♔f6 20 ♔c5 ♔e7 21 ♔c6 ♔d8 22 ♔b7 ♖g7+ 23 ♔b8 ♔d7 24 ♔b7 ♔d6 25 ♔b6 ♖g3!, and Black wins, **0-1**

233 Markowski – Kaidanov
Moscow 2002

How is it possible to lose such a game at grandmaster level? Simplest was to establish the rook on the third rank and play the king to f3. However there followed:

1 ♖a4 e5 2 ♖a6+ f6 3 ♖a3

Better is 3 ♖a8 ♖d4 4 ♖h8!, latching on to the h5 pawn.

3...♖d4! 4 ♔h3 e4 5 ♔g2?

Better was 5 ♖a2 ♖d3 6 ♖e2.

5...f4! 6 gxf4 ♔f5 7 ♖c3?

Correct is 7 f3!, exchanging the remaining pawns.

7...♖d2 8 ♔g1 ♖d3 9 ♖c8 ♖h3 10 ♖a8 ♔xf4, and he can resign, **1-0**

234 **Piket – Kasparov**
Internet 2000

The presence of remaining pawn material on one flank creates the prerequisites for the drawing tendencies of the present endgame. But it is necessary to play very accurately and not allow the activation of the opponent's pieces.

1...♖d3

Better is 1...♖d5 with the idea of undermining the pawn mass by ...g6-g5.

2 ♔h3!

Under cover of his own pawn barrier the white king heads towards the opponent's camp.

2...♖e3?!

He should attack the opponent's pawn from the side: 2...♖a3 3 ♔h4 ♔g7 4 ♔g5 (or 4 ♖c7 ♖a6 5 ♖e7 ♔f8!) ♖a5 5 ♖c7 ♖b5 6 ♖e7, and now bad is 6...♔f8? 7 ♔f6 ♖b6+ 8 e6! winning for White. The more passive 6... ♖b6 7 e6 (or 7 f5 gxf5 8 ♔xf5 ♖b2) 7...♖b5+! (losing is 7... ♖xe6 8 ♖xe6 fxe6 9 ♔h4) leads to a draw after 8 ♔h4 ♔f6 9 ♖xf7+ ♔xe6. But preferable is 6...♖a5! 7 f5 (nothing essentially is changed by 7 h3 ♖b5 8 g4 hxg4 9 hxg4 ♖a5 10 f5 ♖xe5! 11 ♖xe5 f6+ 12 ♔f4 fxe5+ 13 ♔xe5 gxf5, and Black maintains equality, or 7 ♔h4 ♖a6 with the idea of 8...♔f8) 7...gxf5!

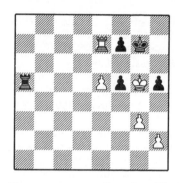

Now on any continuation Black holds, for example, 8 ♔xf5 ♖a2 9 h4 (9 e6 ♖a5) ♖a3; or 8 e6 f4+ 9 ♔xf4 ♔f6 10 ♖xf7+ ♔xe6; or 8 ♔xh5 ♔f8.

3 ♔h4! ♔g7

3... ♖a3 is bad because of 4 ♖c7 ♔g8 5 e6 fxe6 6 ♔g5 winning.

4 ♔g5 ♖e1?

A decisive mistake. He should attack the white pawns from the side by 4... ♖a3! 5 f5 (5 ♖c7 ♖a5) gxf5 6 ♔xf5 (6 ♔xh5 ♖e3 7 ♖c5 ♖e2 8 h4 ♖e3) ♖f3+ 7 ♔g5 ♖e3 8 ♔f4 ♖e1 9 ♔f5 ♖f1+ 10 ♔g5 ♖e1 11 ♖c5 ♖e2 12 h4 ♖e3 13 ♔f4 ♖e1.

5 ♖c7 ♖e2 6 ♖e7!

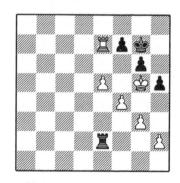

6...♖a2?!

There is also no salvation in other variations: 6...♖e1 7 e6! ♖xe6 8 ♖xe6 fxe6 9 h3 ♔f7 10 ♔h6 ♔f6 11 g4 h4 (or 11...hxg4 12 hxg4) 12 g5 ♔f5 13 ♔g7 ♔xf4 14 ♔xg6 e5 15

&f6 e4 16 g6 e3 17 g7 e2 18 g8=♕
e1=♕ 19 ♕g4 &e3 20 ♕e6 &f2 21
♕xe1+ &xe1 22 &g5, as reached in
a similar endgame in the games,
Ionov-Karasev, Leningrad 1983,
and Stean-Hartston, Brighton 1972.

7 f5!

Inferior is 7 e6 ♖a5+ 8 &h4 &f6
9 ♖xf7+ &xe6, and Black manages
to hold on.

**7... gxf5 8 e6 h4 9 ♖xf7+ &g8 10
&f6**, and Black resigned in view of
the variation 10... ♖a6 11 ♖g7+ &f8
12 ♖h7 &g8 13 ♖xh4. **1-0**

235 **Schchekachev – Kiriakov**
Russia 1996

There is the threat to transpose
into a pawn endgame. A typical
method of defence would be 1 ♖b8,
not allowing the opponent's king
either to f3 or to h3.

1 &g1 ♖f2 2 ♖b1?

Again he needs to go to the
eighth.

1...&h3 3 ♖a1??

But this is a generally incomprehensible threat to the opponent – the
rook must defend from the eighth
rank.

**3...♖d2 4 ♖b1 ♖d3 5 ♖f1 g4 6
♖c1 g2!**,

And there is no defence against
the transposition to a pawn endgame
after ♖d3-f3-f1+, **0-1**

236 **Moisenko – Bezgodov**
Alushta 1999

If the white rook were standing on
b8, the pawn goes on to b7, then the
advance of the passed f-pawn
decides the game. Nevertheless it is
not so complicated to achieve a
draw if we remember the classical
principle of two weaknesses.

1...h4!! 2 gxh4

Or 2 g4 ♖b4.

2...h5!!

After 2...♖b4 3 h5+ White would
activate the king. Now White has
too many weak pawns, while the
loss of any of them is clearly
inadmissible. Let's say 3 f5+ &f6
followed by ♖b2-b4xh4; 3 ♖g5+
&h6 4 &f1 ♖b4 5 ♖f5 &g6; 3 ♖c6+
&f5 – with a draw in all cases.

White now chooses perhaps the strongest continuation.

3 ♔f1 ♖b4 4 ♔e2 ♖xf4 5 b6 ♖xh4!? 6 ♖b5 ♖e4+ 7 ♔f3 ♖e8 8 b7 ♖b8 9 ♔e4 h4

Let us imagine that Black allowed 3 h5 – he would have had to lose several tempi to eliminate it.

10 ♔d5

Or 10 ♔f4 ♔f6.

10...♔g5!

Also possible is 10...♔f5. White's last chance consisted of 10...h3?? 11 ♔c6 h2 12 ♖b1.

11 ♔c6 ♔g4 12 ♔c7 ♖xb7+ 13 ♔xb7 h3 14 ♔c6 h2 15 ♖b1 ♔f3, draw, ½-½

Interesting manoeuvres in rook endgames

It is useful to know some tactical manoeuvres in rook endgames which help to speed up the achievement of a draw or a victory.

237 Hjartarson – Malaniuk
Tilburg 1993

Black threatens to advance the g5 pawn and achieve a draw so the white pawn begins its own advance.

1 ♖h6! ♔xe7 2 a7! g4 3 ♖h8 c2+ 4 ♔xc2 ♔f6 5 a8=♕ ♖xa8 6 ♖xa8 ♔e5 7 ♔d3, and Black resigned, **1-0**

238 Stohl – Korchnoi
Tilburg 1993

Here after **1...♔xf7 2 ♖h8!** with the threat of 3 a7 Black had to play **2...♔g7 3 a7 ♔xh8 4 a8=♕+** and transpose to a hopeless endgame of rook against queen, **1-0**.

But the question arises: how to win after **1...♖d8! 2 ♖h7 ♔f6! 3 ♔e2 ♔g6** and the f7 pawn falls.

This case reminds us of a classical example where a well-known grandmaster resigned in a drawn position.

239 Polugaevsky – Parma
Vrnjacka Banja 1968

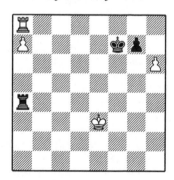

It appeared to him that after **1...gxh6 2 ♖h8** the weakness of the seventh rank is decisive, but he forgot that in chess capturing is not obligatory and after **1...♔g6!** and **2...♔h7!** it's a simple draw!

240 **Shirov – Kramnik**
Belgrade 1999

Shirov pursues a beautiful idea to clear the seventh rank. **1 b6!!** wins at once, but he played:

1 ♖a8 ♖a1 2 a7 ♖d1+ 3 ♔e4 ♖e1+ 4 ♔f3 ♖a1 5 b6!

Only now.

5...cxb6 6 ♖h8, Black resigned, **1-0**

A very famous example on this theme, and indeed a very effective one, was seen forty years ago.

241 **Vistaneckis – Sardarov**
USSR 1961

1 f5!! exf5 2 e6! fxe6 3 ♖h8, and Black has to give up a rook. **1-0**

11 Bishop Endgames

In the first part of our trilogy we looked at specific bishop endgames on one flank and special cases with passed pawns. Here we look at other cases where additional factors come into play. These cases are a little more complicated.

Particularly in the area of bishop endings much came out of Tilburg 1994.

242 Andersson – Lanka
Tilburg 1994

The weakness of h5 is very important, but it is even more important to create a passed pawn.

1 g4! hxg4 2 ♗xg4+ ♔e7 3 h5 ♔f7 4 h6 ♔g8

After 4...♔g6 White would have the blow 5 ♗h5+!.

5 ♗f5 ♔h8 6 ♔e3 ♔g8 7 ♔d4 ♔h8 8 ♔c3 ♔g8 9 ♔d4!

At his disposal White has the roundabout route to b6, but he decides to play more simply.

9...♔h8 10 b5! cxb5 11 ♗xd5 ♗f7+

If 11...♔g8, then 12 ♔d4 with a further itinerary ♔d4-c3-b4 and the transfer of the bishop by ♗f5-d3.

12 ♔d6 ♗h5 13 c6 ♗f3 14 c7 ♗b7 15 ♔c5, Black resigned, **1-0**

243 Bareev – Karpov
Tilburg 1994

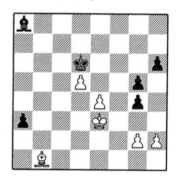

There followed the surprising
1...g3!!
with the idea of creating a passed pawn on the kingside.

2 hxg3 ♔e5 3 ♔d3 ♗b7 4 ♔c4 ♗c8?!

Simpler was 4...h5!? 5 ♔b4 ♗a6 6 ♔xa3 ♗f1 with a draw.

5 ♔b4

Nothing is offered by 5 ♔c5 h5 6 ♔c6 h4 7 gxh4 gxh4 8 d6 h3 9 gxh3 ♗xh3 10 d7 ♗xd7+ 11 ♔xd7 a2.

5...♗g4??
And now the last chance was 5...h5! 6 ♔xa3 ♗a6! 7 ♔b4 ♗f1 8 ♔c5 ♗xg2 9 d6 ♗h3 10 ♔c6 h4, with a draw.

6 ♔xa3 ♗e2 7 ♔b4 ♗f1 8 ♔c5 ♗xg2 9 ♗d3 ♗f3
Or 9...h5 10 d6 ♗h3 11 ♗e2! ♗d7 12 ♗xh5 ♔xe4 13 ♔b6 g4 14 ♔c7 ♗e6 15 ♗f7!, and White wins.

10 d6 ♗g4 11 ♔c6 ♗c8 12 ♔c7 ♗e6 13 ♗c4 ♗g4 14 ♗e2 ♗e6 15 ♗f3 g4 16 ♗g2 h5 17 d7, Black resigned, **1-0**

244 **Khalifman – Hjartarsson**
Tilburg 1994

1...g6?!
White has a great advantage in space, and it is understandable that Black tries somehow to free himself. Upon this, however, he serious-

ly weakens the h6 square. Better was the transfer of the king to d7.

2 g4 gxh5 3 gxh5 a5
Preventing b3-b4 and the approach of the king to b5.

4 ♗d2 ♔h7 5 f5 ♗h4 6 b4!
Managing the break all the same.

6...exf5+
After the double exchange on b4, Black fears the clamp f5-f6 and the transfer of the bishop to e3 with a winning pawn endgame. But there is also no salvation in 6...a4 7 bxc5 bxc5 8 ♗e3 ♗e7 9 f6 ♗f8 10 ♗d2 followed by ♗d2-a5-c7-d6 and a win for White.

7 ♔xf5 cxb4 8 axb4 a4 9 ♗c1! ♗g5 10 ♗a3 ♔g8 11 b5! ♗d8 12 c5 bxc5 13 ♗xc5 ♔h7 14 ♔e4 ♔g7 15 ♔d5 ♗c7 16 b6 ♗b8 17 b7 f5 18 ♗d6 ♗a7 19 ♔c6 f4 20 e6 f3 21 e7, Black resigned. **1-0**

In bishop endgames two basic factors have decisive significance: the arrangement of pawns on squares of the colour of the bishop and, as a consequence of this, zugzwang. One's own pawns should be placed on squares of the opposite colour to the bishop. Then the opponent's pawns will restrict their own bishop.

245 Pytel – Witkowski
Poland 1971

1 ♔c2?

The first mistake. He should play 1 h3, preventing the advance of the opponent's pawn ...g6-g5-g4.

1...♝d8?

Black makes a crucial mistake. Correct was 1...g5! 2 g4! hxg4 3 ♔d3 g3! 4 hxg3 g4!, and things are in order for Black.

2 ♝b2 ♝f6 3 ♝c3 ♔c5

Now 3...g5 is no good because of 4 g4! hxg4 5 ♝e1.

4 ♔d3 ♔b5 5 ♔e3 ♔c5 6 ♔f3 ♔b5 7 h3 ♔c5 8 g4 ♔b5?!

Of course, not 8...hxg4+ 9 ♔xg4 followed by h2-h4-h5 with a win for White. But correct is 8...♔c6.

9 ♝d2

Black can hold the position after 9 ♔g3 ♔c5 10 h4 ♔d6 11 g5 ♝d8 followed by ...♝d8-c7 and ♔d6-c6 -b5.

9...♔c5 10 g5 ♝g7??

A decisive mistake. Correct was 10...♝d8 followed by 11...♝d8-c7 and ♔c5-b5.

11 ♝c3 ♔b5 12 ♔e3 ♔c5 13 ♔d3 ♔b5 14 ♔c2 ♔c5 15 ♔b2 ♔b5 16 ♔a2 ♔c5! 17 ♔a3 ♔b5 18 ♝b4!

Black resigned because of the variation 18...♔c6 19 ♝e7 with a transfer of the bishop to f6, **1-0**

246 Konstantinopolsky – Shtern
Correspondence game 1965

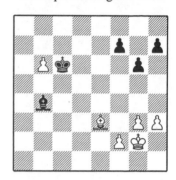

Upon correct play by the opponent, White's extra distant passed pawn ought not lead to victory. This is because his pawns are placed on squares of the colour of his bishop and their advance leads to a reduction of material and an increase in the opponent's chances of a bishop sacrifice to leave White with insufficient potential for a win.

1...♝d6?

Correct is 1...h5! 2 ♔f3 ♝d6 3 g4 hxg4+ 4 hxg4 f5! 5 ♝f4 ♝c5 6 gxf5 gxf5 7 ♝c7 ♝d4 8 ♔g3 f4+! with a draw.

2 g4 f5 3 gxf5 gxf5 4 ♔f3 ♝e5 5 ♝f4 ♝d4 6 ♝c7,

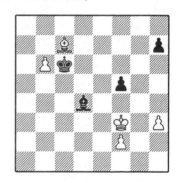

and in view of the transfer of pieces along the itinerary ♔f3-g3, f2-f3, ♔g3-h4, Black resigned, **1-0**

247 **Rozentalis – Smagin**
Odessa 1989

1...d4?
A mistake. In the queen ending arising after 1...♔xc3 2 ♗xf7 ♗xf7 3 ♔xf7 d4 4 g6 d3 5 g7 d2 6 g8=♕ d1=♕ Black's chances are preferable.

2 cxd4 exd4 3 ♗f3?
Returning the compliment. After 3 ♗xf7 ♗xf7 4 ♔xf7 d3 5 g6 d2 6 g7 d1=♕ 7 g8=♕ ♕d5+ 8 ♔f8 ♕xg8+ 9 ♔xg8 there is an obvious draw. Now, however, Black wins.

3...b5 4 g6 fxg6! 5 ♔xe6 a5 6 ♔e5 d3 7 ♔e4 ♔c3 8 ♔e3 d2 9 ♗e2 a4, White resigned, **0-1**

248 **Voitsekhovsky – Kobalya**
Ekaterinburg 1999

With the last move ...e6-e5 Black creates a second weakness for himself (the first is the a5 pawn), and now his position cannot be held. Black made this impulsive move to block any dangerous kingside raid by the white king via the e5 square.

1 ♗g5 ♗c7 2 ♗f6 ♗d6 3 ♗d8 ♗b4 4 ♗h4 ♗c5 5 ♗g3 ♗d6
With a series of accurate moves White has placed Black in a position of zugzwang, provoking the advance of pawns on the kingside. No help is 5...♗d4!? 6 ♗h2! ♗b2 (6...♗a1? 7 ♗g1 ♗b2 8 ♗f2 and 9 ♗e1) 7 ♗g1 ♗c1 (7...♗a3 8 ♗f2 ♗e7 9 ♗g3 ♗d6? leads to variations in the game) 8 ♗f2 ♗d2!? (8...♗g5 9 ♗g3 ♗f6 10 ♗h2 ♗g7 11 g5!) 9 ♗g3 ♔d6 10 ♔b5 ♔d5 11 ♗f2.

6 ♗e1 ♗c7 7 ♗c3!
The first zugzwang!

7...g5
Nothing is offered by 7...h5, as White again – with a 'dance' – produces a zugzwang.

8 ♗d2 ♗d8
Bad is 8...h6? 9 ♗c3!.

9 ♗e3 ♗e7
Or 9...h6 10 ♗c5 11 ♗f8.

10 ♗c1!
The final finesse.

10...♗f6
Unfortunately no good is 10...h6 11 ♗d2 ♗d8 12 ♗e1! with the idea of 13 h4 and yet another zugzwang – this is what Black did not see when he played ...a6-a5.

11 ♗b2! ♔d6
There is also no salvation in 11...♗g7 12 ♗c3.

12 ♗c3 ♗d8 13 ♔b5 ♔d5 14 ♗xa5 ♗xa5 15 ♔xa5 Black resigned, **1-0**

249 **Tukmakov – Timoschenko**
USSR 1969

White's chances lie only in an attack on the f4 pawn. But Black has an additional resource consisting of the fact that the corner square for the promotion of the pawn is of the opposite colour to that of his bishop.

1 g5 hxg5?

Black makes a decisive mistake in a simple endgame, giving the white king the extra square on h4 for manoeuvre. He should play 1...♗h5 2 ♚g2 ♗e2 3 ♚h3 ♗f3 4 ♗g4 ♗e4, holding the position.

2 hxg5 ♗h5 3 ♚g2 ♗g6 4 ♗g4 ♗e4+ 5 ♚h3 ♚g6 6 ♚h4 ♗c6 7 ♗d1 ♗d7 8 ♗c2+ ♚g7 9 ♗e4 ♗e6 10 ♚h5 ♗d7 11 f3 ♗h3 12 g6! ♗d7 13 ♚g5 ♗e6 14 ♚xf4 ♚f6 15 ♚g3 ♚g5 16 f4+ ♚h5 17 f5 ♗b3 18 f6

Also possible is 18 ♚f4 with a passage to f6.

18...♚h6 19 ♚f4, Black resigned, **1-0**

250 **Spiridonov – Spassky**
Sochi 1973

Even such a great player as Boris Spassky made a mistake in the following bishop endgame.

In the game there followed 1...h6? and after 2 ♚e2! c5 3 ♗d2! c4 4 ♗c3 ♗xc3 5 bxc3 ♚e6 the opponents agreed a draw, ½-½

But Black can achieve victory in the following way: **1...hxg6 2 hxg6 c5 3 ♚e3** (Black also wins after 3 ♚e2 ♚e4 4 ♗d2 c4 5 ♚d1 ♗xb2 6 ♗h6 c3 7 g7 c2 or 3 ♚f4 c4 4 ♚f5 ♚d4 5 ♚e6 ♚d3 6 ♚f7 ♗d4 7 g7 ♗xg7 8 ♚xg7 ♚c2) **3...c4 4 ♚f3 ♚e5 5 ♗d2 ♚f5 6 ♗c1 ♗d4!** (inferior is 6...♚xg6 7 ♚e4 and with ♚e4-d5 White holds the position) **7 ♚e2 ♚e4 8 ♚d1 ♚d3 9 ♗h6 c3!.**

251 **Hartston – Suetin**
Hastings 1967/68

1 a4!

An excellent move, fixing Black's pawn weaknesses on the queenside. Also possible was 1 b4.

1...♗d7 2 axb5?

A mistake. White simplifies his opponent's bad structure on the queenside. He should emphasise this weakness by 2 a5 g5 (worth considering is 2...♔d5) 3 hxg5 hxg5 4 ♗f3 ♗c8 5 b4.

2...♗xb5! 3 ♗f3 a5!

As we see, at the first opportunity Black straightens out his structure – placing the pawn on a square of the opposite colour to his bishop.

4 ♗d1 ♔d5 5 ♗g4 ♗e8 6 ♔d3 ♗g6+ 7 ♔e3 ♗b1 8 ♗c8 ♔e5 9 ♗g4 ♗f5 10 ♗f3 ♗c2 11 ♗b7 ♗b3 12 ♗e4 ♗d5 13 ♗d3 ♗c6 14 ♗g6 ♔f6 15 ♗d3 g5 16 hxg5+ ♔xg5

Here White cannot exploit a resource of the weaker side – the transfer to an endgame without pieces and with edge pawns – as his king cannot get into the corner!

17 ♗e2 ♗d7 18 ♗f3 ♗g4 19 ♗c6 h5 20 ♗d5 h4 21 ♗g2 ♗d7 22 ♗f1 ♔g4 23 ♔f2 ♔f4 24 ♗g2 a4! 25 ♔e1

After 25 ♗f1 h3 26 ♗xh3 ♗xh3 27 ♔e2 ♔e4 28 ♔d2 ♔d4 29 ♔c1 ♗f5 Black likewise wins.

25...♔g3 26 ♗f1 ♗c6, White resigned, **0-1**

252 Minić – Piasetski
Karlovac 1977

Black played 1...♔e5? and after 2 ♔h5 ♗c2 3 g5 ♗d3 4 ♗f7! ♗c2 5 ♗g6! ♗xg6+ 6 ♔xg6 a2 7 h7 lost.

On **1...♔e7** he creates not bad drawing chances after **2 ♔h5 ♗c2 3 g5 ♗d3 4 g6 ♔f6 5 g7 ♗g6+! 6 ♔h4 ♗h7**.

253 Oll – Jurtaev
Tallinn 1983

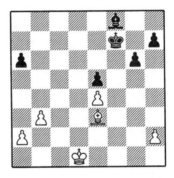

Black's position is probably a little worse in view of the fixing of the black pawn cage on e5.

1 ♔e2?!

Better is 1 a4 ♗b4 (also possible is 1...♔f6) 2 ♗d2 ♗xd2 3 ♔xd2 g5? 4 b4 ♔e6 5 h4! g4 6 h5, and White's position is preferable. Also worth considering is the plan of 1 ♗d2 followed by 2 a4. In the event of 1...♗a3 there follows 2 ♔c2 and then 3 b4 and 4 ♔b3.

1...♔f6 2 ♔d3?

Again he should prefer 2 a4 or 2 ♗d2.

2...g5 3 ♔c4?

White continues the realisation of his mistaken plan. It was still not too late to return to the kingside after 3 h3 h5 4 a4 g4 5 hxg4 hxg4 6 ♗d2 ♗c5 7 ♔e2 followed by ♔f1-g2-g3, b3-b4-b5.

3...h5 4 b4?

And here stronger was 4 ♗f2 or 4 ♔d5, and likewise 4 h3.

4...g4 5 b5?

A mistake in return. Virtually the last possibility of saving the game was 5 a4!.

5...axb5+ 6 ♔xb5

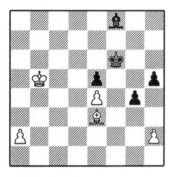

6...♗a3!!

An excellent idea, fixing the pawns on the queenside.

7 ♔c4?

He should all the same prefer 7 ♔a4 ♗b2 8 ♔b3 ♗d4 9 ♗xd4 exd4 10 a4 h4 11 a5 g3 12 hxg3 hxg3 13 a6 g2 14 a7 g1=♕ 15 a8=♕, and it is not easy for Black to win.

7...h4 8 ♔d3 h3! 9 ♗f2 ♗c1 10 a4 ♔e6

More accurate is 10...♗f4! 11 a5 g3! 12 a6 gxf2 13 ♔e2 ♗e3! with a decisive advantage.

11 a5 ♔d6 12 a6 ♔c6 13 a7 ♔b7

With the idea of 14...♗f4. Now White again has the possibility of complicating the struggle by 14 ♗g3 ♗f4 15 ♗xf4 exf4 16 e5 g3 17 e6 gxh2 18 e7 h1=♕ 19 a8=♕+ ♔xa8 20 e8=♕+, and Black will hardly succeed in realising his material advantage.

254 Smagin – Aseev
Moscow 1987

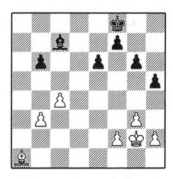

White's position is preferable due to his majority on the queenside, and likewise the fixing of the only black pawn there on the same co-loured square as his bishop.

1...♔e7 2 ♗d4 e5 3 ♗e3 e4?

He should create counterchances on the kingside by 3...f5 4 f3 ♔f6.

4 f3 exf3+

Insufficient to maintain equality is 4...f5 5 fxe4 fxe4 6 ♗f4! ♗xf4 7 gxf4 ♔d6 8 b4 and, in association with the manoeuvre ♔g2-f2-e3, White has the advantage.

5 ♔xf3 ♔d7?

A serious mistake. Obviously better is 5...♔e6 6 b4 f5 7 b5 ♗d8! (with the idea of ...g6-g5) 8 h4 ♗c7 9 c5 bxc5 10 ♗xc5 ♔d5 11 ♗e3 ♗d6 12 ♗f4 ♗b4 13 b6 ♔c6 14 ♗c7 ♗d2 with equality.

6 b4 ♗d6 7 b5 ♔c7 8 ♗g1!

8 ♔e4 is no good because of 8...h4! 9 gxh4 ♗xh2. The last chance was 8...f5.

8...♔b7 9 ♔e4 ♗c7 10 ♔d5 f5

Zugzwang. There is also no salva-tion in 10...♗b8 11 ♗d4! h4 12 ♗e5 hxg3 13 hxg3 ♗c7 14 ♗xc7

♔xc7 15 ♔e5 ♔d7 16 ♔f6 ♔d6 (or
16...♔e8 17 g4 ♔f8 18 c5 winning)
17 ♔xf7 ♔c5 18 ♔xg6 ♔xc4 19 g4
♔xb5 20 g5, and White wins.

**11 ♔e6 f4 12 gxf4 ♗xf4 13 ♔f6
g5 14 ♔g6 h4 15 ♔f5 ♔c7 16 h3,**
and Black resigned in view of the
manoeuvre ♗g1-d4-f6. **1-0**

255 **Ribli – Romanishin**
Leningrad 1977

The white pawns are fixed on
black squares, and so it is quite
complicated to exploit the extra
pawn.

1 e4

Insufficient is 1 f3 gxf3 2 exf3
♔d5 or 1 e3!? ♔d5 2 ♔e2 ♗e7 3 f3
gxf3+ 4 ♔xf3 ♗f6 5 e4 ♔e6 6 ♗c7
♗c3 7 ♔f4 ♗d2+ 8 ♔f3 fxe4+, and
the position is approximately even.

**1...fxe4 2 dxe4 c5! 3 ♔e2 c4 4 f3
gxf3+ 5 ♔xf3 ♗d6! 6 ♗c1**

Of course not 6 ♗xd6 ♔xd6 7
♔e3 ♔e5 8 g4 hxg4+ 9 h5 ♔f6!.

6...♗e7 7 ♗g5

Nothing is offered by 7 g4 hxg4+
8 ♔xg4 ♗xh4 with equality.

**7...♗f6 8 ♗f4 ♗e5 9 ♗e3 ♔f6 10
♔d2 ♔e6 11 ♔c2 ♗d4 12 ♔b1
♗c3 13 ♔a2 ♗b4! 14 ♔b2 ♔f6 15
♔c2 ♔e6 16 ♔d1 ♗c3 17 ♔e2
♗b2 18 ♔e3 ♔f6** with a draw, ½-½

256 **Mikhalchishin – Holzmann**
Budapest 1990

In this position the fact that
White's pawns are on squares of the
same colour as his bishop cannot be
regarded as a defect. The white
bishop occupies an important out-
post where it supports the advance
of the passed h-pawn and controls
its queening square.

1...♗f2

Possibly an attack from the front
is preferable: 1...♗b6!? 2 ♔g5
♗d8+ 3 ♔g4 ♔g6 4 h5+ ♔h6 5
♗c3 ♗b6 6 ♗d2 ♔h7 7 f5 exf5+ 8
♔xf5 ♗d4 9 ♗c3 ♗e3 10 ♔e4 ♗c1
11 ♔d5 ♗xb2 12 ♗xb2 ♔h6 with a
draw. But also in this variation
White has the possibility of improving his play: 7 ♔f3! ♗d4 8 ♗c3
♗b6 (8...♗xc3 9 bxc3 ♔h6 10 ♔g4
winning) 9 ♔e4 ♗c7 10 ♗e5 ♗b6
11 ♗d6 ♔h6 12 ♔e5 ♔xh5 13
♔xe6 ♔g4 14 f5, and White must
win.

2 ♔g5 ♔g8

There is also no salvation in
2...♗b6 3 ♗f6! ♗e3 4 h5 ♗xf4+ 5
♔xf4 ♔xf6 6 h6 ♔g6 7 ♔e5, and
White wins.

**3 ♔f6! ♗xh4+ 4 ♔xe6 ♔f8 5 f5
♔e8 6 f6 ♔d8 7 f7,** Black resigned,
1-0

257 **Szilagyi – C.Horvath**
Budapest 1990

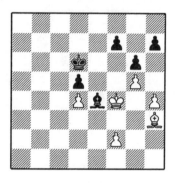

The prerequisities for playing for a win for White are the opponent's fixed pawns on squares of the colour of his bishop and the fact that his own pawns are further advanced. However getting to the black pawns with the king and bishop is very difficult. The play consists of several important stages. In the first stage White pushes the h-pawn to the sixth rank, exploiting the fact that it is unfavourable for the opponent to exchange it as this would only create new objects of attack. In the second stage White breaks through with the king into the opponent's camp, utilising zugzwang. In the third stage he creates the threat to sacrifice the bishop with the aim of clearing the way for his h-pawn and forcing a transposition to a pawn endgame. But even there the outcome of the struggle is unclear:

1 ♗g4! ♗c2 2 h5 ♗e4

After 2...gxh5 3 ♗xh5 ♗g6 White places the opponent in zugzwang by 4 ♗g4! followed by 5 ♗g4-f5.

3 h6 ♗b1! 4 ♔e3

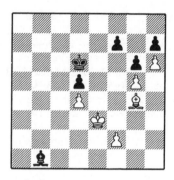

4...♔c6

Losing at once is 4...♗f5? 5 ♗xf5 gxf5 6 ♔f4 ♔e6 7 f3 f6 8 g6. He can resist rather longer by 4...♗e4 5 ♔d2 ♗b1 6 ♔c3 ♗e4 7 ♔b4 ♔c6 8 ♔a5 ♗d3 9 ♗c8! ♗e4 10 ♗a6! ♔d6 11 ♔b6 ♗f5! 12 ♔b7 ♗g4 13 ♔b8 ♗f5 14 ♗c8 ♗d3 15 ♗g4 ♗a6.

In the event of the breakthrough of the white king behind enemy lines by 16 ♔a7! ♗c4 17 ♔b7 – after ♗c8-d8 the best position for Black is with the placement of the bishop on b5. For an analysis of the arising position let us look at the following diagram.

White wins with a breakthrough: 1 f4 ♗c6 2 f5 ♗b5 3 fxg6 fxg6 4 ♗f5! gxf5 5 g6.

Now we return to the position in the game.

5 ♔d2 ♔b5 6 ♗d7+

Inferior is 6 ♔c3 ♗f5 7 ♗e2+ ♔a5, and there is no apparent win.

6...♔c4 7 ♗e8 ♔xd4 8 ♗xf7 ♔e5 9 ♗g8 ♔f4 10 ♗xh7 ♔xg5 followed by **11...♔xh6** and a draw. ½-½

White can win a tempo by **7 ♔e3 ♗f5! 8 ♗xf7** (despite his inventive play White also does not manage to win after 8 ♗e8 ♗e6 9 f4 ♔c3 10 f5! gxf5 11 g6! fxg6 12 ♗xg6 ♗g8 13 ♗xf5 ♔c4 14 ♗b1 ♔c3 15 ♗d3 ♔b4 16 ♔f4 ♔c3!) **8...gxf5 9 ♔f4 ♔xd4 10 ♔xf5**

In this pawn endgame there are three possibilities for Black.

a) 10...♔c5 11 f4 d4 (11...♔d6 12 ♔g4! d4 13 f5 d3 14 ♔f3 ♔e7 15 g6 winning) 12 ♔e4 ♔c4 13 f5 d3 14 ♔e3 ♔c3 15 g6 fxg6 16 fxg6 d2 17 gxh7 d1=♕ 18 h8=♕, and White's chances of a win are not great.

b) 10...♔c4 11 ♔f6 d4 12 ♔xf7 d3 13 g6 d2 14 gxh7 d1=♕ 15 h8=♕, and White wins.

c) 10...♔c3 11 ♔f6 d4 12 ♔xf7 d3 13 g6 d2 14 gxh7 d1=♕ 15 h8=♕ winning.

258 Yudasin – Vaganian
Telavi 1982

In this endgame Black has fair chances of victory thanks to his extra pawn and the fact that the corner square of promotion for his edge-pawn is of the colour of his bishop, which does not give the opponent the possibility of sacrificing his bishop and transposing to a drawn endgame. But all is not quite so simple.

1 ♔e3

Better is 1 ♔f4 f5 2 ♗d5 ♔f6 3 h4 h6 4 ♗b3 g5+ 5 hxg5 hxg5 6 ♔e3 ♔e5 7 ♗f7 f4+ 8 gxf4 gxf4+ 9 ♔f2, and the pawn on c3 gives the black king no chance of breaking through behind enemy lines.

1...f5 2 ♗d5 g5 3 h4?! f4+! 4 ♔f3

After 4 gxf4 gxh4 5 ♔f3 ♗d7 6 ♗e4 h5 7 ♗d5 ♗g4 Black wins.

4...fxg3 5 ♔xg3 ♔f6 6 ♗e4 h6 7 ♗c2 ♗d7 8 ♗b3 ♗e8 9 ♗c2 ♗h5! 10 ♗d3 gxh4+ 11 ♔xh4 ♗g6, and, in view of the manoeuvre of the black king, f6-e5-e4(f4)-e3, White resigned, **0-1**

259 Pigusov – Atalik
Reykjavik 1994

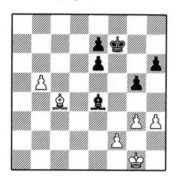

In the present situation White has three possibilities:

a) **1 f3?** (game).

Something like a logical decision: opening, with tempo, a way for the king to go to the queenside and his own passed pawn. In the game, however, White misses a defensive moment, as does his opponent...

1...♗xf3 2 ♔f2 ♗b7 3 ♔e3 ♔e8??

Black is led by his opponent. Better is 3...♔f6 4 ♔d4 e5+ and now either 5 ♔c5 e6 6 ♔d6 (6 ♔b6 ♗d5!) e4 7 b6 ♗d5 8 ♗e2 e3 9 ♔c7 ♔e5, and the chances are equal, or 5 ♔e3 e4! 6 ♔d4 ♔f5 7 ♔c5 ♔e5 8 ♔b6 ♗d5, and the position is drawn. Now, however, White wins.

4 ♗xe6 ♔d8 5 b6, Black resigned, **1-0**

b) 1 b6 ♗b7 2 ♗f1 e5 3 ♗g2 e4 4 ♔f1 ♔e6 5 ♔e2 ♔e5 6 ♔e3, and the position assumes an unclear character;

c) An idea is to create a second passed pawn on the opposite flank: 1 ♗f1! ♔e8 2 ♗g2 ♗d5 3 ♗xd5 exd5 4 f4 gxf4 5 g4! d4 6 ♔f1 d3 7 h4 f3 8 ♔e1 e5 9 b6 ♔d7 10 b7 ♔c7 11 g5 hxg5 12 hxg5 e4 13 g6 e3 14 g7 d2 15 ♔d1 f2 16 b8=♕+ ♔xb8 17 g8=♕+ winning.

260 Taimanov – Wade
Biel 1994

1...e5?

Weakening the position – after the correct 1...f5 2 ♔d4 ♗a2 3 ♗d7 ♔e7 4 c6 ♔d6 there is no apparent win.

2 ♔e4 ♗f1 3 ♔f5 exf4 4 ♔xf4 ♔e7 5 ♗e4 h6 6 ♔d5 ♗h3 7 ♗f3 ♗e6 8 ♗e4 ♔d7 9 g4! ♗c4 10 ♔g3 ♔e6 11 ♔h4 ♔e5 12 ♗f5 ♗e6 13 c6! ♔d6 14 ♔h5, and White wins, **1-0**

261 Bisguier – Arnason
New York 1989

A 'bad structure' usually leads to a bad pawn endgame.

1...h6! 2 ♔c2

Also losing is 2 ♗xh6 ♗xg3 3 ♗g5 f4 followed by ...f3-f2.

2...♗xf4 3 gxf4 ♔e4 4 ♔b3 ♔xf4 5 a4 bxa4+ 6 ♔xa4 ♔e5 7 ♔a5 ♔d6, and Black wins, **0-1**

Zugzwang is one of the basic elements (means) of play in bishop endgames.

262 Lobron – M.Gurevich
Munich 1993

Black's task is to gain access for his king to one of the two distant enemy pawns. This is achieved by a bishop manoeuvre.

1...♗b5+ 2 ♔d2 d4 3 ♗b7 ♗e8 4 ♗f3 ♗g6 5 ♗b7 ♗e4 6 ♗c8 ♗c6 7 ♗a6 ♗d7 8 ♗e2 ♔d5 9 ♗f3+ ♔c4 10 ♗e2+ ♔xb4 11 exd4 a5 12 ♔c2 ♗c6 13 ♔b2 ♗d5 14 ♗d3 a4, and Black wins, **0-1**

263 Brunner – Porper
Lenk 1993

1...♗b6?

Black cannot wait for 2 ♔e7 and 3 ♗c8, though even this should not lead to defeat, for example, 1...♗f3 2 ♔e7 ♔c7, and Black holds his ground.

2 ♔d6 a5 3 bxa5+ ♔xa5 4 ♔c5 ♔a4 5 b4 ♗d3 6 ♗e6 ♔b3 7 ♗f7 ♗c4 7 ♗e8, and Black resigned, **1-0**

264 Timman

Black has two ways to drive the bishop off the e1-h4 diagonal.

a) 1...♔f3? 2 ♔g6 ♔e2 3 ♗h4 ♗f2 4 ♔f5! f3 5 ♗f2 ♗e7 6 ♗g3 ♗c5 7 ♗d6 ♗a7=;

b) **1...♔f5!!** (shouldering) **2 ♔h6 ♔g4 3 ♔g7 f3 4 ♔g6 ♗g1 5 ♔h6 ♗h2 6 ♗f2 ♔h3 7 ♔g5 ♔g2**, Black wins.

A very important factor is a lack of space, linked in the first instance to the placement of pawns on squares of the colour of the bishop.

265 Kallai – I.Farago
Budapest 1994

Here all White's pawns stand on dark squares, and he should occupy himself with improving this structure: 1 h5 and 2 g4 or 1 b3 with the idea of 2 a4, on which the best move for Black is 1...a4 2 b4, 'closing' the flank.

1 ♗d2?! a4 2 ♗b4?

Again correct is 2 h5.

3...h5!

Now Black fixes the white pawns.

3 ♗c5 g6 4 ♗b4 ♗d8 5 f4?

How can a grandmaster commit such 'hara kiri'? Better was 5 f3 ♗c7 6 ♗e1 ♔e6 7· ♔e3 ♔f5 and then ...f7-f6, ...g6-g5, the bishop goes to d6, and upon the move ♗e1-f2 follows ...b5-b4 with the unpleasant restriction of living space.

5...♔e6 6 ♔e3 ♔f5 7 ♔f3 ♗b6 8 ♗c3

Probably White reckoned on 8 ♗c5, but after 8...♗xc5 9 dxc5 ♔e6 10 ♔e3 ♔d7 and then ♔c6 Black has a tempo move with the pawn.

7...♗c7!

But now it's zugzwang – the main cause of defeat in bishop endgames – he has to allow the black king into his camp.

9 ♔e3 ♔g4 10 ♔f2 ♔h3 11 ♔f3 f5! 12 ♔f2 ♔h2 13 ♔f3 ♔g1 14 ♔e3 ♔g2 15 ♗e1 ♗b6!, yet another zugzwang, and so White resigned, **0-1**

266 Grigat – Karker
Germany 1995

Here White makes the mistake of waiting...

1 ♗c6?

After 1 f4+! ♔d6 2 ♔f3 h5 3 gxh5 ♗xh5 4 g4 White holds the draw.

1...♗f7 2 ♗b5?

Again correct would have been 2 f4!.

4...f5! 3 gxf5 ♔xf5 4 g4+

Now he has to make an ugly move in order to prevent ...h6-h5 with the creation of a passed pawn.

4...♔e5 5 ♗a6 ♗g6 6 ♗b5 ♗b1 7 ♗a6 ♗a2 8 ♗b5 ♗b3

The first zugzwang – he has to allow the king in.

9 ♔d3 ♔f4 10 ♔e2 ♗a2 11 ♗a6 ♗b1 12 ♗c8 ♗g6 13 ♗d7 h5!

Now it is necessary to create a weakness on f3.

14 gxh5 ♗xh5 15 ♗c6 ♗f7 16 ♗b5 ♗e6 17 ♗a6 ♗h3 18 ♔f2

On 18 ♗b5 there is 18...♗g2 19 ♗c6 g4, but also now followed:

18...g4! 19 fxg4 ♗xg4 20 ♗b7 ♗e6 21 ♔e2

The last chance was 21 a5! bxa5 22 ♔e2 ♗xc4+ 23 ♔d2 ♗b5 24 ♔c3 ♔e3 25 ♗d5, endeavouring to give up the bishop for the c5 pawn.

21...♗xc4+ 22 ♔d2 ♔e5 23 ♔c3 ♗d5 24 ♗a6 ♗c6 25 ♔b3

Clearly not 25 a5 because of 25...b5!

25...♔d4 26 ♗e2 ♗d5+ 27 ♔a3 ♗c4 28 ♗f3 ♗a6 29 ♔b3 ♔d3 30 ♗g4 c4+, White resigned, **0-1**

267 Ahmadeev – Arkhangelsky
Riazan 1996

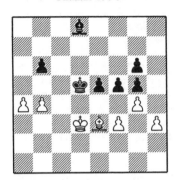

White has the advantage on account of the distant passed pawn and the two weaknesses in Black's camp, though also the opponent has a more active king. White has a choice of two plans.

a) **1 ♗g1**
Playing for zugzwang.
1...♗c7 2 ♗f2 ♗d8 3 ♗e3 e4+ 4 fxe4 fxe4+ 5 ♔e2?
Correct is 5 ♔c3 ♗f6+ 6 ♔c2 ♗d8 (or 6...♗d4 7 ♔d2 winning) 7 ♔b3 ♗c7 8 ♗xg5 ♔d4 9 ♔c2 e3 10 ♗h4 ♔c4 11 ♗e1 and then a4-a5.
5...♔c4 6 ♗d2 ♗c7 7 a5 bxa5 8 bxa5 ♔b5 9 ♔f2 ♗b8
More accurate is 9...♗d6 10 ♗xg5 ♔xa5 11 ♔e3 ♔b5 12 ♔xe4 ♔c6, and the endgame is drawn.
10 ♗xg5 ♔xa5 11 ♔e3 ♔b5 12 ♗f4!
Winning an important tempo.
12...♗a7+ 13 ♔xe4 ♔c6 14 ♗g5 ♔d6
Averbakh reckoned that after 14...♔d7 it's a draw, but what does he do after 15 ♔e5 and 16 ♔f6.
15 ♗e3!
The exchange is inevitable!
15...♗xe3 16 ♔xe3, Black resigned, **1-0**
b) **1 ♗d2!** (immediately creating a passed pawn) **1...e4+ 2 fxe4 fxe4+ 3**

♔e3 ♗f6 4 a5 bxa5 5 bxa5 ♗d4+ 6 ♔e2 and then 7 ♗e3 with a winning endgame.

268 Schneider – Schroder
Eppingen 1996

1...h6!
Preparing ...♗h4-g5 and ...♔f4.
2 ♗xh6 g5!
'Cutting off' the white bishop.
3 ♗f8 ♔f4 4 ♗c5 ♔f3 5 ♔d5 e3, White resigned, **0-1**

269 Shabalov – Varavin
Moscow 1984

Black to move is zugzwang but with White to move it seems impossible to set up zugzwang. However with a 20(!) move manoeuvre White wins.
1 ♗d2! ♗d8 2 ♗e1 ♗b6
Bad is 2...♗c7 3 ♗c3 zugzwang.

3 ♗h4 ♗e3 4 ♗g3 ♗d4 5 ♗h2 ♗b2 6 ♗g1 ♗a3

Not possible is 6...♗c1 7 ♗f2 ♗d2 8 ♗g3, and White wins.

7 ♗f2 ♗e7 8 ♗g3 ♗d6 9 ♗e1 ♗c7 10 ♗c3

It's a zugzwang position. But Black still has pawn moves.

10...h5 11 ♗d2 hxg4 12 hxg4 ♗d8 13 ♗e1 ♗b6 14 ♗h4 ♗e3 15 ♗g3 ♗d4 16 ♗h2 ♗b2 17 ♗g1 ♗a3 18 ♗f2 ♗e7 19 ♗g3 ♗f6 20 ♗h2 ♗g7 21 g5 ♗f8 22 ♗xe5 ♗e7 23 ♗f6 ♗b4?!

More stubborn is 23...♗d6. However after 24 ♗c3 ♗c7 25 ♗d2 ♗d8 26 ♗f4 ♗b6 27 e5 ♗d8 28 ♔d4 ♗b6+ 29 ♔e4 with the idea of e5-e6 White has the advantage.

24 ♗c3 ♗e7 25 ♗xa5 ♗xg5 26 b4 ♗f4 27 b5+ ♔d6 28 ♗c3! g5 29 e5+!

The pawn endgame is hopeless for Black.

29...♔c7 30 ♗a5+ ♔c8 31 ♔d5 g4 32 e6 g3 33 ♔c6 ♗g5 34 b6, Black resigned, **1-0**

270 Taimanov – Tseshkovsky
Minsk 1976

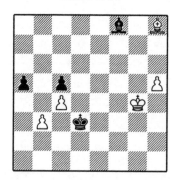

Despite White's extra pawn, chances of victory lie only with Black – in view of his active king.

1 ♔f5 ♔c2!

Inferior is 1...a4 2 bxa4 ♔xc4 3 ♗c3! ♔d5 4 ♔g6 c4 5 ♗b2 ♔c6 6 ♗c1 ♔d5 7 ♔f7 ♗d6 8 h6 ♗e5 with a draw.

2 ♔e4?

There is also no salvation in 2 ♔g6 ♔xb3 3 ♗g7? ♗xg7 4 ♔xg7 a4 with a win. But White has the resource 2 b4!! axb4 3 ♔e4 b3 4 ♔d5 b2 5 ♗xb2 ♔xb2 6 h6!, when he saves himself.

2...♔xb3 3 ♔d5 ♔b4, and Black wins, **0-1**

Yet another case where a lack of space usually leads to zugzwang.

271 Khalifman – Salov
Match, 1994

1 ♗b2?

Correct was 1 ♔f3! ♗e7 (or 1...g5 2 g4+ =) 2 g4+ hxg4 3 hxg4+ ♔e6 4 ♔g3 ♗d6+ 5 ♔f3 g5 6 ♔e2 ♗f4 7 f3 with a draw.

1...g5 2 ♗c1

Now on 2 ♔f3 g4+ 3 hxg4 hxg4+ 4 ♔e3 ♗e7 5 ♔d3 ♗g5 6 ♗a1 ♗c1 7 ♔c2 ♗a3 8 ♔d3 ♗g5 9 ♔e2 f5 10 ♔e3 ♗c1 11 ♔e2 f4 the black king breaks into the opponent's position.

2...g4+ 3 hxg4 ♔xg4 4 ♗d2 f5! 5 ♗e1 f4 6 f3+ ♔h3 7 gxf4 ♔g2! 8 f5 ♗e7! 9 f6 ♗xf6 10 ♗xb4 h4 11 ♗d6 h3 12 b4 ♗e7, White resigned, **0-1**

12 Karpov's Technique in Rook and Bishop Endgames

Rook endgames

The most famous 'technician' in rook endgames was the unforgettable Akiba Rubinstein. Among the greats in subsequent times is undoubtedly Anatoly Karpov for whom technique remains, unreservedly, his main weapon.

272 **Karpov – Korchnoi**
Brussels 1988

White's plan is firstly to centralise his king, and then to get to work on the pawns on Black's queenside.

1 ♔f3 ♔e6 2 ♔e4 ♔d6+ 3 ♔d4 ♔d7 4 g4!

First of all White tries to exploit his majority on the kingside.

4...♖e8 5 e4 b6 6 ♖d5+ ♔e7 7 e5 ♖f8 8 ♖d6!

Now weaknesses are apparent in Black's position.

8...b5 9 ♖xa6!

Inferior is 9 f4 fxe5 10 ♔xe5 ♖xf4!.

9...fxe5+ 10 ♔xe5 ♖xf2 11 ♖a7+ ♔f8 12 h5! ♖f3 13 ♔d4

The objective is the b5 pawn.

13...♖f4+ 14 ♔c5 ♖xg4 15 ♔xb5 ♖g5+ 16 ♔c6 ♖xh5

Black wins back the pawn but now other factors come into play – the white pawns are further advanced and indeed all White's pieces are better placed.

17 b5 ♖h6+ 18 ♔c7 ♖h3 19 b6 ♔e7 20 b7 ♖c3+ 21 ♔b6 ♖b3+ 22 ♔c6, Black resigned, **1-0**

273 **Karpov – Korchnoi**
Biel 1992

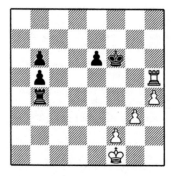

White obviously has the better pawn structure, therefore his chances of victory are very great.

1 ♔g2 ♔g6

On 1...♖b1 simplest is 2 g4 with a win.

2 ♖e5 ♔f6 3 f4 ♖b2+

After 3...♖b1 4 h5 b4 winning is 5 ♖b5.

4 ♔f3 b4 5 ♖b5 b3 6 ♔g4 ♖b1 7 ♔h5! b2 8 g4, Black resigned, since on 8...♖f1 there follows 9 ♖xb2 ♖xf4 10 ♖xb6 ♖a4 11 ♖b7! and 12 g5+ **1-0**

274 Ehlvest – Karpov
Linares 1991

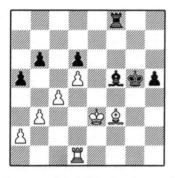

It seems that White has no problems, but there follows a transfer to a rook endgame.

1...♗g4! 2 ♗xg4 hxg4 3 ♖h1 ♖f6!

Brilliant prophylaxis in true Karpov style – inferior is 3...g3 4 ♖h3 ♔g4 5 ♖h6! with counterplay.

4 ♔e2 g3 5 ♖f1 ♖f4!

Transferring to a pawn endgame – only on Black's terms.

6 a3 ♔g4 7 b4 axb4 8 axb4 g2! 9 ♖xf4+ ♔xf4 10 ♔f2 ♔e5!

Namely this, but not 10...♔e4? 11 c5!=.

11 ♔xg2 ♔d4 12 c5 bxc5 13 bxc5 ♔xc5, White resigned, **0-1**

275 Karpov – Ehlvest
Belfort 1988

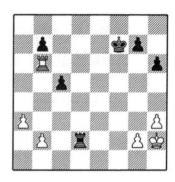

White has the advantage in the arrangement of his pieces, and his king can enter the game.

1...♖d7

After 1...c4 2 ♖xb7+ ♔f6 3 a4 ♖c2 4 a5 c3 5 bxc3 ♖xc3 6 a6 there is nothing to be done.

2 ♔g3 ♔e7

It is better to try and 'cast off' a pawn by 2...♖c7 3 ♔f4 c4 and then ...c3.

3 ♔f4 ♔d8 4 ♖b5! ♖c7 5 ♔e5!

What active pieces White has!

5...♔c8 6 ♔d5 ♔b8 7 g4 ♖e7 8 ♖xc5 ♖e2 9 ♖b5 ♔c7 10 ♖b3!

Now it is necessary to activate the rook.

10... g6 11 ♖c3+ ♔b6 12 b3 h5 13 ♖f3 hxg4 14 hxg4 ♔a5 15 ♖f7 ♖g2 16 ♖xb7! ♖xg4 17 ♔c5 ♖g5+ 18 ♔c6 ♔a6 19 b4, Black resigned, **1-0**

276 Karpov – Gelfand
Linares 1991

Black has a weakness on c6, but this does not look so terrible.

1 g4!

It is important to designate play on his stronger flank.

1...hxg4 2 hxg4 ♔f6 3 ♔g3 ♔e6 4 a4!

Trying to 'cut out' the black rook after a4-a5.

4...♔d7 5 g5!

And now fixing a second weakness on f7.

5...♖a6 6 ♖d4+ ♔e8

After 6...♔e6 7 ♖c5! ♖d7 8 a5 ♖d5! creating some sort of chances.

7 ♖c5 ♖b6 8 ♔f4 ♖d7 9 ♖xd7 ♔xd7 10 ♔e5!

The white king is in play!

10...♔e7 11 f4 ♖b4 12 ♖a5 ♖b7 13 e4!

Now White's plan is clear – to create a passed pawn on the kingside.

13...♖c7 14 ♖c5 ♖c8 15 ♖c3!

Preparing to break through with the rook on the h-file.

15...♖e8 16 ♖c4!

Prophylaxis against the discovered check.

16...♖c8 17 ♖b4 ♖c7 18 a5 ♔d7 19 ♖b3 ♔e7 20 a6 ♔d7 21 ♔f6 ♔c8 22 ♖h3! ♖d7 23 f5 gxf5 24

exf5 c5 25 ♖c3 ♖c7 26 g6 fxg6 27 fxg6 ♔d7 28 g7 ♖c8 29 ♖g3 Black resigned, **1-0**

277 Antunes – Karpov
Tilburg 1994

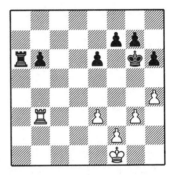

Despite the extra pawn, Black's chances of victory ought not to be high because of the passive position of his rook.

1 e4

Better is 1 g4 ♔f6 2 ♖b5 with the idea of g5.

1...♔f6 2 f4 ♔e7 3 ♔e2 ♔d6 4 g4

After 4 ♖d3+ ♔c6 5 ♖c3+ ♔b7 6 ♖d3 ♖a7! (Karpov prophylaxis!) and Black has all the chances.

4...♖a2+ 5 ♔e3 ♔c6 6 ♖c3+ ♔b7 7 ♖d3 ♖c2 8 h5 b5 9 e5 ♔c7 10 ♖a3 ♔b6 11 ♖a8 ♖c3+! 12 ♔d4 ♖c4+ 13 ♔e3 ♖c7 14 ♖g8 b4 15 ♔d3 b3! 16 ♖b8+ ♔b7 17 ♖c8

He cannot transpose to the pawn endgame – it is lost.

17...♖a7! 18 ♖c1 ♖b5!

A fantastic reconstruction of the black pieces!

19 ♔c3 ♔b6 20 ♔b2 ♖b4 21 ♖f1 ♔c5 22 ♖f3 ♔d5 23 ♖f1 ♔e4 24 ♔c3 ♖b7

The well known Karpov prophylaxis – principally defending the seventh rank.

25 ♔b2 ♔e3, White resigned, 0-1

278 **Kasparov – Karpov**
World championship, Moscow 1984

1...♖a8!

Back to its starting position!

2 ♖a5 ♔b6 3 ♖a2 a5 4 ♔f1 a4 5 ♔e2 ♔c5 6 ♔d2 a3 7 ♔c1 ♔d4 8 f4 ♔e4 9 ♔b1 ♖b8+!

Black exploits the chance to get his rook out of the eighth rank.

10 ♔a1 ♖b2! 11 ♖xa3 ♖xh2 12 ♔b1 ♖d2! 13 ♖a6 ♔f5 14 ♖a7 g5! 15 ♖a6 g4! 16 ♖xh6 ♖g2 17 ♖h5+ ♔e4 18 f5 ♖f2!! 19 ♔c1 ♔f3 20 ♔d1 ♔xg3 21 ♔e1 ♔g2

The position is reminiscent of the ending to the game Fischer-Geller.

22 ♖g5 g3 23 ♖h5 ♖f4 24 ♔e2 ♖e4+ 25 ♔d3 ♔f3 26 ♖h1 g2 27 ♖h3+ ♔g4 28 ♖h8 ♖f4 29 ♔e2 ♖xf5, White resigned, **0-1**

279 **Karpov – Sokolov**
Brussels 1988

1...f5

There was a simple draw by 1...♔g8 2 ♖xb7 h5! and then 3...a5.

2 ♖xb7 h5 3 ♔g2 ♖a2?

Again better was 3...♔h6 4 ♔f3 g6 and then ...a5.

4 h3 ♖b2?

But why this?

5 ♖b6!

Eliminating the threat of ...a6-a5.

5...g6 6 ♔f3 ♖a2 7 e4!

Only in this way is it possible to activate the king.

7...fxe4+ 8 ♔xe4 a5?

Apparently the decisive mistake – after 8...♖xf2 9 ♖xa6 ♖b2 10 ♖b6 ♖b3 there are still drawing chances.

9 b5! a4

After 9...♖xf2 10 ♖a6 ♖b2 11 ♖xa5 the position is lost.

10 ♖a6 ♖xf2 11 b6! h4 12 gxh4 ♔h6

An attempt to include the king in the game.

13 ♔d5 ♖f5+ 14 ♔c6 ♖f6+ 15 ♔b5 ♖f5+ 16 ♔xa4, Black resigned **1-0**

280 **Karpov – Knaak**
Baden 1992

The difficulties in the realisation of such a position are generally well known – the main thing is to find a function for the rook, and Karpov demonstrates this.

1 ♖a3!! g5

Or 1...Rc1+ 2 ♔d2 Ra1 3 ♔c2 winning.

2 ♔d2 ♔g6 3 Rc3 Ra5 4 a3 h5 5 ♔c2 Ra8 6 ♔b3 Rb8+ 7 ♔a2 Ra8

Better is 7...Rd8!? 8 Rc2 Rd3!, somehow preventing the activation of the white king.

8 Rc4! f5 9 a4 ♔f6 10 ♔a3 ♔e5 11 Rc5+

Inferior is 11 h4 g4 12 g3 ♔d6 13 Rf4 Ra5 14 ♔b4 Re5!.

11...♔e4 12 a5 h4 13 ♔a4 ♔f4

After 13...g4 14 hxg4 fxg4 there is 15 Rh5!.

14 Rc4+ ♔e5 15 Rb4 ♔d5 16 Rb5+ ♔e4 17 Rb6! ♔f4 18 a6 g4 19 ♔a5 g3

Or 19...gxh3 20 Rb4+! with a decisive advantage.

20 Rb4+ ♔e5 21 f3 f4 22 Re4+ ♔f5 23 Re2!!,

This is typical Karpov – no counterplay! Black resigned, **1-0**

281 **Karpov – Hort**
Waddinxveen 1979

Black has a 'damaged' structure, and the white rook is obviously more active.

1 Ra3! Re7

Weak is 1...Ra8 2 Ra6, and then the white king takes flight to g5.

2 Ra5!

Now the white rook is as active as it can be on the fifth rank, where it cuts off the black king.

2...♔f7 3 h4 h6 4 g4 ♔f6 5 f4!

Allowing ...g7-g5 would not be desirable.

5...Rb7 6 ♔f3 Rc7 7 Ra6 g6 8 Ra5 Rd7 9 e3 Rb7 10 h5!

Black has a weakness on a7, and he will be saddled with yet another weakness on h6.

10...g5 11 Ra6 gxf4 12 exf4 Rb3+ 13 ♔g2 Rb7 14 ♔g3 ♔f7 15 Ra4!

Defending the king against future possible checks along the fifth rank.

15...♔g7 16 g5 Rc7 17 Ra5 ♔g8 18 Rb5!

Now he has time to activate the rook.

18...♔f7 19 ♔g4 a6 20 Rb8 Rc1 21 g6+ ♔g7 22 Rb7+ ♔f8 23 Rb6!

The pawn will fall!

23...Rg1+ 24 ♔f3 Rf1+ 25 ♔e4 Re1+ 26 ♔d4 ♔e7 27 Rxa6 ♔f6 28 Ra7 e5+ 29 fxe5+ Rxe5 30 Ra6+,

Black resigned, **1-0**

At times, of course, even on the sun there will be spots. The following endgame was presented in the second of our books and Karpov ought to have known the classic game Smyslov-Gligoric, Warsaw 1947, in which Black demonstrated a straightforward winning plan.

282 **Ribli – Karpov**
Budapest 1973

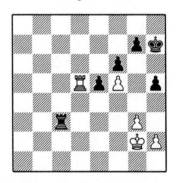

1 h4

Denying the black king any possible access to g5.

1...罝c6

There is apparently no other plan of activating the black king – after 1...e4 2 罝d4 罝c2+ 3 ⬦g1 e3 4 罝e4 the draw is obvious.

2 ⬦f3 g6 3 fxg6+ ⬦xg6 3 罝d8 罝c3+ 4 ⬦f2 ⬦f5 5 罝h8 罝c2+ 6 ⬦e3 ⬦g4 7 罝g8+ ⬦f5

After 7...⬦h3 8 罝g6 罝c3+ 9 ⬦f2 f5 10 罝g5 draw.

8 罝h8 罝c3+?

Here Karpov fails to find Korchnoi's plan 8 e4!.

9 ⬦f2 e4! 10 罝g8

After 10 罝xh5+ ⬦g4 11 罝h6 罝f3+! Black wins.

10...罝a3 11 罝e8 罝a4 12 罝g8 罝a2+ 13 ⬦e3 罝g2 14 罝g7 ⬦e5 15 罝e7+ ⬦d5 16 罝d7+ ⬦e6 17 罝a7 罝xg3+ 18 ⬦xe4 罝g4+ 19 ⬦f3

And clearly without any problem White made a draw in the classical endgame against the f and h-pawns.

½-½

Anatoly Karpov's technique in play with opposite-coloured bishops

283 Ljuboević – Karpov
Milan 1975

The first disciple of Mikhail Botvinnik took much from his teacher, and particularly brought perfection into play with opposite-coloured bishops, where his superiority in exploiting the slightly better piece was truly incredible.

1...⬦h5!

An ingenious transfer of the bishop to b3.

2 ⬦f6 ⬦f7 3 ⬦e5 ⬦b3! 4 ⬦g7 b5 5 ⬦f8 c4 6 ⬦g7 b4!

Here comes the breakthrough.

7 ⬦d4

Or 7 axb4 c3 8 bxc3 ⬦c4! and then a4-a3-a2-a1=♛.

7...c3 8 bxc3 bxa3 9 c4 a2 10 ⬦d5 ⬦b1, and Black wins, **0-1**

284 Karpov – Khalifman
Linares 1995

In the present position Karpov has the possibility of creating threats on different flanks.

1 a5! e6 2 ⬦f3 b5

A struggle on the light squares.

3 d5! bxc4 4 dxe6 ♛xe6 5 bxc4

The whole difference in the power of the bishops is that White's can attack whereas Black's does not get the chance.

5...♛f5 6 ⬦g2 ⬦f6 7 a6 h5 8 罝e1 罝c5 9 ⬦d5 罝b8 10 罝c2 ⬦g7 11

♗e4 ♕d7 12 ♗b7! ♕c7 13 ♕d3 ♖d8 14 ♗d5 ♕a5 15 ♖b1!

From this moment one begins to sense that threats are emerging for White.

15...♕xa6 16 ♖b7 ♖f8 17 ♖e2!

The bishop enters the game.

17...♖a5 18 ♖e3! ♖a1 19 ♖f3

Everything is on f7.

19...♖e1 20 ♖xf6! ♔xf6 21 ♕f3+,

and White gained victory, **1-0**

285 Karpov – Short
Lucerne 1989

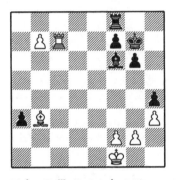

1...♗e5 2 ♖c8 g5 3 ♔e2 f5

Black's chances lie only in the creation of weaknesses on the opponent's kingside.

4 ♔d3 g4 5 f3!

Ending play on the flank.

5...gxh3 6 gxh3 ♗f4 7 ♔d4 ♗d6 8 ♔d5 ♗g3 9 ♔c5 ♗e5 10 ♗a2 ♗f4 11 ♔b5 ♗g3 12 ♔a4 ♗d6 13 ♗c4!

Zugzwang, now on 13...♖h8 follows 14 ♖c6, and the a3 pawn falls.

13...♖f6 14 ♔b3 ♖g6 15 b8=♕ ♗xb8 16 ♖xb8 ♖g3 17 ♖g8+ ♔f6 18 ♖xg3! hxg3 19 ♗f1 ♔g5 20 ♗g2, and White wins, **1-0**

286 Alterman – Karpov
Czech Republic 1997

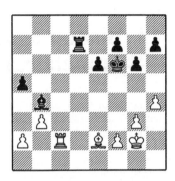

To obtain minimal chances Black should try to exploit his advantage on the kingside.

1...e5 2 h5 ♔g5 3 hxg6 hxg6 4 ♔f1 ♖d6!

For future defence of the weakness on g6.

5 ♔g2 f5 6 ♔f1 ♔f6 7 ♔g2 e4 8 ♔f1?

He should throw caution to the wind by 8 f3 e3 9 f4 and 10 ♔f3.

8...♔e5 9 ♔g2 g5 10 ♔f1 ♖d8 11 ♔g2 f4 12 f3

A principle of Dvoretsky – pawns on the same colour squares of the bishop!

12...e3 14 g4 ♖d2!

A clearly calculated endgame.

15 ♖xd2 exd2 16 ♗d1 ♔d4 17 ♔f2 ♔c3 18 ♔e2 ♔b2 19 ♔d3

After 19 a4? ♔c1 – zugzwang.

19...♔b1!

Not 19...♔xa2 20 ♔c2 with a draw.

20 a3 ♔c1! 21 ♔e2 ♗xa3 22 b4 axb4 23 ♗a4 ♔b2 24 ♔d1 b3 25 ♗c6 ♔a1, White resigned, **0-1**

13 Bishop against Knight with a Symmetrical Pawn Structure

In endgames of this type the knight is usually successful in contending with the bishop. But if the side with the knight faces an opponent with an active bishop then he might encounter quite complex problems.

287 **Kasparov – Salov**
USSR 1987

1...♘xa4?

Black starts with a mistake – correct was 1...♔e6!, controlling the important d5 square, 2 ♗b8 (or 2 ♗xg7 ♘xa4 3 ♗f8 ♘b2 4 ♗a3 ♘d1! 5 ♗c1 ♘f2) 2...a5! 3 bxa6 (3 ♗a7 ♘d7) ♘xa6 4 ♗a7 ♘c5 with a draw.

2 ♗b8!

On 2 ♔d5 Black manages to achieve a draw by 2...♘c5 3 ♔c6 g6 4 ♗d6 ♔e6! 5 ♗xc5 bxc5 6 ♔xc5 ♔d7.

2...♔e6

After 2...h4 3 gxh4 ♔g6 winning is 4 ♗xa7 ♔h5 5 ♔c4 ♔xh4 6 ♔b4

♘c5 7 ♗xb6 ♘d3+ 8 ♔c4 ♘xf4 9 ♗a5 ♘e6 10 ♔d5 ♘f8 11 ♔d6!, cutting off the knight from the passed pawn.

3 ♗xa7 g6

After 3...♔d6 there is 4 ♗b8+ ♔e6 5 ♗c7 ♔d7 6 ♗e5! ♘c5 7 ♔d5 ♘e6 8 ♗b8 g6 9 ♗a7 h4 10 ♗xb6 hxg3 11 hxg3 g5 12 ♔e5 gxf4 13 gxf4 winning.

4 ♔c4 h4 5 gxh4 ♘b2+ 6 ♔c3 ♘a4+ 7 ♔b4 ♘c5 8 ♗xb6 ♘d3+ 9 ♔c4 ♘xf4 10 ♗f2

The b-pawn cuts off the black king, whereas the white king dashes over to the other side.

10...♘h3 11 ♗a7 ♔d7 12 ♔d5 ♘f4+ 13 ♔e5 ♘h5 14 ♗c5 f4 15 ♗f2 ♔e7 16 ♔e4 ♔e6 17 ♗d4 ♔d6 18 ♔f3 ♔d5 19 b6!, and Black resigned, **1-0**

288 **Mikhalchishin – Kupreichik**
Lviv 1986

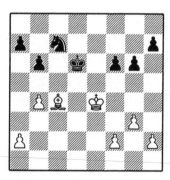

1 g4?

Correct was to immediately define the structure on the kingside by means of 1 ♗g8, without fearing 1...f5+.

1...♘e6 2 h4

The pawn endgame after 2 ♗xe6 ♔xe6 3 f4 promises some chance of victory, but obviously he does not want to exchange the strong bishop.

2...♘g7 3 ♗g8 h6 4 ♗f7 g5 5 hxg5?

A principally incorrect exchange – after 5 h5 the white king would have prospects of travelling to the g6 square.

5...hxg5 6 ♗b3 ♘e8

Now, however, it turns out that the itinerary of the king to g6 is pointless.

7 ♗f7 ♘c7 8 ♗c4 ♘e8, and ½-½

289 **Ivanchuk – Epishin**
Terasn 1992

1...g6?

Correct was to advance 1...h6 and not to place the pawns on white squares.

2 ♗c4+ ♔f6 3 a4 h6 4 h4!

In the game was played 4 h3 g5 5 h4 gxh4 6 gxh4 ♘e6!, and the pawn endgame turned out to be drawn.

4...h5 5 a5 ♔e7 6 ♔e5 bxa5 7 bxa5 ♘e8 8 ♗d5 ♘d6 9 ♔d4 ♔d7 10 ♗f3 with a great advantage.

290 **Kasparov – Karpov**
World Championship, London 1986

Again a symmetrical formation and again the side having the bishop has chances of victory.

1...♘c7

After 1...♘d6+ 2 ♔d5 ♘xc4 3 ♔xc4 ♔d6 (inferior is 3...a6 4 ♔d5 ♔d7 5 g4 a5 6 a4 ♔c7 7 h4 ♔d7 8 h5 ♔c7 9 g5! winning) arises a typically symmetrical pawn endgame, analysed earlier. After 4 ♔b5 ♔c7 5 ♔a6 ♔b8 6 f5 h5 7 h4! ♔a8 8 a3 ♔b8 9 a4 ♔a8 10 a5 bxa5 11 ♔xa5 ♔b7 12 ♔b5 ♔c7 13 ♔c5 ♔d7 14 ♔d5 ♔c7 15 f6! g6 16 ♔c5 ♔d7 17 ♔b5 ♔c7 18 ♔a6 ♔b8 19 b4! the march of the b-pawn decides.

2 ♔e5 f6+ 3 ♔f5 ♘e8 4 ♔e4 ♘c7 5 h4 ♔d6 6 ♔f5 ♔e7 7 ♔g6 ♔f8 8 ♔f5 ♔e7 9 ♔e4

Bad is 9 g4? ♘e8 10 ♔e4 f5!.

9...♔d6 10 g4 ♔e7

Another passive defensive method was 10...♘e6 11 ♔f5 ♘f8.

11 b4?

A serious mistake. Correct was 11 a3! ♔d6 12 ♔f5 ♔e7 13 ♔g6 ♔f8 14 g5 fxg5 15 fxg5 hxg5 16 ♔xg5 with a great advantage.

11...♔d6 12 ♔f5 ♔e7, and since after 13 g5 fxg5 14 fxg5 hxg5 15 hxg5 ♘e8 16 ♔e5 ♘d6 17 ♗d5 a5! the resources of both sides for playing for a win were exhausted, ½-½

14 Positional Draw

This is a very interesting method of defence, usually exploited by chess-players of higher rank. The method consists of the construction of an impregnable position or in the creation of a position where combinational motives make ineffective any superiority in the opponent's forces.

291 Portisch – Kavalek
Montreal 1978

Simplest here was 1 ♗e1 ♔c6 2 b4 with a win. But Portisch played at once

1 b4?, and after 1...♘b8 2 b5 ♘c6! White's bishop and pawn do not win against the lone king, ½-½

An analogous idea in expressed in the following instructive position.

292 Vuković

Bad here is 1 ♔xc4 because of 1...b6, and there is no defence against 2...♔b7. Therefore...

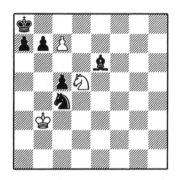

1 c8=♕+!! ♗xc8 2 ♘c7+ ♔b8 3 ♘a6+!! bxa6 4 ♔xc4 and 5 ♔xc5 with a draw.

293 Macieja – Skalik
Poland 1996

Does Black stand to win? Let's see.

1 c5!! ♗xc5

After 1...♖xc5 2 ♖xb4 ♖a5 3 ♖g4+ ♔f7 4 b3 a3 5 b4 the draw is obvious.

2 ♖c4 ♔f7

If 2...a3 then simply 3 b3 and 4 c3 forces a draw.

3 b3! axb3

After 3...♔e6 4 bxa4 ♔d5 5 ♔b3 follows 6 c3 with an exchange of the last pawn.

4 ♔xb3 ♔e6 5 c3, reaching a drawn endgame , ½-½

294 **Gdanski – Macieja**
Poland 1999

A very unpleasant endgame for Black. The g7 pawn is hanging and the approach of the white king to g6 is threatened.

1...♔d6! 2 h5

After 2 ♖xg7 ♖h6 3 ♖g4 ♖h5 Black marshals his defence.

2...♖e7 3 ♖g6+ ♔c7 4 h4

Black's position now looks lost, but he finds a splendid chance.

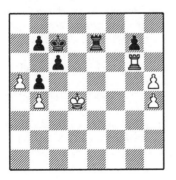

4...b6! 5 a6 ♔b8! 6 ♖xc6 ♔a7 7 ♔d5 ♔xa6 8 h6 gxh6 9 ♖xh6 ♖h7!!,

Black's drawing resource lay precisely in this stalemate idea.

½-½

295 **Granda – Stefansson**
Las Vegas 1997

1...♖h1+!!

Black's only chance of salvation can be without rooks and with a blockading knight.

2 ♔xh1 ♘g3+ 3 ♔g1 ♘xe4 4 ♔f1 ♔g6 5 ♔e2 ♔f5 6 ♔d3 ♔e5 7 ♔c4 ♔e6 8 ♗f4 ♔f5 9 ♔d4 ♘f6 10 ♗b8 ♘e4 11 ♗c7 ♘f6 12 ♗d8 ♘e4 13 ♗c7 ♘f6 14 ♗b8 ♘e4 15 ♗e5 ♘f2 16 ♔d5 ♔g4?

It is incomprehensible what Black had in mind by needlesly lifting the blockade.

17 ♔e6! ♘e4

Clearly not 17...♔xh4 because of 18 ♔f5, and the black king is arrested.

18 ♗f6 ♘c5+ 19 ♔d5 ♘d3 20 ♗g5!, and the blockade is broken and there is no defence against e3-e4, **1-0**

296 Sveshnikov – Nikolić
Bled 2000

Black has a knight for just one pawn, and White's only chance is the distant passed a-pawn.

1...♕b5+ 2 ♔c1 ♔e8 3 ♕a8+ ♔d7 4 ♕a7+ ♔d8 5 a6 ♘c8?

Possibly 5...♘c6 is also not winning, but undoubtedly it was more active and deserved the preference.

6 ♕b7!

Here also the key position is reached. Now bad is 6...♘d6 because of 7 ♕a8 and 8 a7 with the threat of 9 ♕b8.

6...♕c5 7 ♕a8 ♕e3+ 8 ♔d1 ♕b6 9 ♕b7 ♕c7 10 ♕b4!

Preparing to meet 10...♘b6 with 11 a7!.

10...♕d7 11 ♔c1 ♕d5 12 ♕b7!

Again a drawn setup.

12...♕d4 13 ♕c6 ♕d7 14 ♕b7 e5 15 ♕b4 ♕e7 16 ♕b7 ♕c5 17 ♕b8 e4 18 a7! ♕e3+ 19 ♔d1 ♕xa7 20 ♕xa7 ♘xa7 21 ♔e2 ♘b5 22 ♔e3 ♘d6 23 c4! and because of the threat of 24 c5 it's a draw, ½-½

297 Leko – Beliavsky
Istanbul 2001

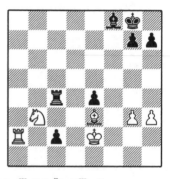

1...♖c3 2 ♘c1 ♖c4!

Black defends against ♖a4. Now both the c2 and e4 pawns are defended, and it is very difficult for White to break through the defence.

3 ♖a7 ♗d6 4 ♖d7 ♗a3!

Not allowing ♖d7-d4.

5 ♖b7 ♖c3 6 ♗d2 ♖xg3 7 ♔f2 e3+!

Transposing to a classical endgame of rook against bishop which is a draw with the correct arrangement of pawns.

8 ♗xe3 ♖xe3 9 ♔xe3 ♗xc1+ 10 ♔d3 h5!

It is very important not to allow g2-g4.

11 ♔xc2 ♗h6 12 ♔d3 g6, and Black establishes the basic fortress in this endgame – draw, ½-½

298 Cebalo – Mikhalchishin
Ptuj 1995

1 ♘xb3! ♖xb3 2 ♖d6+ ♔e5 3 ♖d3

It seems that the bishop must be stronger than a pawn but surprisingly the fortress cannot be breached.

3...h6 4 ♔g2 ♔e4 5 ♖g3 ♔d4 6 ♖e3 ♖b6 7 ♖g3 ♗d2 8 ♖f3 ♔e4 9 ♖a3 ♖g6+ 10 ♖g3! ♖c6 11 ♖f3 ♗f4 12 ♖a3 ♖g6+ 13 ♔f1 ♗e5 14 ♖e3+ ♔f4 15 ♖g3! ♖d6 16 ♔g2 ♔f5 17 ♖f3+ ♗f4 18 ♖a3 ♖g6+ 19 ♔f1 ♗h2 20 ♔e2 ♖g1 21 ♖d3 ♔g5 22 ♖d1 ♖xd1 23 ♔xd1 ♔f4 24 ♔e2 h5 25 ♔f1 ♔f3 26 h4!, and ½-½.

299 Rodriguez – Mikhalchishin
Belgrade 1988

A positional draw is very often achieved with the help of tactics. Here the white knight is cut off and

Black threatens simply to 'eat' it, therefore White must do something.

1 g4! ♔b5 2 gxf5 gxf5 3 ♘c3+! ♗xc3 4 ♔f4, and a draw, ½-½

300 Mikhalchishin – Ivanchuk
Lviv 1987

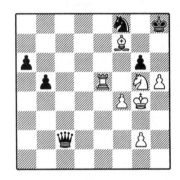

White's position does not look good, and the only chance is to play against the black king.

1 h6!! ♕xg2+ 2 ♔h4 ♕h2+ 3 ♔g4 ♕xh6 4 ♖e8 ♔g7 5 ♗d5 ♕h5+ 6 ♔g3 ♕d1 7 ♖e7+ ♔h8 8 ♘f7+! ♔g7 9 ♘g5+, and it turns out that around the black king is woven a drawing net of white pieces, ½-½

301 Romanishin – Beliavsky
Erevan 1975

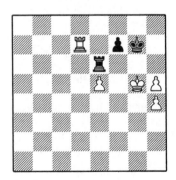

White has two extra pawns and it seems chances of victory. But Black finds a chance to fight for a draw.

1 h6+ ♔g8 2 h7+ ♔h8!

The corner is the best place for the king.

3 ♔f5 ♖g6 4 h5

After 4 ♖xf7 the black rook becomes 'wild' 4...♖g5+!!, and the white king cannot get away.

4...♖g1 5 ♔f6 ♖f1+ 6 ♔e7 ♖f5!

A typical 'trailer' in the rook endgame.

7 ♔d6 ♖f1 8 ♖e7 ♖f2 9 h6 ♖d2+ 10 ♔c6 ♖d1 11 ♖e8+

After the capture on f7 the rook again becomes 'wild'.

11...♔xh7 12 ♖e7, draw, ½-½

302 **Kasparov – Kramnik**
London 2000

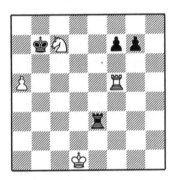

1 ♖xf7?!

Incredible but this natural move is not the best. Correct is 1 ♘d5 ♖e4 (or 1...♖a3 2 ♘b4 f6 3 ♖b5+ ♔c7 4 ♔c2 etc.) 2 ♔c2 g6 3 ♖f6 ♖a4 4 ♖b6+ ♔a7 5 ♖b5, and then again the approach of the king.

1...♖e5?

The only way of constructing a fortress was by 1...♔c6 2 ♘a8 ♖e5! 3 a6 ♖a5 4 a7 g5, and it is unclear how White can overcome Black's defence.

2 a6+?

Correct was again to coordinate his pieces by 2 ♘d5+ ♔c6 3 ♘b4+ ♔b5 4 ♖f4.

2...♔b6 3 ♖xg7 ♖a5!

Now the white pieces occupy inconvenient positions.

4 ♔d2 ♖a1 5 ♔c2 ♖h1??

Unbelievable, but this only shows how difficult is the theme of the positional draw. It is necessary to hold the a6 pawn literally by the teeth with 5...♖a5! and not let it go!

6 ♔b2??

Correct is 6 ♖g8! ♖a1 7 ♘d5+ ♔c5 8 ♖g5 and at the right moment to transfer the knight to b4.

6...♖h8! 7 ♔b3 ♖c8 8 a7 ♔xa7, and a draw ½-½

303 **Hasin – Bronstein**
Moscow 1957

A game position which is a real study. It turns out that Black cannot win this position:

1 ♔c4 ♗h6 2 ♔b4 ♗f8+ 3 ♔c4 ♗e7 4 ♔d5 ♔xb5 5 ♔e6 ♗d8 6 ♔d7 ♗a5 7 ♔e6 ♗c3 8 ♔f7 – draw. ½-½

304 Filip – Bronstein
Moscow 1967

In the game Black played 1...♗c2, avoiding variations which lead the endgame to a position similar to the previous one.

1...gxf2+ 2 ♔xf2 ♔g4 3 ♔e3 ♗b5 4 ♔d4 ♔f3 5 ♔c5!

Losing is 5 a4 ♗a6 6 a5 ♔e2.

5...♗a6 6 ♔b6 ♗c8 7 ♔c5 ♗e6 8 ♔d4 ♔e2 9 a4 ♔d2 10 a5 ♔c2 11 a6 – draw. ½-½

15 Computers and Endgames

Computer programs have entered seriously into opening theory and work on opening theory is now simply impossible without the use of ChessBase. Situations with endgames are rather different – here the direction is changed. The computer is like a bulldozer working out all positions till the end, where the amount of material allows – this relates, for example, to five-piece positions such as rook against one pawn. John Nunn even wrote a book with the objective of elucidating computer analysis, but chessplayers are not very interested in this work... Another direction is to play a program in an endgame and generally assess the positions through analysis gained with the help of Fritz, Crafty and other monsters.

Here is one interesting example:

305 **Rogozenko-Morozevich**
Istanbul 2000

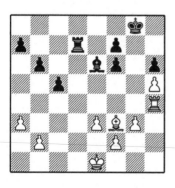

This is what Morozevich wrote: "Strange – all the chess programs considered that White stood better *(in the evaluation function doubled pawns have a very strong influence on the assessment – A.M.)*. In fact, however, Black has the advantage – his control of the d-file and queenside pawn majority might begin to tell. Now best was to transfer to a rook endgame by 1 ♗g4! ♖d5 2 ♗xe6 fxe6 3 ♔e2 ♔f7 4 e4 ♖d4 5 ♖g4 with equality.

In the game, however, there followed:

1 ♗e2?! ♗b3! 2 ♖f4 ♔g7 3 g4 ♖d6 4 ♖e4 ♔f8 5 ♖f4 a5 6 ♖e4

Better looks 6 ♗c4 ♖d1+ 7 ♔e2 ♖b1 8 ♔d3.

6...♖d8 7 ♖f4 ♔e7 8 ♖e4+ ♔d6 9 ♗d1 ♗e6! 10 ♗e2?

Again better is 10 ♖f4.

10...f5 11 gxf5 ♗xf5 12 ♖f4 ♔e5 13 ♖f3 b5!

The advance begins.

14 e4?

Correct is 14 ♖f4 b4 15 ♖c4 ♔d6 with a slight advantage for Black.

14...♗e6!

Now White stands badly, for example, 15 ♗xb5 ♗g4 16 ♖d3 ♖xd3 17 ♗xd3 ♗xh5.

15 ♖c3 c4 16 f3 ♔f4 17 ♖c2 ♖d4 18 ♗d1 b4 19 axb4 axb4 20 ♗e2 ♔e3 21 ♖c1 ♖d2 22 ♗xc4 ♖h2, and it is time to resign, **0-1**

Computers have carried out analyses of all five-piece endgames

– and endgames of two bishops against knight were assessed as winning; however several grandmasters have found that with the production of a position with the knight on b2,b7,g2,g7 there is no win.

306 Oll – Gelfand
Polanica Zdroj 1998

1 ♘e3! ♗d4 2 ♔f4 ♗f6 3 ♘g2 ♔d4 4 ♔f3 ♗d5+ 5 ♔f2 ♔e4 6 ♔g3 ♗e5+ 7 ♔f2 ♗b7 8 ♘h4 ♗h8 9 ♘g2 ♔f5 10 ♘e3+ ♔f4 11 ♘g2+ ♔g4 12 ♘e3+ ♔h3 13 ♘d1 ♗d4+ 14 ♔e2 ♔g3 15 ♔d2 ♔f3 16 ♔c2!

Now to the other setup in the other corner.

16...♔e2 17 ♘c3+ ♔e1 18 ♔b3 ♔d2 19 ♔c4 ♗e3 20 ♘a4 ♗c6 21 ♘c5 ♗g2 22 ♘b3+ ♔c2 23 ♘d4+ ♔b2 24 ♔d3 ♗g5 25 ♔e2 ♗d5 26 ♘f3!

And now forward!

26...♗f6 27 ♔f2 ♔c3 28 ♔g3 ♔d3 29 ♘h4 ♔e2 30 ♘f5 ♗e6 31 ♔f4 ♗d7 32 ♘g3 ♔d3 33 ♘f5 ♔c4 34 ♘e3+ ♔d4 35 ♘g2 ♔d3 36 ♔f3 ♗c6+ 37 ♔f2 ♗g5 38 ♘e1 ♔e4 39 ♘g2 ♔f5 40 ♔g3, draw, ½-½

In the endgame it is possible to display resourcefulness and surprise the soulless machine.

307 Anand – Fritz
Frankfurt 1999

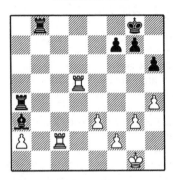

1 ♖d7!

Feeling threatened, Black exchanges rooks or attacks the a2 pawn, but White does not want to play passively by 1 ♖dd2.

1...♗b2 2 ♔g2! ♖xa2? 3 ♖dd2!, and the bishop is in a cage – a positional draw.

An interesting endgame arose in the game:

308 Bareev – Junior 6
Dortmund 2000

Bareev sacrificed a pawn right in the opening. Everybody knows that computers particularly like to accept sacrifices. And White now makes one more...

1...g5!

White reckoned on 1...♘xg2 2 ♘xd5+ ♚b8 3 ♘e7! ♘f4 4 ♚d4 g5 5 ♘xf5 ♘xh3 6 ♚e3 ♘f4 7 ♘h4 ♘d5 8 ♚f3 gxh4 9 ♚g4 with a draw.

2 ♚d4 g4!

In any other case a draw is again achieved: 2...♘xg2 3 ♚xd5 g4 4 ♚e5 g3 (4...gxh3 5 ♘d3 ♘e1 6 ♘f2) 5 ♘xd5+ ♚c6 6 ♚xf5 ♘e1 7 ♘e3 g2 8 ♘xg2.

3 ♚c5!

Fantastic! By sacrificing both **pawns** on the kingside, White **coordinates** his scant forces and obliges Black to force a draw.

3...d4 4 ♚xd4 ♘xg2 5 ♘d3 gxh3

Or 5...g3 4 ♘e5 f4 (4...♘f4 5 ♚e5 ♘xh3 6 ♚f5) 5 ♘f3 ♘e3 6 ♚e4 or 6 ♘xh4 with a draw.

6 ♘f2 h2 7 ♚e5 f4 8 ♚e4 ♚b6, and a draw, ½-½

Clearly it is pointless to analyse endgames over the board with computers, and possibly it only teaches young players incorrect assessments. Material in the evaluation function of all programs is so predominant that when there is an advantage of a pawn or even just doubled pawns a correct assessment is impossible.

16 Exploiting Analogous Thoughts When Playing Endgames

For qualified chessplayers, this is a very important method of struggle in endgames, based on intuitive thinking. Here an active role is played by a knowledge of methods of play in endgames and familiarity with the classical legacy.

309 Anderssen – Steinitz
London 1866

Knight endgames are the same as pawn endgames, as taught by the great Botvinnik, and a relationship of 3:2 on one flank offers the greatest chance of a win in pawn endgames and, after that, in those with knights.

1 ♘e5+?

A mistake. According to an analysis by Fine, leading to a draw is 1 ♔g2! ♔f5 2 f3 g5 3 ♔f2 ♘c5 4 ♘e7+ ♔e6 5 ♘c6! ♔d5 6 ♘e7+ ♔c4 7 ♘f5 h5 8 ♘xg7 h4 9 ♔e2 ♔d4 10 ♘e8 etc.

1...♔f5 2 ♘d3 g6 3 ♘e1 ♘d4+ 4 ♔g2 ♔e4 5 ♔f1 f3 6 ♔g1 g5 7 ♔h2 h5 8 ♔g3 ♘f5+

But here winning is 8...♘e2+! 9 ♔h2 h4 10 ♘c2 ♘f4 11 ♘e3 ♔d3 and 12...♔e2.

9 ♔h2 g4?

How, in such an endgame, could he exchange to the small pawn majority which will now remain?

10 hxg4 hxg4 11 ♔g1 ♔d4 12 ♘c2 ♔d3 13 ♘a3?

To the edge of the board – shame! After 13 ♘b4+! ♔e2 14 ♘d5 the win is not easy.

13...g3! 14 ♘b5 g2, and there is no defence against ...♘f5-d4-e2, therefore Black wins, **0-1**

The history of the following endgame is very entertaining. It came about during a match between two of the strongest players in the West at that time. Fine worked as a psychologist in a New York hospital and did not want to spend his free day playing off this endgame. He phoned Najdorf and said: "This is a draw – look at my book". Najdorf looked at the book and did not agree!

310 Fine – Najdorf
New York 1949

The further continuation of the game was:

1...♘c2!

With the threat of 2...♘c2-e1, h6-h5, and zugzwang.

2 ♔g2 ♘e1+ 3 ♔f2 ♔xh3! 4 ♔xe1 ♔g2!

After the typical piece sacrifice the march of the h6 pawn is inevitable.

5 ♔e2 h5 6 ♘g5 h4 7 ♘e6 g5! 8 ♘xg5 h3 9 ♘xh3 ♔xh3 10 ♔f2 ♔h2, and White resigned, **0-1**

311 Sermek – Beliavsky
Portoroz 2001

1 ♔h3?

Correct was to go with the king to the first rank 1 ♔g1! ♕xa2 2 ♕c3+ ♔g8 3 ♔f1, moving the king over to the distant pawn – this is a rule of queen endgames.

1...♕xa2 2 b5 ♕f2!

A double function for the queen – cutting off the king and also the passed pawn. Draw! ½-½

An analogous case occurred some years later in the following game:

312 Beliavsky – Gelfand
Linares 1993

1...♔h6?

Again in the wrong direction – the king should go to the distant pawn 1...♔f8, then 2...♕d6 and 3...♕c5, threatening to advance the b6 pawn, and after the checks by the white queen, the king gets out via d6 with chances of a win. But now follows a typical cutting-off move.

2 ♕f7! b5 3 f4 ♕h8 4 ♔h2 ♕g7 5 ♕e8 b4 6 ♕b8 h4 7 gxh4 ♕e7 8 ♔g3 ♕e3+ 9 ♔g4, and a draw. ½-½

17 The Connection of the Opening and the Endgame

In two games of Palatnik arose the following position, deep in a rook endgame.

313

We begin with the later game.

Palatnik – Rashkovsky
Palma de Mallorca 1989

28...♚e7 29 ♖a6
The white rook occupies an ideal position, forcing both black pieces to defend their weaknesses. The black rook cannot abandon the c7 square, where it simultaneously defends the pawns on a7 and c5, while the black king cannot leave the e6 pawn undefended. For Black there remains only to move the king along the squares d7, e7, f7 or advance the pawns on the kingside. At the same time White has a clear plan to win. It consists of the following: firstly the activation of the king, and then a minority attack, in order to create additional pawn weaknesses or weak squares for the penetration of the white king. However, if this plan is not crowned with success White still has in reserve play on the queenside by a2-a3, b3-b4.

29...e5??
A very big positional mistake. True, Black frees his king from the defence of the e6 pawn, but he considerably weakens the d5 square.

30 ♚g2 ♚f7 31 ♚f3 f5
A forced advance, otherwise the white king penetrates into Black's camp.

32 h3! g6 33 g4 ♚e7 34 ♚e3 ♚f7 35 gxf5 gxf5 36 ♖h6
After 36...♚f8 37 ♖e6 ♖e7 38 ♖c6 Black loses a pawn, therefore he resigned.

There was a more interesting development of events in the game:

Palatnik – Maksimenko
Kherson 1989

28...f5 29 f4 h6 30 h4 ♚e7 31 ♖a6 ♖d7
An attempt to activate the rook fails. This would work only in the case of 32 ♖c6? ♖d1+ 33 ♚f2 ♖d2+ 34 ♚e3 ♖xa2 35 ♖xc5 ♖b2 with counterplay.

32 ♚f2 g6
There was the threat to paralyse the pawn structure by h4-h5.

33 ♚e3 ♖c7 34 ♚d3

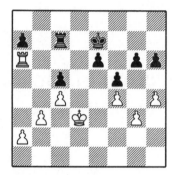

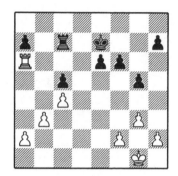

The situation on the kingside has been established in White's favour – his three pawns without difficulty hold the four pawns of his opponent. Black has no chances at all of counterplay, and it is possible to proceed with the next stage of the plan.

34...♔f6 35 a3 g5 36 hxg5+ hxg5 37 b4!

White sticks to the main line. Later on, in certain cases, the black pawns could be a source of unpleasantness for White.

37...cxb4

There is also no salvation in an attack on the f4 pawn: 37...gxf4 38 gxf4 ♖d7+ 39 ♔c3 ♖d4 40 bxc5 ♖xf4 41 ♖xa7 ♖g4 (41...♔e5 42 ♖d7!) 42 c6 ♖g8 43 ♖d7 e5 44 c7 ♖c8 45 c5 ♔e6 46 c6, and White wins.

38 axb4 ♖h7 39 fxg5+ ♔e5 40 ♖a5+ ♔d6 41 ♔d4

The struggle is at an end. After a few moves Black resigned, **1-0**

Palatnik's clear and logical play in this endgame demonstrates White's possibilities, but did not give a simple answer to the question whether it is a win or not. Probably the best defence would have been:

28...♔e7 29 ♖a6 g5!

Sample variations are:

a) 30 f3 ♖d7 with counterplay;

b) 30 f4 g4 with the idea of f6-f5, ♔d6, h7-h5-h4;

c) 30 ♔f1 f5! 31 ♔e2 ♔f6 32 ♔d3 h5 33 a3 ♖b7 34 ♔c3 ♔e5 with counterplay – 35 b4 cxb4+ 36 axb4 h4;

d) 30 g4 h5! (30...♔d7 31 ♔g2 f5 32 gxf5 exf5 33 h4! gxh4 34 ♔h3) 31 gxh5 (31 h3 hxg4 32 hxg4 ♔d7 33 ♔g2 f5) 31...f5 (with the idea of ♔f6-e5) 32 ♔g2 ♔f6 33 ♔g3 ♔e5 34 f3 ♖h7 35 ♖c6 ♖xh5 36 ♖xc5 ♔d4 37 ♖c6 e5 38 ♖d6 ♔e3, and at the cost of a pawn Black has succeeded in activating all his forces.

Now, however, let us see a position reached by two different move orders:

Palatnik – Maksimenko
Slav Defence

1 c4 c6 2 d4 d5 3 ♘f3 ♘f6 4 ♕c2 e6 5 g3 ♗b4+ 6 ♗d2 ♗e7 7 ♗g2 b6 8 0-0 ♘bd7 9 b3 0-0 10 ♖d1 ♗b7

Palatnik – Rashkovsky
Bogoljubow Defence

1 d4 ♘f6 2 c4 e6 3 g3 ♗b4+ 4 ♗d2 ♗e7 5 ♗g2 d5 6 ♘f3 0-0 7

0-0 c6 8 ♕c2 b6 9 b3 ♗b7 10 ♖d1 ♘8d7

Further play in both games was identical.

314

11 ♘c3 ♖c8 12 e4 dxe4 13 ♘e5 c5 14 ♗f4 cxd4 15 ♖xd4 ♗c5 16 ♖xd7! ♘xd7 17 ♖d1 ♖c7 18 ♘b5 ♕e7 19 ♘xc7 ♘xe5 20 ♗xe5 f6 21 ♗d4 ♕xc7 22 ♗xc5 bxc5 23 ♗e4 ♗xe4 24 ♕xe4 ♖e8 25 ♕d3 ♖e7 26 ♕d8+ ♔f7 27 ♕xc7 ♖xc7 28 ♖d6

Let us have a look at the following game:

Rashkovsky – Platonov
USSR 1980

1 d4 ♘f6 2 c4 e6 3 ♘f3 b6 4 g3 ♗a6 5 b3 ♗b4+ 6 ♗d2 ♗e7 7 ♘c3 c6 8 e4 d5 9 ♕c2 dxe4 10 ♘xe4 ♘bd7 11 ♗g2 0-0 12 0-0 c5 13 ♖ad1 ♗b7 14 ♘xf6+ ♗xf6 15 ♘g5 ♗xg5 16 ♗xb7 ♖b8 17 dxc5 ♗xd2 18 ♖xd2 ♖xb7 19 c6 ♖c7 20 ♖fd1 ♖xc6 21 ♖xd7 ♕b8 22 ♕e4 ♖c7 23 ♖1d6 h6 24 h4 ♕c8 25 ♕d4 ♖xd7 26 ♖xd7 ♕a6 27 a4 ♕a5 28 ♕d2 ♕xd2 29 ♖xd2

Once again the rook endgame has arisen. The enormous difference in the activity of the rooks indicates that White has a decisive advantage.

315

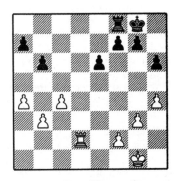

29...a6 30 ♖d7 ♖c8 31 ♔f1 b5 32 cxb5 axb5 33 a5 ♖c1+ 34 ♔e2 ♖a1 35 b4 ♖a4 36 h5 ♖xb4 37 a6 ♖a4 38 a7 ♔h7 39 ♖xf7, Black resigned, 1-0

316 **Ivanov – Lengyel**
Sarajevo 1980

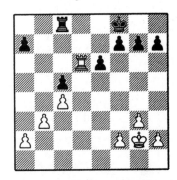

An insignificant difference between the present position and the endgame in Palatnik-Rashkovsky lies not only in the position of the white king, but mainly in the position of the black pawn on f7 instead of f6. Now the pawn on e6 is invulnerable, which frees the black king, and the result of the game amounts to a draw.

31...♔e7 32 ♖a6 ♖c7 33 ♔f3 ♔d7

Worth serious consideration is the plan to advance the g-pawn: 33...g5 34 ♔e4 ♖d7 35 ♔e3 ♖c7 36 g4! h5, but then dangerous is 37 h3! hxg4 38 hxg4 f5 39 gxf5 exf5 40 ♖g6, and White has a decisive advantage.

34 ♔e4 ♔c8

In the event of 34...♔e7 White would apply the plan with a2-a3, b3-b4.

35 ♔e5 ♔d7?!

Black stops half-way. He should play 35...♔b7! 36 ♖d6 (36 ♔d6 ♖c8 37 ♖a5 ♖c6 38 ♔e7 ♖c7+ 39 ♔f8 f6 40 h4 h5) 36...♖e7! with a draw.

In the game after 35...♔d7?! White won by carrying out the following plan:
1) advancing the pawns on the kingside to provoke ...f6;
2) advancing f4-f5 to enable him to occupy the d5 square;
3) as a result of these moves the c5 pawn will fall.

To conclude, a short excursion to the past.

317 Flohr – Maroczy
Bled 1931

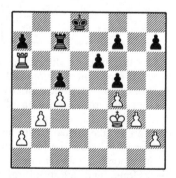

The difference between this position and the preceding one is the structure of the black kingside. This redoubles Black's problems.

34 ♔e3 ♔c8 35 ♖a5 f6?

Passive defence likewise does not bring results: 35...♔b7 36 ♖b5+ ♔c8 37 ♔d3 followed by a2-a3, b3-b4.

36 ♖a6 ♔d7 37 g4! fxg4

No help either is 37...♔e7 38 gxf5 exf5 39 ♔d3.

38 f5! ♖c6 39 ♖xa7+ ♔d6 40 ♔f4! h5 41 ♖f7 ♖a6 42 ♖xf6 ♖xa2 43 ♖xe6+ ♔d7 44 ♔g3, and White wins. **1-0**

We encounter such endgames also in our day.

318 Stohl – Skembris
1992

1 d4 d5 2 c4 c6 3 ♘c3 ♘f6 4 ♘f3 e6 5 e3 ♘bd7 6 ♕c2 ♗d6 7 ♗e2 0-0 8 0-0 ♖e8 9 ♖d1 ♕e7 10 b3 b6 11 e4 ♘xe4 12 ♘xe4 dxe4 13 ♕xe4 ♗b7 14 ♗f4 ♗xf4 15 ♕xf4 c5! 16 ♕c7 ♖ab8 17 ♘e5 ♘xe5 18 ♕xe7 ♘f3+! 19 ♗xf3 ♖xe7 20 ♗xb7 ♖exb7 21 dxc5 bxc5 22 ♖d6 ♖c7 23 ♖ad1 ♔f8 24 ♖a6 ♔e7 25 ♖dd6

A well known position? And the plan of defence is also well known. 25...♖d8 26 ♖xd8 ♔xd8 followed by ...♔d8-c8-b7 with a draw.

Transfer to an endgame with doubled pawns

The great Botvinnik and Smyslov had in their technical arsenal an interesting weapon – transfer to an endgame with doubled pawns (which, in principle, is not encouraged in the endgame). But they saw its advantage in the exploitation of open lines. It is very interesting to evaluate this element with modern computer programs (Fritz, Crafy and others) – in these doubled pawns are installed as a negative element. But in chess everything is concrete!

319 Botvinnik – Sorokin
Moscow 1931

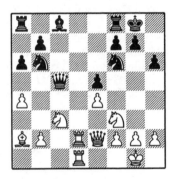

1 ♕e3! ♕xe3

Black's reply is practically forced, since on 1...♕c7 there is 2 ♘xe5.

2 fxe3 ♗g4 3 a5 ♘c8

After 3...♘bd7 4 h3 ♗xf3 5 gxf3 ♘c5 6 b4 ♘e6 7 ♗xe6 fxe6 8 ♘a4 and White has a great advantage lnked to the threat of ♘c5.

4 ♖c1! ♗xf3 5 gxf3 ♘e6 6 ♘d5! ♘c6 7 ♘xf6+ gxf6 8 ♖d7 ♖ab8 9 ♔f2!

With the idea of ♖g1.

9...♘xa5 10 ♖cc7 ♖bc8 11 ♖xf7 ♖xc7 12 ♖xc7 ♔h8 13 ♗d5! b5 14

b3 ♖d8 15 ♔g3 f5 16 ♔h4!, and White has a decisive advantage.

320 Botvinnik – Euwe
The Hague 1948

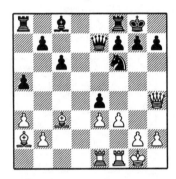

1...♘d5

No good is 1...exf3 2 ♗b1! h6 3 ♖xf3 ♘d5 4 ♖g3, and White wins.

2 ♕xe7 ♘xe7 3 fxe4 b6

After 3...♗e6 4 ♗xe6 fxe6 5 ♖xf8+ ♔xf8 6 ♖f1+! ♔g8 7 ♖d1 White has the advantage in view of the threat ♖d7.

4 ♖d1 ♘g6 5 ♖d6 ♗a6 6 ♖f2 ♗b5

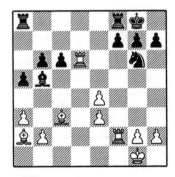

7 e5!

Black's main weakness is the f7 square, and the e-pawn serves as a battering ram!

7...♘e7 8 e4!

With control over all the central squares.

8...c5 9 e6! f6 10 ℤxb6 ♗c6 11 ℤxc6! ♘xc6 12 e7+ ♔f7 13 ♗d5, and White wins, **1-0**

321 Smyslov – Tal
Candidates tournament,
Yugoslavia 1959

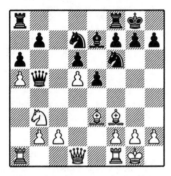

1 ♕d3! ℤfc8 2 ℤfc1 ♕xd3 3 cxd3 g6

Bad is 3...♘c5 4 ♘xc5 dxc5 5 d6 with a win for White.

4 ℤc3! ℤxc3 5 bxc3 ℤc8 6 c4 e4!

The only chance of counterplay against the latent threat of 7 ℤb1xb7.

7 dxe4 ℤxc4 8 ♘d2 ℤc2 9 ♗d1 ℤc3 10 ♔f1! ♘c5 11 ♗d4 ℤd3 12 ♗xc5 dxc5

There is no change in the assessment after 12...ℤxd2 13 ♗e3 ℤb2 14 ℤc1, and White has the advantage.

13 ♔e2 ℤxd2+

After 13...ℤd4 White has 14 f3.

14 ♔xd2 ♘xe4+ 15 ♔c2 ♘d6

There is no salvation in 15...♘xf2 16 ♗f3 f5 17 ℤb1, when White wins.

16 ♗e2 ♘f6 17 ℤb1 ♔f8 18 ♔b3 ♔e7 19 ♗d3 ♔d7 20 f4 ♗d4 21 ℤf1 ♗e3 22 f5, and White has a great advantage.

322 Rashkovsky – Loginov
Moscow 1995

1 ♕b3! ♕xb3 2 axb3

White's advantage is defined by his knight in the centre, while the doubled pawns only help him.

2...a6 3 ℤfc1 ♘d5 4 g4 g6 5 ℤc4 ♗g7 6 ℤa5 ℤcd8 7 ♘e2! ♘f6 8 g5 ♘g4 9 ♘c3 ℤd2 10 ♘xe4 ℤxb2 11 h3 b5 12 ℤc7 ♘e5 13 ℤxa6 ℤe8 14 ℤf6 ℤd8 15 ♘d6 h6 16 ♘xf7 hxg5 17 ℤd6 ℤxd6 18 ♘xd6+ ♔f6 19 ♘xb5 ♘f3+ 20 ♔g2 ♘e1+ 21 ♔g3 ♘d3 22 ℤc6+ ♔e7 23 ♘d4 ℤxf2 24 ℤc2!, and White won, **1-0**

323 Glek – Groszpeter
Paris 1996

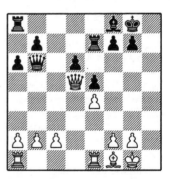

1 ♕b3! ♕xb3 2 axb3 ℤd7 3 ♗c4 g6 4 c3 ♔g7 5 b4!

Improving his formation – with White on black squares.

5...♖c8 6 ♗d5 ♗e7 7 ♖e3! ♗d8 8 ♖d3 ♖a8

With the idea of ...a5.

9 ♗c4 ♗c7 10 ♖d2 ♖dd8 11 ♗d5 ♖ab8 12 ♖d3 ♖f8 13 ♔f1! ♖h8 14 ♔e2 ♖h2 15 ♖f3 f6 16 ♖h3! ♖xh3 17 gxh3 f5 18 h4 ♔f6 19 ♖h1! a5 20 bxa5 ♗xa5 21 h5 ♖h8?

Better is 21...gxh5 22 ♖xh5 with the idea of ♖h6 or b2-b4 with advantage to White.

22 h6! f4 23 b4 ♗b6 24 ♗xb7!, and White won, **1-0**

324 Oral – Fedorov
Leon 2001

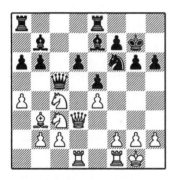

Modern young chessplayers have adopted this technical method from the veterans.

1 ♕e3!

The weaknesses on b6 and on d6 determine White's advantage.

1...♕xe3 2 fxe3 b5 3 axb5 axb5 4 ♘b6 b4 5 ♘cd5!

There is no tactical device – only the d5 square.

5...♖a6 6 ♗c4 ♗xd5 7 ♘xd5 ♘xd5 8 ♖xd5 ♖c6 9 ♗b3

Now it turns out that Black has an exceptionally weak f7 square.

9...♗g5 10 ♔f2 ♖c5 11 ♔e2 f5!?

Risky but insufficient.

12 exf5 ♖xd5 13 ♗xd5 gxf5 14 ♖xf5 ♖c8

Black plans 14...♖f8, but the bishop endgame is lost in view of the fact that White can create passed pawns on different flanks.

15 ♔d3 ♖f8 16 ♖xf8 ♔xf8 17 ♔c4! ♗xe3 18 ♔xb4 ♔e7 19 ♔b5 ♔d7 20 g4 ♗f2 21 ♔a6 ♔c7 22 b4 ♗e1 23 b5 ♗f2 24 h3, zugzwang – Black resigned, **1-0**

18 Endgames in Super-Tournaments

Endgames at the Olympiad in Erevan 1996

Every Olympiad, where practically all the strongest players of the world contribute a great deal that is new in chess, features in the first instance many opening ideas and good combinations – indeed quite simply a large number of excellent games. Play at an Olympiad is very interesting also from the point of view of instructive endgames, a review of which will give chess spectators great satisfaction and can also be of great use in their own practice. Precisely from this angle we look at the most interesting endgames from the Olympiad. In the first place we are struck by the great number of mistakes, even in games by all the strongest players.

We start with the incredible.

325 Kazhgaleyev – Hellsten

'Everything' wins – simplest is 50 h4, but White had a contract to kill

'everyone': **50 ♕xg4??**, and after **50...♕g2+!** it was stalemate.

326 Kobese – Tu

Now after 64...♔g6 and then 65...h5 and 66...g4 the draw was obvious. But why did Black think he had to play more actively and continue **64...♔h4? 65 ♗g4 h5 66 ♔f5!**, when the pawn endgame is hopeless for Black.

327 Norri – Svidler

It's an elementary draw – White should simply wait, but he decided to make a draw in a more active way: **44 f5? gxf5 45 ♖h7 ♔g8 46 ♖xh5 ♖e5 47 ♔f3 f4!**, and he had to resign – the pawn endgame is hopeless.

But this lucky break for Svidler pales by comparison with the next example.

328 Svidler – Lobron

Here Lobron simply resigned, not seeing the obvious **61...♔g2 62 ♔c5 h1=♕ 63 ♖xh1 ♔xh1 64 ♔d4 ♔g2 65 ♔e5 ♔f3 66 ♔xf5 ♔e3**, and the king captures the c-pawn.

329 Bologan – J.Polgar

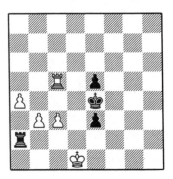

Leading to a draw here is 62 a5 ♔f3 63 ♖xe5 ♖a1+ 64 ♔c2 e2 65 b4 e1=♕ 66 ♖xe1 ♖xe1 67 ♔d3, but Bologan made the terrible move **62 ♖c8?**, and after **62...e2+!** just resigned – there is no defence against mate, **0-1**

330 Djurhuus – Sousa

There followed:
65...♔d7?
Correct was 65...♖a3! 66 ♖xe5 ♔d6 67 f4 ♖a8 68 ♔f5 ♖f8+ 69 ♔g5 ♖g8+ 70 ♔h6 ♖f8 71 ♖e4 ♔d5
There followed:
66 ♖xe5 ♖a3?!
Better is 66...♖a8 67 f4? ♖e8, with a draw.
67 ♔f4! ♖a1?.
Again in the wrong direction, but the impression is that Black has learned only the position of the rook behind and has not heard about the 'frontal attack' 67...♖a8 and 68...♖f8.
68 ♔g5 ♖f1
Now it is too late for 68...♖a8 69 f4 ♖g8+ 70 ♔h6 ♖f8 71 f5 ♔d6 72 ♖e6 etc.
69 f4 ♖a1 70 f5, and it was time for Black to resign, **1-0**

331 Mas – Hernandez

Now simplest was 60...♖b2 and 61...♖b6+ with an elementary draw, but Black played:

60...♖a1? 61 ♔e7 a4?

Again best was to return with the rook by 61...♖b1.

62 ♖g3+ ♔h7 63 e6 a3 64 ♖d3! a2 65 ♖d2!.

After this it's hopeless for Black.

65...♔g6 66 ♔d7 ♔f6 67 e7 ♖e1 68 ♖f2+ ♔g7 69 ♖xa2 ♖d1+ 70 ♔e8 ♔f6 71 ♔f8 ♖h1 72 ♖a6 Black resigned, **1-0**

332 Xu – Alterman

It looks like a draw, but there followed:

61...♖a2+?

Correct is 61...♔b6 62 ♖d3 ♔c6 63 ♔e3 ♖a8 64 ♔f4 ♖f8+ 65 ♔g5 ♖e8 66 ♖d4 ♔c5 67 ♖d5+ ♔c6, and White cannot strengthen his position.

62 ♔f3 ♔b7 63 ♔f4 ♔c7 64 ♖d3 ♖a8 65 ♖d4!

Clearly not 65 e5? ♖d8!=.

65...♖f8+ 66 ♔g5 ♖g8+ 67 ♔f5 ♖f8+ 68 ♔e6 ♖f4

Or 68...♖e8+ 69 ♔f7 ♖e5 70 ♔f6 etc.

69 ♖d7+ ♔c8 70 e5 ♖h4 71 ♖d1 ♖h6+ 72 ♔f7 Black resigned, **1-0**

333 Ricardi – Kotronias

There followed:

75...♔g7?!.

Why not 75...♖a4+ 76 ♔f3 ♔g7 77 ♔e3 ♖a3+ with an easy draw.

76 ♔f5 ♔f7?

Still leading to a draw, according to an old analysis by Romanovsky, was 76...♖a5+! 77 ♔e6 (77 ♔e4 ♖b5 78 ♖a7+ ♔g6 79 ♖b7 ♖a5 80 a7 ♔f6 81 ♔d4 ♔e6 82 ♔c4 ♔d6 83 ♔b4 ♔c6=) 77...♖h5!! 78 ♔d7 ♖h6 79 ♔c7 ♖f6 80 ♔b7 ♖f7+, etc.

77 ♔e5 ♔g7 78 ♔d5 ♖f1 79 ♖b8 ♖a1 80 ♖b7+ ♔f6 81 a7 Black resigned, **1-0**

334 Lauritsen – Kutirov

White must enter a pawn end-game, but what's the assessment?

Correct was 38 ♕xe6 fxe6 39 ♔f2 ♔g7 40 ♔f3 ♔f6 41 g4 hxg4+ 42 ♔xg4 b6 43 ♔g3 ♔f5 44 ♔f3 b5 45 ♔g3 ♔e4? 46 ♔g4, and it is only Black who can have problems. In the game was played:

38 ♕e5 ♕xe5 39 dxe5?

After 39 fxe5 ♔g7 40 ♔f2 f6 41 exf6+ ♔xf6 42 ♔e3 ♔f5 43 ♔f3 b6 44 ♔e3 ♔g4 45 ♔f2 ♔h3 46 ♔f3 ♔h2 47 ♔f2 b5 48 ♔f3, and dangerous is 48...♔g1 49 g4.

39...♔g7 40 ♔f2 f6 41 ♔e3

After 41 exf6+ ♔xf6 42 ♔e3 b6 43 ♔d4 ♔e6 Black has the chances.

41...fxe5 42 fxe5 ♔f7

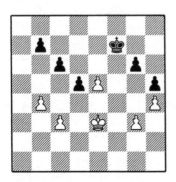

43 ♔f4

After 43 ♔d4 ♔e6 44 ♔c5 ♔xe5 45 ♔b6 d4 46 cxd4 ♔xd4 47 ♔xb7

c5! 48 bxc5 ♔xc5 49 ♔c7 ♔d5 50 ♔d7 ♔e4 51 ♔e6 ♔f3 Black wins.

43...b6! 44 g4 hxg4 45 ♔xg4 c5 46 bxc5 bxc5 47 ♔g5 c4! 48 e6+ ♔xe6 49 ♔xg6 d4 50 cxd4 c3, and it is time for White to resign, **0-1**

It is very easy to win a knight endgame...

335 Azmaiparashvili – Mitkov

There followed:

42 ♔e3 ♔e7 43 ♔d3!

Threatening, when the opportunity arises, to break through with the knight on b4.

43...h5 44 ♘c2! ♔e6 45 ♔d4 g5

On 45...♘b7 follows 46 ♘a3 b4 (46...♘a5 47 ♔c3) 47 ♘c4! with the threats of ♘d2 and ♔c4.

46 f3 g4 47 f4 ♘b7?

Better is 47...h4, though after 48 gxh4 ♘f5 49 ♔e4 ♘xh4 50 ♘d4 White has all the chances.

48 b4! f6 49 ♘e3 f5 50 ♘d5 ♘d6 51 ♘c3!

Zugzwang.

51...♘e4 52 ♘xe4, and Black resigned, **1-0**

Indeed, generally speaking, besides mistakes, in Olympic end-games we detect other tendencies such as shunning a tactical decision.

336 **Lobron – Blatny**

Losing is 62...axb6 63 ♔b5!, and there is no defence against a6-a7, but Black found the splendid chance **62...♗xb6! 63 ♘xb6 ♔c7 64 ♘d5+ ♔b8 65 ♔b5 ♔a8**, and the black king cannot be smoked out of the corner.

337 **J.Polgar – Antunes**

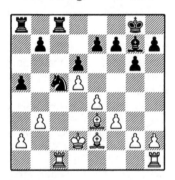

It seems that White has a comfortable position, but suddenly there followed **19...a4! 20 b4 ♘b3!! 21 axb3 ♖xc1 22 ♖xc1 a3!**, and it becomes clear that the pawn cannot be held. Judit began to search for counterchances.

23 ♗b5 a2 24 ♔d3 a1=♕ 25 ♖xa1 ♖xa1 26 ♗c6! ♖b1 27 ♔c4 ♖b2 28 ♗xb7 ♖c2+ 29 ♔d3

Really it is better to go *va banque* with 29 ♔b5.

29...♖c3+ 30 ♔e2 ♖xb3 31 ♗d2 ♗c3 32 ♗xc3 ♖xc3 33 b5 e5! 34 dxe6 fxe6 35 h4 ♔f7 36 g4 ♔e7 37 ♔f2 h6 38 f4

He cannot allow himself to be blockaded by ...g6-g5.

38...♖h3 39 e5 dxe5 40 fxe5 ♖c3!

There is no sense in falling into the trap after 40...♖xh4 41 ♔g3 g5 42 ♗f3.

41 b6 ♖b3 42 ♗e4 ♖xb6 43 ♗xg6 ♖b5 44 ♔f3 ♖xe5 45 ♔f4 ♔f6 46 ♗d3 ♖a5 47 ♗e4 e5+ 48 ♔e3 ♖a3+ 49 ♗d3 ♖b3 50 ♔e2 ♖b4 51 ♔f3 ♖f4+ 52 ♔g3 ♖d4! 53 ♗h7 ♖a4 54 ♔f3 ♖a3+ 55 ♔e4 ♖h3! 56 g5+ hxg5 57 hxg5+ ♔xg5 58 ♗f5 ♖a3 White resigned, 0-1

We would like to make a note of Black's technique in the following game:

338 **Bouaziz – Yusupov**

There followed:

34...♘f5! 35 ♕xa5 ♕xd4 36 ♕c7+ ♘e7 37 ♕c2 ♕g4 38 ♕d3 h4!

For the present creating some threats.

39 f3 ♕e6 40 ♔f2 ♘f5 41 g4

It is worth trying 41 b4 and 42 a5.

41...♘e7 42 ♕e3 ♕d6 43 f4 g5! 44 ♘f3

He has to give up a pawn.

**44...gxf4 45 ♕d2 h3 46 g5 ♘c6
47 ♕d3 ♔c5+ 48 ♔e2 ♕e7+! 49
♔f2 ♕e4 50 ♕c3 d4 51 ♕c4+ ♔g7
52 gxf6+ ♔xf6 53 ♕e2 ♕e3+ 54
♔f1 ♔f5**, and White resigned. **0-1**

And, to conclude, one more interesting rook endgame.

339 Soppe – Malishauskas

Here Black should refrain from the capture 60...♖h1 61 ♖a5 (threatening 62 ♔g7) ♔e6 62 ♔g6 ♖g1+ 63 ♔h7 ♖h1 64 h6 ♖h2 65 ♔g7 ♖g2+ 66 ♔h8 ♖h2 67 h7 ♖g2 68 ♖a8 ♔f7 69 ♖g8 ♖h2 70 ♖g7+ ♔f8 71 e6, exactly what occurred in the game Mikhalchishin-Kluger, Pecs 1978.

In our main game, however, was played:
60...♔xe5 61 ♔g5 ♖h1 62 ♖e8+ ♔d6 63 h6 ♖g1+

If 63...♔d7, then 64 ♖e4! with the threat ♖h4.

64 ♔f6 ♖f1+ 65 ♔g7 ♖g1+ 66 ♔h8 ♖h1

No help is 66...♔d7 67 ♖g8 ♖h1 68 h7 ♔e7 69 ♔g7 with an easy win.

67 h7 ♔d7 68 ♖a8 ♔e6

Trying to complicate the exit of the white king, but after
69 ♔g7 ♖g1+ 70 ♔f8 ♖f1+ 71 ♔e8 ♖h1 72 ♖a7

he had to resign, since there is no defence against the approach of the white king to g8. **1-0**

Endgames from the world championship in Groningen 1997

Let us look at endgames from the tournament in Groningen in two categories

1 Rook endgames
2 All other endgames

1 Rook endgames

We begin with a game betwen the winners at Groningen: Vishy Anand against Alexander Khalifman.

340 Anand – Khalifman

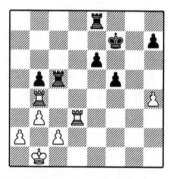

Black has two passed pawns in the centre and the better king, therefore he plays actively for the win.
36...e5 37 a4 e4 38 ♖d7+

The check looks silly, but on 38 ♖d1 follows 38...bxa4 39 ♖xa4 f4.
38...♔e6 39 ♖d1

It is clear that after 39 ♖xh7 e3 40 ♔c1 e2 41 ♔d2 ♔f6 42 ♔e1 ♖d5 he has to resign.
39...bxa4 40 ♖xa4 ♔e5 41 ♔c1 ♖ec8?!

Why? – after the reply the black rook on c5 will be badly placed.

After 41...e3 or 41...♚f4 White will be close to surrender.

42 c4 e3 43 ♖a7 ♖8c7 44 ♖a8 ♚e4 45 ♖8d8 f4?

But this is already the decisive error – better was 45...♖e5!, maintaining every chance of victory.

46 ♖1d4+ ♚e5

No use is 46...♚f3 47 ♖f8.

47 ♚d1 ♖c8 48 ♖8d7 ♖8c7?

Why? – after 48...♖a5 he still has chances. But now it's a draw.

49 ♖d8 ♖c8 draw, ½-½

341 Hansen – Miladinović

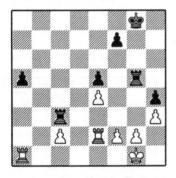

After the normal 28...♖c5 Black has a fortress position, while the exchange of the a5 pawn for that on h3 looks suicidal.

28...♖xh3? 29 ♖xa5 ♖c3 30 ♚h2 ♖c6 31 ♖d2 ♚g7 33 ♖ad5 ♖cg6 34 f3 ♖g3

How otherwise to contend with the advance of the c-pawn?

35 ♖f2!

Preventing h4-h3.

35...f6 36 c4 ♚h6 37 c5 ♚h5 38 ♖d7 ♖g8 39 c6 ♖3g7 40 ♖fd2 ♚g6 41 ♚h3 Black resigned, 1-0

An interesting endgame was seen in the next encounter:

342 Bareev – Malaniuk

36 h3

It is necessary to create a passed pawn.

36...♖f7 37 g4 hxg4 38 hxg4 ♖h7 39 f5 gxf5 40 gxf5 ♖f7?

When there is a choice – activity or passivity – then one should always prefer activation: 40...♖h1 with the threats of ♖d1 or ♖f1.

41 ♖f4 ♚e7 42 ♚d5 ♚f6 43 ♖f1 ♖e7 44 ♚c6 ♖h7 45 ♚b7 ♖g7

And here White waited with the rook instead of deciding on

46 ♖e1! ♚xf5 47 ♖e8 ♖g4 48 ♚xc7 ♖c4+ 49 ♚xb6 ♖xa4 50 ♚c6 ♖b4 51 b6, and Black has to resign, since on 51...d5 follows 52 b7 d4 53 b8=♕ ♖xb8 54 ♖xb8 d3 55 ♚c5 ♚e4 56 ♚c4 d2 57 ♖d8 ♚e3 57 ♚c3.

Another interesting game which the superior side failed to win came in one of the principal encounters of the Women's Candiddates tournament.

343 Chiburdanidze – Galliamova

White's position looks miserable, but Maia finds a splendid defence.

44 ♖f1+! ♔d2 45 ♖xf7! e4 46 ♔g2 e3 47 ♖e7 ♖d3 48 g4!

Creating chances for a passed pawn on the kingside.

48...♖d8

Other moves such as 48...♖d4 are no help because of 49 ♔f3.

49 ♔f3 ♖f8+ 50 ♔g2 ♖f4

After 50...e2 51 ♖d7+ ♔e1 52 ♖d6! ♖f2+ 53 ♔g1 ♖f4 54 h3 White threatens to take on h6.

51 ♖a7!

Transferring into known positions: the rook attacks the opponent's king with checks from the side.

51...e2 52 ♖a2+ ♔d1 53 ♖a1+ draw, ½-½

344 Ehlvest – Van der Wiel

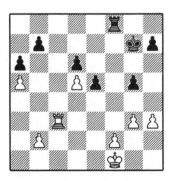

White stands a little better, and Black should occupy himself with all-round defence 30...h5 and 31...♖f7, awaiting White's action. Instead of this Black displays inappropriate activity.

30...♔f6? 31 ♔e2 e4 32 ♖c7 ♖b8 33 ♔e3 b6

Bad is 33...♔e5 34 ♖xh7 ♔xd5 35 ♖g7.

34 ♖xh7 bxa5 35 ♔xe4 ♖b4+ 36 ♔f3 ♖xb2 37 ♖h6+!

Now Black has the unpleasant choice – to give up the pawn on d6 or g5.

37...♔e5 38 ♖g6 ♔xd5 39 ♖xg5+ ♔c6 40 ♖xa5 ♔b6 41 ♖a1 ♖b3+ 42 ♔g4 d5 43 h4 d4 44 h5 d3 45 h6 ♔c5 47 h7 ♖b8 48 ♔f5 ♔c4 49 g4, Black resigned, **1-0**

2 Other endgames

Several times we have encountered very interesting knight endgames, one of which had a great influence on the course of the world championship.

345 Van Wely – Adams

62 ♘d4?

Correct was the transfer to a pawn endgame: 62 ♘d6! ♔e6 63 ♘e4 ♘xe4 64 fxe4 ♔xe5 65 ♔f3 ♔f6 66 h4! gxh4 67 ♔xf4, and then the king goes over to h3.

62...♘d7 63 e6 ♘e5 64 ♔d2 ♔d6 65 ♔c3 ♔e7 66 ♔b4 ♔d6 67 e7

What else is there to do – he has to give up the pawn – though it was possible to try to break through with the king to the d8 square but then on king e7 the knight from e5 goes to d3, and what then?

67...♔xe7 68 ♔c5 ♔f6 69 ♔d5 ♘d3 70 ♘c6 ♘e1 71 ♔e4 ♘g2 72 ♘d4 ♘e3 73 ♘f5 ♘c4 74 ♔d3 ♘e5+ 75 ♔e2 ♘g6 76 ♔f2 ♔e5 77 ♔g2 ♔f6 78 h3 ♘e5 79 ♘d6 ♔g6 80 ♘e4 ♔h6 81 ♔f2 ♔g6 82 ♔e2 ♔h6 83 ♘c5 ♔g6?

Black must have the possibility on ♘d3 to reply ...♘g6, defending the pawn on f4.

84 h4?

Correct was 84 ♘d3! ♘c4 85 h4, obtaining a winning position. The transposition of moves gives Black the possibility of saving himself.

84...gxh4 85 ♘e6 h3! 86 ♘xf4 ♔g5 87 ♘xh3+ ♔h4 88 ♘f2 ♔g3!

The black king breaks through to the white pawns, and a draw is inevitable.

89 g5 ♘xf3 90 g6 ♘d4+ 91 ♔d3 ♘e6 92 ♔e3, draw, ½-½

Despite his extra pawn Black surprisingly lost the next game...

346 Epishin – Sokolov

Black played
33...♘a8??

It is clear that correct was 33...♗b5 34 ♗xb5 ♘xb5 35 ♔b3 ♘c3 36 ♗b6 a4+ 37 ♔xb4 ♘xa2+ 38 ♔a4 ♘c1 39 ♔b4 ♘d3+, and the knight jumps out of the white camp. But with the knight on a8 the game does not last long.

34 ♗a6! ♗c6 35 ♔b3 ♔f8 36 ♔c4 ♘c7 37 ♔c5! ♗d7

After 37...♗xe4 38 fxe4 ♘xa6 39 ♔b6 the black pawn falls.

38 ♗c4 ♘e8 39 ♔b6 a4 40 ♗c5+ ♔g8 41 ♗xb4, Black resigned, since the loss of the a4 pawn is inevitable. **1-0**

And what did Milov do against Georgiev after declining a draw in the better position?

347 Milov – Georgiev

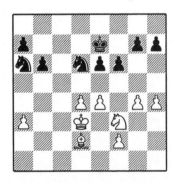

Correct was 23 e5, but White played

23 a4? e5! 24 ♗c3?

Correct is 24 a5! with equality.

24...exd4 25 ♗xd4 ♘b7!

And it is clear that he cannot defend the pawn – ♘c5 attacks it in two moves.

26 ♔c4 ♘ac5! 27 e5 ♘xa4 28 h5 ♘ac5 29 h6 gxh6 30 exf6+ ♔e6 31 ♔b5 ♔d5! 32 ♗e3 ♘d6+ 33 ♔b4 a5+, and it was time to resign. **0-1**

Black conducted the knight endgame very strongly in the game:

348 Glek – Nijboer

Black has the advantage on the queenside, and it is very important to devalue White's advantage on the kingside.

31...g5! 32 ♘f3 gxf4+ 33 ♔xf4 a5 34 g5 ♘e5!!

A beautiful trick. After 35 ♘xe5 fxg5+ 36 ♔xg5 ♔xe5 37 ♔h6 b4 Black queens the pawn. He has to step back.

35 ♘d2 fxg5+

Very good was 35...♘d3+ and 36...♘c1.

36 ♔xg5 b4! 37 cxb4 axb4

Now the march of the c-pawn is threatened.

38 ♔h6 c4 39 ♔xh7 c3 40 ♘b3 ♘f3+ 41 ♔g6 ♔e5 42 ♔h5 ♔xe4

43 ♔g4 ♘d4! 44 ♘c1 ♔e3 45 h4 ♔d2 46 h5 ♔xc1 47 h6 ♘c6! 48 h7

After 48 ♔f5 ♔b1 Black has simply an extra knight.

48...♘e5+ 49 ♔f5 ♘f7 50 ♔f6 ♘h8, and White resigned. **0-1**

Galliamova played very convincing chess, based on real preparation (she trained that year with Khalifman, Rublevsky and Bareev) and demonstrated very consistent technique.

349 Galliamova – Peng

30...♔e8

After 30...♗e7 31 ♗c3 ♗d6 32 ♗e5 ♗xe5 33 fxe5 and 34 a5 the pawn endgame is won for White.

31 f5 ♔f7

Another option was 31...gxf5 32 exf5 ♔d7 33 fxe6+ (33 f6!? looks interesting) 33...♔xe6 34 g5 followed by g6 trying to penetrate Black's queenside after forcing ...♔e6-f6.

32 ♗g5!

With the threat of 33 ♗d8.

32...exf5 33 gxf5 gxf5 34 exf5 ♔e8 35 ♔d5 ♔d7 36 ♗d8!?

A very good option was 36 ♗e3 followed by 37 a5.

36...b5 37 ♗b6 c4 38 bxc4 bxc4 39 ♔xc4 ♘c6

Now Black intends to give up her bishop for the f-pawn.

40 ♗d8 ♗e5 41 ♗a5 ♗f6 42 ♗c3 ♗h4 43 ♔d4 ♗f6+ 44 ♘d3 ♗h4 45 ♘e4 ♗d8 46 ♔e5 ♗h4?

Under no circumstances should Black allow the white king to penetrate the e6 square. It was necessary to play 46...♔d7.

47 ♔e6 ♗g5 48 ♗f6 ♗e3 49 ♗h4 ♗d4 50 ♗g3!

Now everything is clear.

50...♗g7 51 ♗e5 ♗f8 52 f6 ♗h6 53 f7 Black resigned.

A very clear positional exploitation of an advantage in space.

350 Rublevsky – Spraggett

Black is cramped, but it is not easy for White to achieve victory – he must create some sort of weaknesses in the opponent's camp.

1 b4! axb4 2 axb4 cxb4

After 2...♘c8 3 bxc5 bxc5 4 ♗e3 the c5 pawn is hopelessly weak.

3 ♗xb4 hxg4 4 hxg4 ♗c2 5 ♘d6 ♘g6 6 ♔e3 ♗e7 7 ♗c3!

Threatening to transfer the bishop to where it can attack the b6 pawn.

7...f6 8 ♗e4! ♗xe4 9 ♔xe4 fxe5

After 9...♗xd6 10 exd6 ♘f8 11 ♗d4 ♘d7 12 ♗xb6! ♘xb6 13 c5 the white pawns are irrepressible, but there were chances in 10...♔f7!?

11 ♗d4 ♔e8 12 ♗xb6 ♔d7, blockading the white pawns.

10 ♗xe5! ♘f8

After 10...♘xe5 11 ♔xe5 he sheds the e6 pawn, while there is the threat 11 ♘c8.

11 f5!

Unusually reducing the remaining material, but this captures a maximum amount of space.

11...exf5 12 ♘xf5 ♗f6 13 ♗c7 ♘d7 14 ♘d6 ♗h4 15 ♔f5 ♗f2

There is also no salvation in 15...♗g3 16 g5.

16 g5! ♔f8 17 ♘e4 ♗e3 18 ♔e6!

Black has no future.

18...♘c5+ 19 ♘xc5 bxc5

If 19...♗xc5, then 20 ♗d6+ with a winning pawn endgame.

20 g6 ♔g8 21 ♗d6 ♗f2 22 ♔d5 ♗e3 23 ♗xc5 ♗d2 24 ♗d4 ♗b4 25 ♗e5!

Avoiding the trap 25 c5? ♗xc5!, with a draw.

25...♔h8 26 ♗d6 Black resigned, 1-0

Endgames from the European Championship 1999 in Batumi

In all competitions of high rank are played many interesting and instructive games, and particularly interesting is the play of leading grandmasters in the opening and the endgame. Not without reason the great Mikhail Botvinnik said that there can be no fully-fledged game without an endgame.

In Batumi we come across splendid technical endgames, and likewise simple, but instructive mistakes. In women's games we find these more often, but here we limit ourselves to one example.

351 Babaeva – Medic

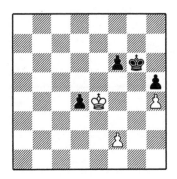

After the correct first move
1 f4! ♔f7
If 1...d3, then 2 f5+ ♔f7 3 ♔xd3
♔e7 4 ♔c4! ♔d6 5 ♔d4 with a
draw. Now White makes a fatal
mistake...
2 f5??
Correct is 2 ♔xd4 ♔e6 3 ♔e4,
with a draw.
**2...♔e7 3 ♔d3 ♔d7! 4 ♔c4 ♔c6
5 ♔xd4 ♔d6**, and White loses the
f5 pawn and with it the game, **0-1**

Men also make mistakes in simple
situations...

352 Rocha – Socko

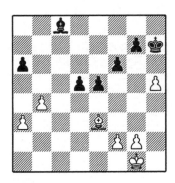

There would be an easy draw after
1 f3 d4 2 ♗c1 f5 3 g3 etc. However
White played
1 ♔f1? ♗g4 2 ♗c5?

Why not 2 a4 ♗xh5 3 b5 with a
draw?
2...♗xh5 3 ♔e1 ♗e8!, and Black
wins, **0-1**

In the next game Black failed to
realise his extra pawn.

353 Lputian – Yusupov

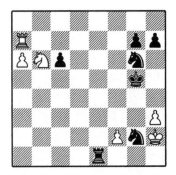

Winning is 1...♘2f4 2 ♖xg7 ♘d5,
but there followed:
**1...♖b1? 2 ♖b7 ♘2h4 3 a7 ♘f3+!
4 ♔g3 ♘gh4 5 ♖xg7+ ♔f5 6 ♖f7+**,
with a **draw**.

White realised a positional advantage in good style in the game

354 Aleksandrov – J.Polgar

Black has problems with her
knight, and she is playing 'without
the king'.

1 ♘d5 c5+ 2 ♔c3 ♘a4+ 3 ♔c4 a6 4 ♘c7 b5+ 5 ♔d3 ♔g7 6 ♘xa6 ♔f6 7 h4! ♔f5 8 h5 b4 9 ♔c4 ♘c3 10 a3 ♘b1 11 a4 ♘d2+ 12 ♔d3 ♘b3 13 ♔c2 ♘d4+ 14 ♔b2 ♘e2 15 ♘xc5 ♘xf4 16 a5 ♘d5 17 a6, and Black resigned, **1-0**

Socko distinguished himself twice...

355 **Anastasian – Socko**

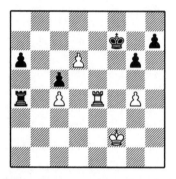

White is a pawn down though the strong d6 pawn compensates for the material loss – but how to play for the win?

There followed:

1...♖a2+?

Why drive the king forward? Correct is 1...♖b4 2 ♖e7+ ♔f8 with the threat of ♖b6.

2 ♔e3 ♖a3+?

Again better is 2...♖b2.

3 ♔f4 ♖d3 4 ♔e5 g5 5 ♖e1! ♖d4 6 ♖a1 ♖xc4 7 ♖xa6 ♖xg4 8 ♖a7+, and White wins, **1-0**

356 **Socko – Gallagher**

1...♖d4+?

What's the point of this check? If he wants to play for a win, then 1...♔g5 or 1...♖d1, preparing 2...g3, and likewise moving the rook round to a1.

2 ♔b5 ♖d2?

Again better is 2...♖d1.

3 c4 g3 4 a6 g2?

Why? Correct is to continue checking 4...♖b2+ 5 ♔c6 ♖a2 6 ♔b6 ♖b2+, for the time being not touching the precious passed pawn.

5 ♖e1 ♖b2+?

Why not 5...♔g5, drawing closer to the pawn, and after 6 a7 ♖a2 7 ♔b6 ♔f4! 8 ♔b7 ♖b2+ 9 ♔c7 ♖a2 it's a simple draw.

6 ♔c6 ♖a2 7 ♔b7 ♖b2+ 8 ♔c7 ♖a2 9 ♖g1 ♔g5 10 ♔b7! ♖b2+ 11 ♔c6! ♖a2 12 a7 ♔f5 13 ♖xg2 ♖xa7 14 ♔xd6, and Black resigned, **1-0**

357 Krakops – Dautov

A typical endgame, somewhat worse for White, where the best method of defence is the sacrifice of the a3 pawn together with the activation of the rook. Black should play 1...g6, but he continued

1...a4?! 2 ♔f1 g6 3 ♖e1 ♖c3 4 ♖e3!

The pawn endgame is drawn, therefore

4...♖b3 5 ♔e2 ♖b2+ 6 ♔f3?

But this is anti-activation – the correct move is 6 ♔e1!.

6...h5

7 h4?

And this is technically incorrect – it was necessary to play 7 h3 followed by 8 g4, to try and create objects for attack.

7...♔g7 8 g3 ♔f6 9 ♔g2 ♖b3 10 ♖e8

Forced – after 10 ♔f3 ♔f5 11 ♔e2 ♖xe3+ 12 ♔xe3 ♔g4 13 ♔e2 f6! 14 ♔e3 f5! and 15...f4 Black wins.

10...♖xa3 11 ♖a8 ♔e5 12 ♖a7 ♔d5 13 f3 f5 14 ♖a6 ♖a2+ 15 ♔h3 a3 16 g4 f4 17 gxh5

After 17 ♖xg6 ♖a1 18 ♖a6 a2 19 ♔g2 hxg4 20 fxg4 f3+ Black wins at once.

17...gxh5 18 ♖a5+

No help is 18 ♖h6, since the black king proceeds to the second rank.

18...♔c4 19 ♖xh5 ♖a1 20 ♖a5 a2 21 ♔g4

Or 21 ♔g2 ♔b3.

21...♖g1+ with an easy win, **0-1**

Another similar catastrophic case with an extra pawn.

358 Danner – Zelcić

White has compensation for the opponent's extra pawn – but no more. Now he should play 1...h5! but in the game there followed:

1...♔f6? 2 ♔f2 ♔e7 3 ♔e3 ♔d7 4 ♔xe4 ♔c7 5 ♖b5 f6

After 5...♖xb7 6 ♖xb7+ ♔xb7 7 ♔e5 the pawn endgame is lost.

6 f5! e5 7 ♔d5 ♖xb7 8 ♖xc5+ ♔d7 9 ♖c6! ♔e7 10 ♖e6+ ♔f7 11 c5!

White has it all – a passed pawn plus an active rook and king.

11...♖d7+ 12 ♔c6 ♖d4 13 ♔b7 ♖xg4 14 c6 ♖b4+ 15 ♔c8 h5 16 c7 h4 17 ♔d7 ♖d4+ 18 ♖d6 ♖c4, and White wins, **1-0**

359 Kiroski – Berg

Simplest here is 1....g6!, with an elementary draw, but let us see what happened.
1...♔f6 2 ♔c3 ♖c1+?
Again possible was 2...g6.
3 ♔b2 ♖h1 4 ♖b5 g6
Now this is bad – necessary was 4...♖h2+ 5 ♔a3 ♖h3+ 6 ♔b4 ♖h4+ 7 ♔a5 ♖f4, again a simple draw.
5 fxg6 ♔xg6 6 a5 ♔f6 7 a6 ♖h8 8 ♔b3 ♔e6 9 ♔b4 ♔d6 10 ♔a5 ♔c7 11 ♖b7+ ♔c6 12 ♖b6+ ♔c7 13 a7 ♖h5+
Or 13...♖h1 14 ♖a6!.
14 ♔a6 ♖h8 15 ♖b7+, and Black resigned, **1-0**

360 Smirin – Emms

Black has two pawns for the exchange, and defeat seems unlikely, but
1...♔f7?
Why not 1...b3 2 ♖b5 ♔e6, and the king comes to the defence.
2 ♔f5 ♔g7?
Again why not 2...b3, trying to transfer the king to the queenside.
3 ♔e6 ♔g6 4 ♖b5 ♔g7 5 ♖g5+ ♔h6 6 ♔f5 b3 7 ♖g6+ ♔h7 8 ♖g3 b2 9 ♖b3 ♗d4 10 ♔e4 c5
Better is 10...♗f6.
11 ♔d3 ♔g6 12 ♔c2 ♔f5 13 ♖b5 ♔e5 14 ♖xa5 ♔d6 15 ♖b5 ♔c6 16 ♔d3 ♔c7 17 ♔c4 ♔c6 18 a5 ♗c3 19 ♖b6+, Black resigned, **1-0**

361 Nisipeanu – Lputian

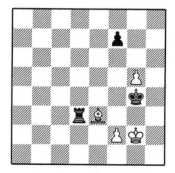

In this completely drawn position there surprisingly followed
1 g6?
Why? It was necessary to simply mark time with 1 ♗c1 and wait. He should give up the pawn only in an extreme case.
1...fxg6 2 ♗b6 ♖b3 3 ♗c5 ♔f5 4 ♗d6 ♔e4 5 ♗c5 ♖b5 6 ♗e3 ♖b1 7 ♗a7 ♔d3 8 ♗e3 ♔e2 9 ♗c5 ♖b5 10 ♗e3 ♖d5 11 ♔g3 ♔d3 12 ♔f3 ♖f5+ 13 ♔g3 ♔e4 14 ♔g2 ♖b5 15 ♔g3 ♔f5 16 ♔g2 ♖b4 17 ♗d2 ♖g4+ 18 ♔f3?

Better is 18 ♔h3! ♖g1 19 ♔h2, not losing contact with the g2 square.

18...♖g1 19 ♗f4 g5 20 ♗h2 g4+ 21 ♔e3 ♖b1 22 ♗c7 ♖b3+ 23 ♔d4

Bad is 23 ♔e2 ♔e4, and the white king is driven to the first rank.

23...♖b1 24 ♔e3 ♖b7 25 ♗h2 ♖e7+ 26 ♔d3 ♖e1 27 ♔d4 ♖b1 28 ♗c7 ♖b4+ 29 ♔e3 ♖b3 30 ♔d4 ♖f3 31 ♗g3 ♔e6!

Finally Black picks the right plan – going round the whole board with the king.

32 ♔e4 ♔d7 33 ♔d5 ♔c8 34 ♔c6 ♖f6+ 35 ♔c5 ♔b7 36 ♔c4 ♖f3 37 ♔b5 ♖c3 38 ♔b4 ♖c1 39 ♔b3

If 39 ♔b5 Black plays 39...♔c8!, and the king hurries to e4.

39...♔c6, and Black wins, 0-1

Examples of the highest technique

362 Kir. Georgiev – Milov

Black is not only a pawn down but the knight on one flank is stronger than a bishop, but Black can put up stubborn resistance by 1...♗f6 or 1...♖b5. In the game came the weaker

1...♖a2? 2 ♖c5! ♔f6 3 ♘h7+ ♔e6 4 ♘f8+ ♔d6 5 ♖b5!

Threatening 6 ♘g6, therefore there followed:

5...f4 6 ♘g6 ♖e2 7 ♔f3 fxg3 8 ♔xe2 g2 9 ♖b1 ♗h2 10 ♔f3, and Black resigned, 1-0

363 Fedorov – Korchnoi

After 1...♔c5 followed by 2...a4 Black has a strong position, but he decides to simplify his task and play

1...♖e6?

and after

2 ♖f7! ♖e7 3 ♖xe7 ♔xe7 4 ♔e3 ♗a4 5 c3 bxc3 6 bxc3 ♔d6 7 ♔d4

there arose a difficult bishop endgame with an isolated pawn.

7...♗c6 8 g3 h6 9 ♗g2 g5 10 hxg5 hxg5 11 ♗f3

It turns out that Black is in zugzwang – if the black bishop were on e6, it would be a draw.

11...♗b7 12 c4 ♗c8 13 ♗xd5 ♗g4 14 c5+ ♔c7 15 ♔e5 ♗e2 16 ♔f5 g4 17 ♔f4 ♔d7 18 a3 ♗d1 19 ♗e4 ♔c7 20 ♗f5 ♔c6 21 ♗xg4 ♗a4 22 ♔e5 ♔xc5 23 ♗e6, and Black gave up resistance, 1-0

Black saved himself beautifully with a surprising transfer to a pawn endgame in the next encounter.

364 Lautier – Mitkov

1...♘xb7! 2 ♗xb7 ♖xb7 3 ♖xb7+ ♔xb7 4 ♔d6 ♔b6!

The white king is nearer to the enemy pawns, however White's 'twice doubled' pawns are weaker.

5 ♔e6 ♔c5 6 ♔f7 ♔c4 7 ♔xg7 ♔d3 8 ♔xf6 ♔xe4 9 ♔g6 ♔xe3 10 ♔xh6 e4 11 g5 ♔f2 12 g6 e3 13 g7 e2 14 g8=♕ e1=♕ 15 g4 ♕h1+ 16 ♔g7 ♕a1+ 17 ♔f7 ♕a2+, and the white king cannot get out of perpetual check. ½-½

365 Palac – Nikolić

The bishop covers the 'bad' corner, but it is not so simple for Black to give up his pawns. By

hurrying with the king to h8, the chances of a draw are enormous.

1 ♔c7 f5 2 ♔d8 ♔f6

He should try 2...♔f7, breaking through to the corner.

3 ♔e8 ♔g5 4 ♔f7 ♔xh5 5 ♗xf5 ♔g5 6 ♗g4 ♔h6 7 ♔g8!

This is where the problem is – he cannot get to h8.

7...♔g6 8 ♗d7 ♔f6 9 h4! ♔g6 10 ♗e8+ ♔h6 11 h5, and Black resigned, **1-0**

366 Zelcić – Psakhis

This endgame looks even, Black's position is only a little more active.

1 ♔e2?

Stronger is 1 c4 followed by ♔c3.

1...♔e6 2 h3 ♔d5 3 c3 ♔e4

Perhaps, in the endgame, it is possible to allow the opponent's king behind his lines.

4 g3 h4! 5 gxh4

Or 5 g4 ♘g3+! winning.

5...♘ce7 6 ♗g1 ♘g3+ 7 ♔d2 ♘ef5 8 ♗f2 ♘h5 9 ♘e5 f6 10 ♘c6 a5 11 c4 ♘xf4 12 ♔c3 ♘xh3 13 ♗e1 ♘f4 14 b4 axb4+ 15 ♘xb4 c5 16 ♘a6 ♘d3, and it was time for White to resign, **0-1**

**Endgames from the Olympiad
at Elista 1998**

367 Mihevc – Kim

Here simplest is to make a draw by 1 ♔c2 or 1 c5, but White played...

1 ♔b4?! ♖b7+ 2 ♔a5?!

Correct is 2 ♔a4 e3 3 c5 ♖c7 4 ♔b4 ♖xc5 5 ♖xe3 with a draw.

2...e3 3 ♔a6?

White sees that the planned 3 c5 is impossible because of 3...♔xc5 threatening mate, but he can make a draw by 3 ♖xe3!! ♔xe3 4 c5 ♔d4 5 c6 ♖b1 6 c7 ♖c1 7 ♔b6 ♔d5 8 ♔b7.

3...♖b3!

And White has to give up the pawn and with it the game.

0-1

368 Batceceg – Grosar

White refuses a draw and quite disheartens Black. He should have played 1...a4! 2 ♔e4 b5! 3 cxb5 (3 ♔d5 b4!) 3...c4, creating a passed pawn, while his rook is ideally placed. However there followed:

1...♖f7? 2 ♔e4?

Correct is 2 a4!, denying Black the chance of creating a passed pawn.

2...a4 3 ♖f6 ♖e7+?

Again it was not too late to return to the correct plan 3...♖c7! and 4...b5!, creating a passed pawn.

4 ♔d5 ♔a6?

Really it was better to play 4...a3.

5 ♖f8 ♖e2 6 ♖a8+ ♔b7 7 ♖h8 ♖xa2 8 ♖xh7+ ♔a6 9 ♔e6 a3 10 ♖h8 ♔b7 11 ♖d8 ♖h2

Up to here we have had a practically forced variation, but now White has a problem: how to position the rook – on the first rank or the a-file? Thinking about it logically, we see White's plan is to go with the king to g6 and advance the h6 pawn. Black's plan, after b5, is to create a passed c-pawn. And it is necessary for the rook to keep hold from the first rank – here is a variation 12 ♖d1 a2 13 ♔f6 b5 14 cxb5 c4 15 ♔xg6 c3 16 ♔g7 c2 17 ♖f1 ♔b6 18 h7 ♔b5 19 h8=♕ ♖xh8 20 ♔xh8 ♔b4 21 g6 ♔b3 22 g7

&b2 23 g8=♕, and the end. But
White decides to play more
cleverly.

12 ♖d7+? ♔c6?

After 12...♔a6! Black, in the
previous variation, would have an
extra tempo and draw. White could
now play 13 ♖d6+! and 14 ♖d1,
winning.

**13 ♖a7? a2 14 ♔f6 b5 15 cxb5+
♔b6!**

Here this refusal to capture saves
Black.

**16 ♖a8 c4 17 ♔xg6 c3 18 h7
♖xh7! 19 ♖xa2 ♖c7 20 ♖c2 ♔xb5**

And a draw, but so many instructive mistakes. ½-½

369 Klimova – Alieva

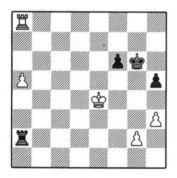

Correct here was 1...♖a3 2 a6 ♖a2
3 ♔d5 ♔f5! – this is where the king
takes refuge – 4 ♔c6 ♔f4 5 ♔b7
♖b2+ 6 ♔a7 ♖xg2 with a draw. In
the game Black went passive with
the king.

1...♔g7? 2 a6 ♖c2?

Better is 2...♖a3!.

**3 ♖b8! ♖a2 4 ♖b7+ ♔g6 5 a7
♖a6 6 ♔d5 ♔f5 (too late) 7 ♔c5
♔f4 8 ♔b5 ♖a1 9 ♔b6 ♔g3 10
♖g7+ ♔f2 11 ♔b7** Black resigned,
1-0

We came across a couple of interesting pawn endgames.

370 Anastasian-Yu

At first glance Black has the advantage because he has the possibility of creating a passed pawn on the
queenside, however the black king
will not break White's defence on
the other flank.

**1 ♔e4 a4 2 ♔d4 b4 3 ♔c4 a3 4
bxa3 bxa3 5 ♔b3 ♔f5 6 f3 g5 7
hxg5 hxg5 8 g4+!**

Defending against ...g5-g4.

**8...♔e5 9 ♔xa3 ♔d5 10 ♔b4
♔d6 11 ♔c4 ♔c6 12 ♔d4 ♔d6 13
f4**

He cannot avoid this exchange.

13...gxf4 14 exf4 f6!

Now it's a draw after

15 f5 ♔c6! 16 ♔e3 ♔d6 17 ♔f3

Nothing is offered by 17 ♔f4 ♔e7
18 g5 fxg5+ 19 ♔xg5 ♔f7.

17...♔e7 18 ♔f4 ♔f7 19 ♔g3

Or 19 ♔e4 ♔e7 20 ♔d5 ♔d7=.

**19...♔g7 20 ♔g2 ♔f7 21 ♔f2
♔e7 22 ♔e3 ♔d7,** and a draw, ½-½

371 Yurtaev – Temirbaev

Usually a pawn endgame with an
isolated pawn is very difficult for
the side having the isolani, but here
Black manages to hold on. White's
chances consist of carrying out at an
appropriate moment e3-e4 and exploiting the more active position of
the king.

1 h4 h5!?

Limiting both his own and his opponent's play on the kingside.

2 a4 ♔e6 3 a5 ♔d6 4 a6

A dangerous attempt at playing for a win – now on 4...♔c6 there is 5 ♔e5 ♔b5 6 ♔xd5 ♔xb4 7 e4.

4...♔e6 5 e4

It is not possible to delay further.

5...dxe4 6 fxe4 fxe4 7 ♔xe4 g6 8 ♔f4 ♔f6 9 g3 b5! 10 g4 hxg4 11 ♔xg4 ♔e6 12 ♔f4 ♔f6, and a draw could be agreed.

372 **Dervishi – Makarov**

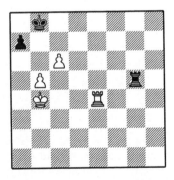

On the board is a well-known theoretical draw, if only according to the game Gelfand-Karpov, Reggio Emilia, 1991. In the game followed:

1...♖g1 2 ♔c5 ♖g5+ 3 ♔d6 ♖g6+ 4 ♖e6 ♖g8 5 ♖h6 ♖d8+?

The correct plan of defence was to keep the rook on the eighth by 5...♖f8, and on 6 ♔d7 ♖c8!, to defend against c6-c7.

6 ♔c5 ♖g8

Here after 6...♖d1 7 ♖h8+ ♔c7 8 ♖h7+ ♔b8 9 ♖b7+ ♔a8 10 ♖d7 ♖c1+ 11 ♔d6 White wins.

7 b6!

This is the whole point – after 7...axb6+ 8 ♔xb6 White wins.

7... ♖g5+ 8 ♔d6 ♖g8 9 b7 a5 10 ♖h5! ♖f8 11 ♖e5

Against the threat of ♔d7 and ♖e8 there is no defence, Black resigned, **1-0**

373 **Forster – Oblitas**

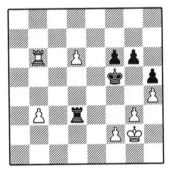

White has two extra pawns, and the task looks simple.

1 ♔f1 g5 2 ♔e2 ♖d5 3 ♔e3 gxh4 4 gxh4 ♖d1 5 ♖c6

Simpler is an immediate advance of the b-pawn or to play 5 f3.

5...♔e6 6 d7+ ♔xd7 7 ♖xf6 ♖b1 8 ♖b6 ♖h1 9 ♖b4 ♔e6 10 ♔f3?

Correct is 10 ♖e4+! ♔d5 11 f3 and 12 b4 with an ideal position.

10...♔f5 11 ♖b5+ ♔f6 12 ♔g3 ♖g1+ 13 ♔h2 ♖g4 14 ♔h3 ♖f4!

Black strives for the endgame with f- and h-pawns.

15 ♖b6+ 18 ♔f3 ♖xh4 19 ♔e3 ♖h1 20 ♔e4 h4 21 ♖b6+ ♔g7 22 ♔f5 h3 23 ♖g6+ ♔f7 24 ♖h6 h2 25

f4 ♔g7 26 ♖g6+ ♔f7 27 ♖g2 ♖b1, draw, ½-½

Even outstanding grandmasters not infrequently demonstrate mediocre defensive technique. Here are a few quite simple examples.

374 **Krasenkov – Topalov**

Black has an extra pawn, but it is not very easy to realise it – however White should carefully watch for ...f5-f4, in order to have a check on the fifth rank. He should play 1 ♖d4 h3 2 ♗b7 ♖f1+ 3 ♔e3, but White simple-mindedly went

1 ♖b2??

and after **1...f4!** there is no defence against 2...fxg3+ 3 hxg3 h3.

375 **Borgo – Kochetkov**

White has a winning position on account of zugzwang – Black must allow the white king to pass on one or other side, for example: 1 g4! hxg4 2 fxg4 ♖b5 3 ♔c3 with the idea 4 ♖f2.

But White played

1 ♔c3 ♖c6+ 2 ♔b3?!

It was still possible to return to d3.

2...♔d4 3 ♖d2+?

Necessary was 3 b5 ♖b6 4 ♔b4 followed by ♔a5.

3...♔e3 4 ♖d5 f6 5 ♖c5!?

After 5 ♖f5 ♔f2 6 b5 ♖e6 7 ♔b4 ♔g2 8 ♔c5 ♔xh2 9 b6 ♔xg3 10 b7 ♖e8 11 ♖xf6 h4 Black's chances are not worse.

5...♖e6 6 b5 ♔xf3 7 ♖c6 ♖e5 8 ♖xf6+ ♔g2 9 ♔c4 ♔xh2 10 ♖f3 ♔g2 he had to agree to a draw, ½-½

376 **Stanojovski – Volkov**

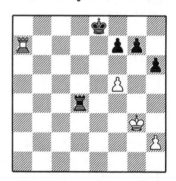

Black threatens, after 1...♖d7, to transfer the king to f6, but here with the white rook on a6 and the black king on e7 simplest is f6 with check. However White decides to take the bull by the horns.

1 f6? g5! 2 h3

A check on e7 offers nothing – after ...♔f8 and ...♔f8 – the threat is ♖f4 transferring the king to g6.

2...♖f4 3 ♖a6 ♔d7 4 ♖b6 ♖d4+!

Danger draws closer.

5 ♖a6 ♖d6 6 ♖a8 ♖d3+!?

Also possible is an immediate capture on f6.

7 ♔g2

Or 7 ♔g4 ♔e6 8 ♖a6 ♔e5 and then ♖d6.

7...♖d4 8 ♖a6 ♖d6 7 ♖a8 ♖xf6 8 h4 ♖f4!

Material is not appropriate here.

9 ♖a7+ ♔e8 10 hxg5 hxg5 11 ♖a5 f6 12 ♖a7 ♖e4 13 ♔f3 ♖e7 White resigned, **0-1**

But there were of course good endgames...

377 **Beliavsky – Spraggett**

1 g4

This looks logical and correct, however, taking into account Black's defensive resources, he should have tried 1 f3, creating a passed e-pawn.

1...hxg4 2 ♖xg4 ♖e5 3 ♔f1 ♔h5 4 ♖f4 ♖e6 5 ♔e2 ♖e5 6 ♔e1

A cunning move – after 6 ♔d2 there is an immediate 6...♖f5. Now Black's reply is forced.

6...♔h6! 7 ♔d2 ♖f5!

A transfer to a pawn endgame looks sheer folly but Black has calculated everything well.

8 ♔c3

Rather better is 8 ♖e4.

8...♖xf4 9 exf4 ♔h5 10 ♔d4 ♔xh4 11 ♔xe4 ♔g4 12 ♔e3

On 12 ♔e5 there is 12...♔f3!.

12...♔h3 13 ♔f3 ♔h2!

Losing is 13...♔h4? 14 f5! gxf5 13 ♔f4.

14 ♔e3 ♔g2 15 ♔e2 ♔h3, draw, ½-½

378 **Brestian – Beliavsky**

Black's position, of course, is winning in view of the presence of the far advanced passed pawns and active position of the king. However it requires definite accuracy, since tempi can have decisive significance.

1...♘f8?

A mistake, almost fatal. He should go with the knight to the other side: 1...♘h4+! 2 ♔g4 ♘f3 3 g6 ♘e5+ 4 ♔f5 ♘xg6 5 ♔xg6 ♔xe3 6 ♔f5 c5 winning.

2 ♖c1?

Black does not exploit the twist of fate. The game could have been saved by 2 ♖a3+!! ♔d2 3 ♖a2 ♔d1 4 ♖a1+ c1=♕ 5 ♖xc1+ ♔xc1 6 ♔xe4 ♘e6 (in the case of 6...♔d2 7 ♔d5 ♔xe3 8 ♔c6 ♘e6 9 g6 – draw) 7 g6 ♔d2 8 ♔d5 with a draw.

2...c5!

Winning a decisive tempo.

3 ♔e5

There is also no salvation in 3 ♖xc2 ♔xc2 4 ♔xe4 c4 winning for Black.

3...c4 4 ♖h1 ♔xe3 5 ♔d5 ♔d3 6 ♔xc5 ♘e6+ 7 ♔b4 ♘xg5 8 ♔a3 ♘f3, White resigned, **0-1**

Endgames from the world championship in Las Vegas 1999

We begin with a very simple pawn endgame.

379 Andersson – Mohammed

Black has a good king position but, together with this, simplest is 1...f5 2 exf5 ♔xf5 3 ♔d4 ♔e6 4 b5 b6 with a draw. However there followed the inaccurate:

1...b5? 2 cxb5 d5 3 b6 dxe4+ 4 ♔c4 ♔d6 5 ♔b5! e3 6 ♔a6 e2 7 b7 e1=♕ 8 b8=♕+

The queen endgame should be drawn, but let us see what Black did.

8...♔d7 9 ♕b7+ ♔d6

Better is 9...♔e6.

10 ♕b6+ ♔d7 11 ♕d4+ ♔c7 12 ♕c5+ ♔d7 13 b5 ♕e4 14 ♔a7 ♕a4+ 15 ♔b7! ♔e6 16 b6 ♔f7 17 ♔c7 ♕f4+ 18 ♕d6 ♕c4+ 19 ♕c6 ♕f4+ 20 ♔c8, and the win is easy.

380 P.N.Nielsen – J.Polgar

There follows a transfer to a pawn endgame.

1...♖xg4 2 fxg4+ ♔e4

After 2...♔xg4 follows 3 e4! dxe4 4 d5 ♔f5 5 d6 ♔e6 6 ♔e3.

3 ♔e2! stalemate!

381 Khalifman – Barua

1 f5! gxf5 2 ♔f4 ♔f6 3 ♘c2!

After the pawn sacrifice White begins a complicated transfer of the knight.

3...♗d7 4 ♘e1 ♗c8 5 ♘d3 ♗e6 6 ♔f3 ♔e7 7 ♔g3 ♔f6 8 ♘c5 ♗c8 9 ♔f4!

Zugzwang.

9...♔g6 10 ♔e5 f4 11 ♔xf4 ♔f6 12 ♔g3!

Again in search of zugzwang.

12...♔g7 13 ♔f3 ♔g6 14 ♘d3 ♗g4+ 15 ♔e3 ♗e6 16 ♘f4+ ♔f5 17 ♘xh5 ♔g4 18 ♘f4 ♗f7 18 ♘d3 ♗e6 20 ♘c5 ♗c8 21 h5! and Black resigned, **1-0**

382 Nisipeanu – Khalifman

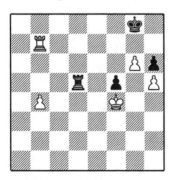

1 ♔e3?
Why not at first 1 b5?

1...f4+! 2 ♔xf4 ♖xh5 3 b5 ♖g5 4 g7 ♖c5 5 ♔e4 h5 6 ♔d4 ♖f5 7 ♔c4 h4 8 b6 ♖f4+ 9 ♔b5 ♖f2 10 ♖e7 ♖b2+ 11 ♔c6 h3 12 b7 h2 13 ♖e1 ♔xg7, draw, ½-½

383 Akopian – Khalifman

1...♖h8?

There is a draw by 1...♔f6! 2 ♖h2 ♔g7 3 ♔b7 ♖h8 4 ♔c7 ♖xh7 5 ♖xh7+ ♔xh7 6 ♔d6 ♔g7 7 ♔xe6 (7 ♔xe5 ♔f7 8 ♔d6 e5!=) 7...♔f8 8 ♔xe5 ♔e7.

2 ♖h2 ♔d6

Now there is no time for ...♔f6.

3 ♖d2+! ♔e7 4 ♔c7! ♔f6 5 ♖h2 ♔g5 6 ♔d6 ♔f6 7 ♔d7 ♔f7 8 ♖h4 ♔f6 9 ♖h1 ♔f7 10 ♖f1+ ♔g7 11 ♔e7 ♖a8 12 h8=♕+!,

With a transfer to a winning pawn endgame.

384 Shirov – I.Sokolov

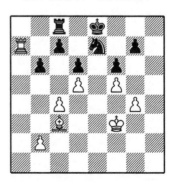

Winning is not very easy, but Shirov demonstrates splendid technique.

1 ♗d4 ♚f8 2 ♚e4 ♚f7 3 b4 ♚e8 4 ♗e3 ♚f7 5 c5!

A decisive plan.

5...bxc5 6 bxc5 dxc5 7 ♗xc5 g6

8 d6!

By opening the seventh rank right up, White increases the advantage of bishop over knight.

8...gxf5+ 9 gxf5 cxd6 10 ♗xd6 ♖e8 11 ♚d4 ♚f8 12 ♖xe7 ♖xe7 13 ♚d5 ♚f7 14 ♗xe7 ♚xe7 15 ♚c6, and in a hopeless pawn endgame Black resigned, **1-0**

According to theory this endgame is a draw, but in practice this has to be shown.

1...♖a3+?

Why drive the white king to the centre? Black could immediately apply Petrosian's plan of ...f7-f6 and ...g6-g5.

2 ♚d4 f6 3 ♖a7+ ♚h6 4 a5 g5 5 ♚c5! gxh4 6 gxh4 ♖a4?

Better really is 6...♖f3 or 6...♚g6, though even this will not save him.

7 a6 ♖a2

After 7...♖xh4 8 ♖d7 ♖a4 9 a7 h4 10 ♚b6 h3 11 ♖d3 and White wins.

8 ♖a8 ♚g6 9 ♚b6 ♖b2+ 10 ♚a7 ♖f2 11 ♖b8 ♖f4

Threatening the transfer of the white rook to the fourth rank.

12 ♖b5 ♖xh4 13 ♚b6 ♖e4 14 a7 ♖e8 15 ♖a5 h4 16 a8=♕ ♖xa8 17 ♖xa8 ♚g5 18 ♚c5 h3

18...♚f4 19 ♚d4 h3 20 ♖h8 ♚g3 21 ♚e3 h2 is the game position.

19 ♖h8! ♚g4 20 ♚d4 ♚g3 21 ♚e3 ♚g2 22 ♚e2 h2 23 ♖g8+ ♚h3 24 ♚f2 h1=♘+ 25 ♚f3 ♚h2 26 ♖g2+ ♚h3 27 ♖g6, Black resigned, **1-0**

Rook endgames

385 Akopian – Kir. Georgiev

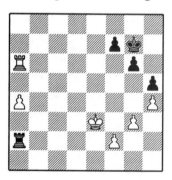

386 Kramnik – Topalov

1 ♚g3!

The only chance is the breakthrough of the king.

1...b3 2 ♔f4 ♖a2 3 ♔f5 ♖xa4?

But why not the simpler 3...♖f2+ 4 ♔e6 ♖e2+ etc., driving away the white king?

4 ♖b7+ ♔g8 5 g4! ♖a6

The threat was 6 ♔g6, while on 5...h5 winning is 6 g5!.

6 ♖xb3 ♔g7 7 ♖b7+ ♔g8?

Stronger is 7...♔f8, not allowing the rook to e7.

8 ♖e7 ♖a5+ 9 ♖e5 ♖a4 10 ♖e4 ♖a7 11 ♔f6 ♖g7 12 ♖e8+ ♔h7 13 ♖e7 ♖xe7 14 ♔xe7 ♔g7 15 h5, Black resigned, **1-0**

387 Azmaiparashvili – Nisipeanu

How could White lose this? Well, very simply!

1 ♖c7?

He should play 1 ♔f1, bringing the king to the centre.

1...♖a8 2 ♔f1 g5 3 ♖b6 ♖a2 4 ♔e1 ♖a1+ 5 ♔e2 ♖a2+ 6 ♔e3 ♖a3+ 7 ♔d4?

Nothing at all – only forward and then where?

7...♔g7 8 ♖b8 ♖f3 9 h3 h5 10 ♖cc8

Playing for mate – White's only chance.

10...♖xf2 11 ♖g8+ ♔h6 12 ♔c5 ♖g2 13 ♖bf8 c3! 14 ♖h8+ ♔g6 15 ♖hg8+ ♔f5 16 ♖xf7+ ♔e4 17 ♖xg5 ♖g1!

Prophylaxis – not giving White control of the first rank.

18 ♖f2 ♔e3 19 ♖h2 ♗g2! and White resigned, **1-0**

The majority was exploited technically in the next game:

388 Kramnik – Korchnoi

1 ♔e3! a6 2 a4 ♗c4 3 b4 g5

Black advances his pawns but, probably, worthy of more consideration is 3...♖d3 4 ♔e4 ♖d8, attacking the white king.

4 ♖c7! ♗b3

He cannot hold the diagonal – 4...♗d3 5 ♖c3 ♗f1 6 ♖c1 ♗d3 7 ♖d1.

5 a5 ♗a4

Threatening b4-b5 a6xb5, ♗f3-c6, and the march of the a5 pawn.

6 ♗e2 h6 7 ♗c4 f5

If 7...♖f6, then 8 ♔d4, and the approach of the king decides.

8 ♖f7+ ♔e8 9 ♖xf5, and Black resigned, **1-0**

In the following position Alexei Dreev exploited his superiority in piece activity very technically.

389 **Dreev – Rublevsky**

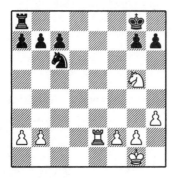

1 ♖e3!!

On 1 ♘e6 there is 1...♖e8! 2 ♖e3 ♖e7 with a draw.

1...♖d8 2 ♘e6 ♖d1+ 3 ♔h2 ♖d7

Better was to activate his pieces: 3...♖d6! 4 ♘xc7 ♖d2 with some chances of a draw.

4 ♖f3 ♖f7 5 ♔g3!

In the knight endgame White has simply a more active king, but nevertheless Black will be forced to try 5...♖xf3+ 6 ♔xf3 ♘b4 7 a3 ♘d3 8 b4, though as before it is not easy for him.

5...♘e5 6 ♖xf7 ♔xf7 7 ♘xc7 ♘d3 8 ♘b5 ♘xb2 9 ♘xa7 ♔e6 10 ♘b5 ♔d5?

But now this activation is mistaken, better was 10...♘d3!, preparing 11...♘c1 and 11 ♔f3 is no good because of 11...♘e1+!.

11 ♘c7+ ♔c4 12 ♘e8 b5 13 ♘xg7 ♘a4 14 f4 ♘c3 15 f5 ♔d5 16 ♔f4 ♘xa2 17 f6 ♔d6 18 ♔f5 ♘c3 19 ♘e6 ♘d5 20 f7 ♘e7+ 21 ♔e4 Black resigned, **1-0**

High technique is demonstrated in single flank endgames (and, naturally, weak defence).

390 **Khalifman – Barua**

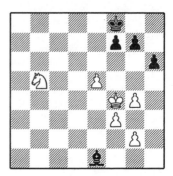

1 ♔e4 ♔e7 2 ♔d5 ♗d2 3 ♘d4 ♗c1 4 ♘e2 ♗d2 5 ♘g3 ♗c1 6 ♘h5 ♔f8?

Black avoids ...g7-g6, and it is not quite clear why?

7 ♔e4 ♗d2 8 f4 g6 9 ♘f6 ♗c1 10 ♘d5 ♗d2 11 f5 ♗c1 12 ♘f4 ♔g7 13 ♘d3! ♗a3 14 f6+!

White's plan is not the creation of a passed e-pawn, but the restriction of the black king.

14...♔g8 15 ♔d5 g5 16 e6! fxe6 17 ♔xe6, and since there is no defence against the transfer of the knight to d7 and march of the f6 pawn to f8 with conversion to a winning pawn endgame, Black resigned, **1-0**

391 **Adams – Dreev**

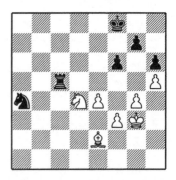

Well, fancy a blunder like this cropping up.

1...♘c3?? 2 ♘e6+ ♔e7 3 ♘xc5 ♘xe2+ 4 ♔f2 ♘f4

And now follows the 'highest' technique.

5 ♘b3 ♔f7 6 ♘d4 ♘d3+ 7 ♔e3 ♘e5 8 ♘f5 ♘c4+ 9 ♔f2 ♘e5 10 ♔g3 ♘c4 11 ♘d4 ♔e7 12 ♔f4 ♔f7 13 ♘c6 ♔e6 14 ♘d4+ ♔e7 15 ♔g3 ♔f8 16 ♔f2 ♔f7 17 ♘e2 ♘e5 18 ♘f4 ♘c4 19 ♘g6 ♔e6 20 ♔e2 ♘d6 21 ♔d3 ♘f7 22 f4!

At last!

22...♘d6 23 ♘h4 ♔f7 24 ♘f5 ♘b5 25 ♔c4 ♘c7 26 ♘d4 ♔e7 27 ♔c5 ♘a6+ 28 ♔b5 ♘c7+ 29 ♔c6 ♘e8 30 e5! fxe5 32 fxe5, and Black can resign. **1-0**

Endgames from the Olympiad in Istanbul 2000

In the endgame chessplayers display their technical mastery (something like a performance of ice figure skaters). However even in the encounters of the greats we witness surprising, if at the same time typical mistakes. Why not learn from these mistakes? We hope that the reader will derive benefit from the following examples which reflect only a hundredth of the Olympic harvest. Here, for example, is a classical endgame from the encounter

392 **Vera – Baburin**

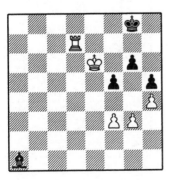

The Cuban grandmaster did not know the classical winning plan, and marked time for 30 moves before playing here 1 ♖f7 ♗d4 2 g4 hxg4 3 fxg4 fxg4 4 ♖f4 ♗c3 5 ♖xg4 ♔h7 6 ♔f7 ♔h6! 7 ♖g5 ♗e1!, and Black managed to exchange the g6 for the h4 pawn and easily make a draw. But the winning plan is simple – to play f3-f4, then transpose to the game Radev-Pribyl, published in every book on the endgame.

We recall the method of realising the advantage – 1 f4 ♗c3 2 ♖d3 ♗b2 3 g4! hxg4 (after 3...fxg4 follows 4 f5! gxf5 5 ♔xf5 ♔f7 6 ♖d7+ ♔e8 7 ♖h7 wins) 4 h5! ♔g7 (on 4...gxh5 follows 5 ♔xf5 ♔g7 6 ♖d7+ ♔h6 7 ♖d6+ ♔h7 8 ♔g5 ♗c1 9 ♖d7+ ♔g8 10 ♔g6 ♔f8 11 f5 wins) 5 hxg6 ♔xg6 6 ♖d5 ♗c1 7 ♖xf5 ♗xf4 8 ♖xf4 ♔g5 9 ♔e5 g3 10 ♔e4 g2 11 ♖f8 ♔g4 12 ♖g8+ ♔h3 13 ♔f3 winning.

In this example the grandmaster did not know the method of winning a quite simple classical position, while in the next he chose a completely incorrect realisation of the advantage.

393 **Perez – Mohr**

A natural and correct plan was 1 ...♔d5 2 ♖b2 c4 3 ♖b6 c3 4 ♖xa6

♗f5 – and then d3. However Black played

1...♗c4+? 2 ♔e1 ♔d5?

Still possible was to return to the plan with 2...♗e6.

3 h4 f5 4 f3 f4!?

Here 4...♗b5 fails to 5 g4 fxg4 6 fxg4 c4 7 h5 gxh5 8 gxh5 c3 9 h6! winning.

5 g4! fxg3 6 ♖g2 ♗d3 7 ♖xg3 ♔e5?

But this is an oversight – why not the natural 7...c4?

8 f4+ ♔e4 9 f5! gxf5 10 h5 f4!

A decisive blow!

11 ♖h3 f3 12 ♔f2! c4 13 h6 ♔d5 14 ♖h5+ ♔d6 15 h7, and it is time for Black to resign. **1-0**

394 Braga – Gunnarsson

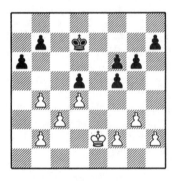

At first sight the endgame looks equal – both sides have doubled pawns on opposite flanks. However White's chances on the queenside are far higher.

1 b3! b5

A debatable move, he should all the same follow the rule and not play where he is weaker. Here is an example: 1...♔c6 2 ♔d3 g5 3 c4 h5 4 ♔c3 ♔d6 5 ♔b2 ♔c6 6 ♔a3, and against the threat ♔a3-a4 and b4-b5 there does not seem to be a good defence.

2 ♔d3 ♔d6 3 c4 g5?

He should keep the pawn on g6, creating for the white king an insurmountable fence.

4 c5+ ♔e6 5 ♔e3! h6 6 ♔f3 ♔e7 7 ♔g2 ♔d7 8 ♔h3 ♔e7 9 f4 ♔e6 10 g4!

His whole position is indefensible.

10...fxg4+ 11 ♔xg4 f5+ 12 ♔h5 gxf4 13 ♔h4!, and the white king captures all the pawns, **1-0**

395 Cilia – Gajadin

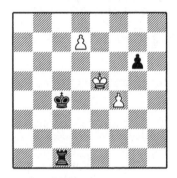

1...♖d1 2 ♔e6 ♔c5?

Though natural, correct is to pass 'behind the rook' by 2...♖d5! or 2...♖d4 3 ♔e7 ♔d3 with an approach to the f4 pawn and a win.

3 ♔e7 ♖e1+ 4 ♔f6 ♖d1, and a draw, **½-½**

396 Amir – Abdulla

And here a chessplayer with a 2400 rating did not know in which corner his king should take refuge in the endgame of bishop against rook.

1...♗e7?

Better to run a little further 1...♗d2 2 ♖a7+ ♔e8, and strive for the a8 square.

2 ♖a7 ♔f8 3 ♔e6 ♗b4?

Correct is not to allow the opponent's king to f6 – by playing 3...♗g5.

4 ♖f7+ ♔g8 5 ♔f6 ♗c3+

Better nevertheless is 5...♗e1 6 ♔g6 ♗h4, though even then the win is just a matter of time.

6 ♔g6, Black resigned, **1-0**

397 **Blehm – Cramling**

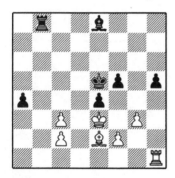

1 f3?

Correct was the transfer to a rook endgame by 1 ♗xh5 ♗xh5 2 ♖xh5 a3 3 ♖h1 a2 4 ♖a1 ♖a8 5 f3! etc.

1...a3 2 fxe4 fxe4 3 ♖a1 ♖a8 4 ♗c4 ♖c8 5 ♗b3 ♖xc3+ 6 ♔f2 ♖f3+ 7 ♔g2 ♗c6 8 ♖xa3 e3! 9 ♖a5+ ♔d6 10 ♖a1 e2, and it's hopeless for White. **0-1**

Rook endgames

Rook endgames are the most common of all types of endgame

(specialists reckon that as the rook is the last to enter play it therefore has a good chance of surviving to the endgame). Besides the knowledge of a sufficiently great number of precise theoretical positions, a chessplayer should possess knowledge of the methods of playing these endgames. The most complexities are experienced by a player during defence – this happens because the defending side usually has several alternatives and the continual choice heightens the tension – and he often cannot stand this.

398 **Gelfand – Mikhalchishin**

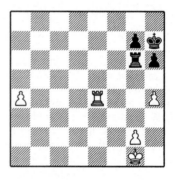

Black's pieces are poorly placed, whereas the white rook on e4 is in a splendid position – defending all its own pawns, therefore Black must transfer his rook to an active position.

1...♖g3! 2 ♔f2 ♖a3 3 g4 ♔g6 4 ♖f4!

Cutting off the black king from the queenside.

4...♖h3! 5 a5 ♖a3!

After 5...♖xh4 6 ♔g2! h5 7 a6 hxg4 the preliminary 8 ♖f8! wins.

6 ♖f5 ♔h7 7 ♖b5 ♖a4 8 ♔f3 ♔g8 9 h5

The second critical position arises from this theoretically important endgame. Black now has three possibilities:

a) passive defence I rejected – White will sacrifice the g4 pawn to control the a-pawn with his king. It is too late for Black's counterplay ...g7-g5;

b) to play 9...g5!?, but it seemed to me that after 10 ♖b6 ♖xa5 11 ♖xh6 ♔f7 12 ♖d6 and a subsequent march of the king and the move ♖d6-d5, the endgame could not be held, but I did not notice that Black keeps the rook on e5 and makes a draw – this also shows poor knowledge of a theoretical position.

c) the game

9...♔f7!? 10 ♖b7+ ♔f6 11 ♖b6+ ♔e5 12 a6 ♖a3+ 13 ♔e2 ♔d4 14 ♖d6+ ♔e4 15 ♔d2 ♔e5 16 ♖g6 ♔d5

17 ♔c2

It is clear that 17 ♖xg7? ♖xa6 leads to a draw, since after 18 ♖g6 ♖a4 the rook endgame is drawn. It occurred to me that Black is in zugzwang – after 17...♖a4 there is 18 g5 hxg5 19 ♖xg5+ ♔c6 20 ♖xg7, and the a6 pawn is indirectly defended. But correct was 17...♔c5! 18 ♖xg7 ♖xa6 19 ♖g6 ♖d6! 20 ♔c3 (on 20 g5 there is 20...♖d5!=) 20...♖d4! – I had not seen this move – the pawn endgame after 21 ♖c6+ is drawn. But in the game it was all very prosaic:

17...♔c4? 18 ♔b2 ♖a5 19 ♖xg7 ♖xa6 20 ♖g6, and it was time to resign. **1-0** Indeed, much still needed to be learnt!

399 Sepp – Hracek

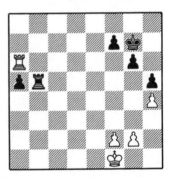

1 g3

Not a bad plan of play was 1 f3, and then 2 ♔f2 and 3 g4, trying to create weaknesses on the kingside.

1...♔f8 2 ♖a7 ♔e8 3 ♔e2

Even better is 3 ♔g2, preparing the above-mentioned plan of f2-f3, g3-g4.

3...♖e5+ 4 ♔f3 ♔d8! 5 ♔g2

It is clear that the pawn endgame is lost without much calculation and White returns to his original plan.

5...♖f5 6 f3 ♔c8 7 g4 ♔b8 8 ♖e7 ♖f6 9 gxh5

9 ♖e5 at once was stronger, then
9...♖a6 (after 9...hxg4 10 fxg4 ♖a6
11 h5 gxh5 12 gxh5 a4 13 ♖e1 ♔c7
14 ♖h1! with an immediate draw)
10 gxh5 gxh5 11 ♖xh5 ♔c7 12 ♖f5!
a4 13 ♖xf7+ ♔c6 14 ♖e7 a3 15 ♖e1
a2 16 ♖a1 ♔d5 17 ♔g3, and in this
typical endgame of rook against
pawn White calmly makes a draw.
   9...gxh5 10 ♖e5 ♖g6+! 11 ♔f1
   After 11 ♔h3 ♖a6 12 ♖xh5 a4 13
♖b5+ ♔c7 14 ♖b2 a3 15 ♖a2 ♔d6
16 ♔g4 ♔e7 17 ♔f5 ♔f8 18 ♔g5
♔g7 19 f4 ♖a5+ 20 ♔g4 ♔g6 21
♔g3 ♔f5 Black eventually wins.
   11...♖a6 12 ♖xh5 ♔c7
   After 12...a4 13 ♖c5 a3 14 ♖c1 a2
15 ♖a1 ♔c7 16 h5 is a draw.

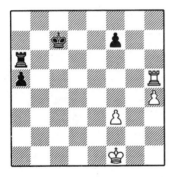

13 ♖d5?
   A decisive mistake, the draw is
held by 13 ♖f5! a4 14 ♖xf7+ ♔c6
15 ♖e7! a3 16 ♖e1 a2 17 ♖a1 ♔d5
18 ♔g2 ♔c4 19 ♔g3 ♔b3 20 ♔g4
♔b2 21 ♖xa2+ ♖xa2 22 h5 ♔c3 23
♔f5 ♖h2 24 ♔g4 etc.
   **13...a4 14 ♖d1 ♔c6 15 ♔e2 a3
16 h5 ♔c5 17 ♔e3 a2 18 ♖a1 ♔c4
19 ♔f4 ♔b3 20 ♔g5 ♖a5+!**
   The only move and sufficient for
victory.
   **21 ♔g4 ♔b2 22 ♖xa2+ ♖xa2 23
h6 ♔c3 24 f4 ♖h2 25 ♔g5 ♔d4**,
White resigned, **0-1**

400 Kunte – Mikhalchishin

1 ♔xe5?
   In such situations it is correct to
take with the rook, 1 ♖xe5+ ♔f7 2
♖h5!, speculating on a transfer to a
pawn endgame and threatening to
break through to the seventh.
   **1...♖h2 2 ♔f5+ ♔f7 3 ♖d1 ♖f2+
4 ♔g5 ♔e6**
   On 4...♖b2 unpleasant was 5 ♖d4.
   5 ♖d4
   On 5 ♔g6 good was 5...♖b2 6
♖d4 ♔e5 7 ♖c4 ♔d5 8 ♖c5+ ♔d6,
and there is no draw for White.

5...♖b2?
   A passive move hoping for 6 ♔g6
♔e5 leading to the previous note.
Correct is 5...c5! 6 bxc5 (6 ♖c4
cxb4 7 ♖xc7 ♖a2 8 ♖xb7 ♖xa5 9
♔h6 ♖a4 10 g5 ♔d5 11 g6 ♔c4 12
g7 ♖a8=) ♖a2 7 ♖b4 ♖xa5 8 ♖xb7
♖xc5 with an easy draw.

6 ♖e4+! ♔d5

Better really was 6...♔f7.

7 ♔f5! b6?

Clearly not 7...♖f2+ 8 ♖f4 with a win, but 7...c5! 8 ♖e5+ ♔c4 9 bxc5 ♖a2 still retains drawing chances.

8 g5 ♖h2 9 g6! ♖h5+

10 ♔f6

White had clearly calculated the rook sacrifice which transposes to a winning pawn endgame.

10...♔xe4 11 g7 ♖f5+ 12 ♔g6 ♖f1 13 g8=♕ ♖g1+ 14 ♔f7 ♖xg8 15 ♔xg8 bxa5 16 bxa5, and the c6 pawn hinders Black from catching the pawn – therefore he resigned, **1-0**

401 **Bauer – Gonzales**

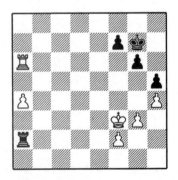

It is dangerous to play such an endgame without a plan – Petrosian's scheme is well-known,

...f7-f6 and ...g6-g5 – to create weaknesses at any price. Waiting is possible but dangerous.

1...♔h7? 2 a5 ♔g7 3 ♖a8 ♖a4?!

Better to go with the king to f5 and play ...f7-f6.

4 a6 ♔f6 5 ♔e3 ♔f5 6 ♖a7 ♔f6?

Why not 6...f7-f6 and ...g6-g5 ?

7 ♔d3 ♖a2 8 ♔c4!

This is a typical pawn sacrifice, offering the possibility of repositioning the rook.

8...♖xf2 9 ♖b7 ♖a2 10 a7 ♔f5 11 ♔b3 ♖a6 12 ♖xf7+ ♔g4 13 ♖f4+ ♔xg3 14 ♖a4 ♖xa7 15 ♖xa7 ♔xh4 16 ♔c3 ♔g3 17 ♔d3 h4 18 ♔e2 h3 19 ♔f1!, and Black resigned, **1-0**

402 **Majoob – Vescovi**

1...♖a1?!

Simpler was 1...e3+ 2 ♔e2 ♔g3 3 ♖c5 f4 4 ♖g5+ ♔h2 5 ♔f3 (5 ♖g4 ♖a2+ and 6...♖f2 leads to the game continuation) 5... ♖a2! 6 ♔xf4 e2 7 ♖e5 ♔xg2, and Black wins.

2 ♖b2?

Better is 2 ♖e2.

2...♔g4 3 ♖c2?

Again 3 ♖e2 is better.

3...♖a8 4 ♖b2 f4 5 ♖b7 ♖a2+ 6 ♔f1 ♖a1+ 7 ♔f2 e3+ 8 ♔e2 ♖a2+ 9 ♔f1 ♖a1+ 10 ♔e2 ♔g3 11 ♖g7+ ♔h2 12 ♖g4 ♖a2+ 13 ♔f1 ♖f2+ 14 ♔e1 ♔g1, and White resigned, **0-1**

403 Cave – Watanabe

Well, how is it possible to win this? The most accurate method of defence is to cut off the opponent's king by 1 ♖a5!, but in the game there came

1 ♖b6 ♖g1+ 2 ♔f3 ♔h5 3 ♖b5+

But here why allow the opponent's king forward, an easy draw was secured by 3 ♖b2 ♖h1+ 4 ♔g3.

3...♔h4 4 ♖b7 ♔h3 5 ♔e4?

This is unjustified activity – good is the simple 5 f5 or 5 ♖f7.

5...g6 6 ♖g7 ♖g3!

The point – the king is cut off!

7 ♖g8 g5! 8 ♖g6

Bad is 8 ♔f5 ♖f3! 9 ♔xf6 ♖xf4+ 10 ♔xg5? ♖g4+, and Black wins.

8...♖g4 9 ♖xf6 ♔g3!

White overlooked this.

10 ♔e3 ♖xf4 11 ♖g6 g4, and 0-1

404 Martinelli – Ovalli

White has a very simple choice, but he contrives to make a mistake.

1 ♔e4?

After 1 ♔xg4 ♖xd3 2 ♔f4 ♔f2 3 ♔e4 the draw is obvious.

1...g3 2 ♔xd4 ♖a8 3 ♖g6?

On principle it is necessary to prepare the advance of the pawn by 3 ♔e5.

3...♖e8 4 ♔c5 ♖e3 5 d4 ♔f2 6 d5 g2 7 d6?

But what is this? – White does not see the check from g1. After 7 ♖xg2+ ♔xg2 8 d6 ♔f3 9 d7 ♖d3 10 ♔c6 it's an elementary draw.

7...♖g3 8 ♖xg3 ♔xg3 9 d7 g1=♕, White resigned, **0-1**

405 Bastidas – Lie

But this is a generally disgraceful example – Black does not know how to make a draw by the frontal attack 1...♖g8! 2 b4 ♖c8+ 3 ♖c5 ♔d7, and ½-½!

There followed:

1...♖g3? 2 b4 ♔e6 3 ♖d1 ♖g5 4 b5 ♔e7 5 ♔b4

Simpler is 5 b6.

5...♔e8 6 ♔a5, Black resigned, **1-0**

406 Lputian – Anageldiev

This position is winning for White, but a very accurate advance of the pawns is necessary.

1 e4?

Obviously stronger is 1 ♔e3!.

1...c3 2 ♔e3 ♖c1 3 ♔f4?!

Stronger is 3 f3!, and there is no move for Black.

3...♔e8 4 ♔f5

After 4 ♖xg7 ♖f1 (on 4...♔d8? winning is 5 ♖a7! c2 6 ♖a2) 5 ♖c7 ♖xf2+ 6 ♔g3 and White has great chances of victory.

4...♖f1!

Black switches his rook to fulfil a double function.

5 f4 ♖f3! 6 e5?

Better really is to capture 6 ♖xg7 ♔d8 7 ♖a7 and then play g4-g5.

6...♔d8 7 ♖c4

By now there is no time to capture the pawn on g7.

7...♔e7 8 e6

Better is 8 g5 hxg5 9 ♔xg5 ♖g3+ 10 ♔f5 ♖h3 11 ♔e4 with chances of a win.

8...♖e3 9 ♖c6 ♖g3 10 ♖c7+?

He should play 10 g5 and try to create yet another passed pawn.

10...♔d8 11 ♖d7+ ♔c8 12 ♖d4 ♖e3 13 ♖c4+?

Preferable was again the plan with g4-g5.

13...♔d8

14 ♔g6?

A kind of bewitching move, White simply does not notice the possibility of 14 g5!.

14...♖xe6+ 15 ♔xg7 ♖e7+!

White overlooked this.

16 ♔xh6 ♖c7! 17 ♖d4+ ♖d7, draw! ½-½

Endings from the world championship in Delhi-Teheran 2000

It should be mentioned at once that the number of mistakes has a tendency to remain at the same level. This could signify that leading chessplayers do not occupy themselves with improving their endgame knowledge.

Rook endgames

A very large number of mistakes were made precisely here.

407 Anand – Khalifman

Three years before, these rivals had also played a rook endgame in which Khalifman had missed 100% of the chances.

1 hxg5 hxg5?

An automatic capture, which seems logical as it does not spoil the pawn structure, but more important was the approach of the king: 1...♔xg5! 2 ♔g2 ♔g4 3 ♖f2 h5 (Also good is 3...♖d8 4 ♖f4+ ♔g5 5 g4 fxg4 6 ♖xe4 h5 7 ♖d4 ♖b8 winning) 4 ♖f4+ ♔g5 5 ♖f2 ♖d8 6 ♔h3 ♖d3 7 ♖e2 ♖d1!, and White has enormous problems.

2 g4!

Anand does everything to prevent the approach ...♔g6-h5-g4.

2...f4 3 ♖d6+ ♔g7 4 ♖d4 ♖xb2+ 5 ♔e1 ♖b3 6 exf4 ♖xa3 7 ♔d2 e3?

Better really was 7...gxf4 8 ♖xe4 f3 9 ♖f4 f2, trying to exploit the passed pawns on a4 and f2.

8 ♔xe3 ♖xc3+ 9 ♔e4 gxf4 10 ♔xf4 ♖c1

No help either is 10...a3 11 ♖d7+ ♔f6 12 ♖a7.

11 ♔e3 a3 12 ♖d7+ ♔f6 13 ♖a7 ♖g1 14 ♔d4! ♖xg4+ 15 ♔c3

Black has two extra pawns, but he cannot realise them.

15...♔e5 16 ♖a5+ ♔d6 17 ♔b4, and a draw was inevitable.

½-½

408 Khalifman – Leitao

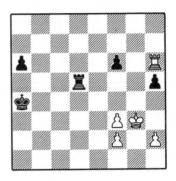

1...♖g5+?

Too complicated – he should sacrifice the pawn by 1...a5!, and try to hurry as quickly as possible.

2 ♔f4 ♖g2 3 ♖xh5 ♖xf2?

Again materialism – after the correct 3...♔b4 4 h4 a5 5 ♖h8 a4 6 h5 ♖h2 7 h6 a3 8 ♔f5 a2 9 ♖a8 ♔b3 10 ♔g6 ♖g2 it is a draw.

4 h4 a5 5 ♖h8 ♔a3 6 h5 ♖h2 7 h6 a4 8 h7 ♖h5 9 ♔g4 ♖h1 10 f4 ♖h2 11 ♔f5 ♖h4 12 ♔e4 ♖h5 13 f5 ♔a2

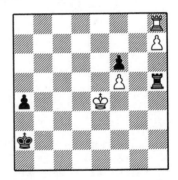

14 ♖a8!

A transfer to a winning classical endgame.

14...♖xh7 15 ♖xa4+ ♔b3 16 ♖a6 ♖e7+ 17 ♖e6 ♖f7 18 ♔d5 ♔c3 19 ♖e8 ♖a7 20 ♔e6 ♖a6+ 21 ♔f7 ♔d4 22 ♖e6, and 1-0

409 Macieja – Krasenkov

1 ♔c6?

Correct was 1 ♔b6! and 2 ♔b5 followed by 3 b3-b4.

1...♖c1+

2 ♔b7?

Again the wrong direction – after 2 ♔b6 ♖c8 3 ♖h3! ♖b8+ 4 ♔c7 ♖b4 5 ♖e3+ ♔f5 6 ♔d6 ♔f4 (or 6...♖b5 7 ♖h3 ♔g6 8 ♔c6 ♖b8 9 ♖d3! ♔f6 10 ♖d6+ ♔e5 11 ♖d5+ ♔e6 12 ♖b5!, with a theoretically winning position) 7 ♖h3 ♔g4 8 ♔c5 ♖b8 9 ♖d3 ♖c8+ 10 ♔b6 ♖b8+ 11 ♔c7 ♖b4 12 ♖c3 ♔f5 13 ♔c6 ♔e5 14 ♔c5 ♖b8 15 ♖e3+ ♔f4 16 ♖h3 ♔g4 17 ♖c3 ♖c8+ 18 ♔b4 ♖b8+ 19

♔a5 ♔f5 20 b4 ♖a8+ 21 ♔b6 ♖b8+ 22 ♔c5 ♖c8 23 ♔d4 ♖b8 24 ♖c5 ♔e6 25 b5 ♖d8+ 26 ♔c4, and wins according to Grigoriev.

2...♖b1?

There is a draw by 2...♔e5 3 ♔b6 (3 b4 ♖b1!) ♖c8 4 ♖h3 ♖b8+ 5 ♔c7 ♖b4 6 ♔c6 ♔d4, and the white king is cut off from its pawns.

3 ♔b6! Black resigned, **1-0**

410 Shirov – Anand

Black has problems here. The natural 1...♖hc8, after 2 ♖cxb7 ♖xb7 3 ♖xb7 gxf4 4 gxf4 ♘d4 5 ♔f2 and then 6 ♔e3, leads to a difficult position. It is necessary to create weaknesses for White.

1...h5!! 2 ♖bxb7

After 2 h4 gxf4 3 gxf4 the assessment is rather less favourable for White in view of the weakness on h4, but nevertheless this was the best decision.

2...♖xb7 3 ♖xb7 h4 4 ♔g2 hxg3 5 hxg3 gxf4

One more exchange than he should; after 5...♘d4 6 b4 ♖c8! 7 bxa5 ♖c3 8 ♗b5 ♘xb5 9 ♖xb5 ♔g6! White's pawns are very weak, and Black has the advantage.

6 gxf4 ♖h4 7 ♔g3 ♖h1 8 ♔g2

After 8 ♗b5? ♘d4! 9 ♗e8 ♔f8 10 ♗xf7 ♖h7 White stands badly.

8...♖h4, draw, ½-½

411 Macieja – Beliavsky

White stands worse but it is not clear how Black would win after 1 ♘e2 ♘d5+ 2 ♔d2, but Macieja went for a bluff.

1 ♘a4+? ♔b4 2 ♔d4 f4?

Winning simply, but more elegant was 2...♘c6+ 3 ♔d5 ♘e5!! 4 ♘b2 c3.

3 ♘b2!

Black counted on 3 gxf4 ♘f5+ 4 ♔d5 ♘e3+ 5 ♔d4 ♔xa4 6 ♔xe3 ♔b3 with a win.

3...♘f5+ 4 ♔e4 ♘xg3+ 5 ♔xf4 c3 6 ♘d3+ ♔c4 7 ♘c1 ♘f1 8 g4, draw, ½-½

A fantastic find in an elementary endgame

412 Krasenkov – Macieja

1...c4?

Winning simply is 1...b4! 2 h6 ♔f7 3 ♔h8 c4 4 h7 ♔f8! 5 bxc4 b3.

2 bxc4 bxc4

No help is 2...b4 3 ♔g8! ♔g5 4 c5 b3 5 c6, with a draw.

3 h6 ♔f7 4 ♔h8 c3 5 h7 c2, and stalemate.

413 Krasenkov – Macieja

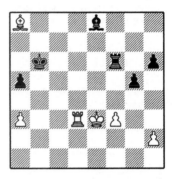

A draw is not bad for White, and with the simple 1 ♗e4 he would easily make a draw, but White 'bungles things' by an exchange of rooks.

1 ♔d4? ♖d6+ 2 ♔c3 ♖xd3+ 3 ♔xd3 ♔c5

And it turns out that the transfer of the bishop to g2 is threatened, followed by ...g5-g4. However White's position, in principle, does not look lost.

4 ♗e4 ♗d7 5 ♔c3 ♗h3 6 ♗d3 ♗d7 7 ♗c2 ♗c6 8 ♗d1 ♗b5 9 ♗c2 ♔d5!

At last revealing the threat to transfer the king.

10 ♗d3 ♗d7! 11 ♗e4+ ♔e5 12 ♗b7 ♗b5! 13 ♗a8 h5!

Time to improve the pawn structure.

14 ♗b7 h4 15 ♗a8 ♗f1!

Creating the threat of ♗g2.

16 ♔d2 ♔d4 17 ♔e1 ♗b5 18 ♔d2 ♔c4! 19 ♔e3

On 19 ♔c2 follows 19...♗a4+!, and White is forced to allow the opponent's king to get to his own pawns.

19...♔b3 20 f4 gxf4+ 21 ♔xf4 ♔xa3 22 ♔g4 a4 23 ♔xh4 ♔b2 24 ♗d5 a3, and there is no defence against the threat of ...♗b5-a4-b3, White resigned, **0-1**

Endgames from the European championship in Leon 2001

The tendency of all these is: the impossibility of holding a slightly inferior position and very poor technique in realising a decisive advantage.

414 Van den Doel – Kovacević

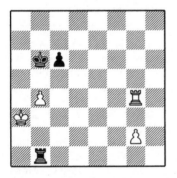

Here Black is a pawn down, but he does not risk losing after 1...♖g1 since White must transfer the king to the kingside, after which Black will attack the b4 pawn. However Kovacević decides on a tactical reduction of material and this is what comes out of it.

1...c5? 2 ♖c4!
Now the pawn endgame is hopeless for Black.

2... ♖a1+ 3 ♔b2 ♖b5 4 ♖c2! ♖a6 5 bxc5 ♖c6 6 ♔b3!, and again the pawn endgame is lost, and Black has to resign, **1-0**

415 Gaponenko – Johansson

Black has a choice – a draw is made by both 1...♔f8 and 1...♔f6 2 g5+ ♔e6 3 ♖g7 ♖a4+ 4 ♔g3 ♖a3+ 5 ♔g2 ♔f5. But he played

1...♔g8? 2 ♖e7 ♖b5 3 ♖e5 ♖b6?
Correct is 3...♖b7!, defending the seventh rank, 4 ♔g5 ♔g7, and the white rook cannot leave the fifth rank because of the check of the rook.

4 ♔g5 ♔f7 5 ♖a5 ♖e6?
Again he should strive for activity by 5...♖b4, though after 6 ♖a7+ ♔f8 7 ♖a6 the problems are enormous.

6 ♖a7+ ♔f8 7 ♔h6 ♖e4 8 g5!, and Black resigned, **1-0**

416 Agrest – Dervishi

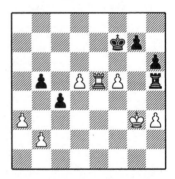

Black brilliantly defends this difficult endgame by the move

1...Rg5+! 2 Kh2

On 2 Kf3 there is 2...Kf6, and 3 d6 does not work because of the fact that the black rook manages to hold up the white pawns, while 2 Kf4 Rg2 gives Black sufficient counterplay.

2...g6!

This is a principal move.

3 h4 Rxf5 4 Rxf5+ gxf5 5 Kg3 Ke7 6 Kf4 Kd6 7 Kxf5 Kxd5 8 Kg6 Kc5 9 Kxh6 b4 10 axb4+ Kxb4 11 h5 Kb3 12 Kg5 Kxb2 13 h6 c3 14 h7 c2, with a draw in a theoretical endgame. ½-½

417 Seitaj – Heidenfeld

But how is it possible to lose this, since 1...Qd2+ gives an immediate draw. It turns out that it is very simple...

1...g4? 2 hxg4 hxg4 3 a6 Qa1?

And this is where – better really is 3...Qd2+, though after 4 Qf2 problems arise for Black. Nevertheless 4...Qd5 looks sufficient.

4 Qd7+ Kh6 5 a7, and the white king draws close to the a7 pawn with a win, **1-0**

And here a young and talented Yugoslav player contrives to lose...

418 Vucković – Upton

White is playing for a win, and normal would be the transfer of the knight to f3 via e1, but

1 Ne5?? Bxd4+ 2 Kxd4 c5+, and he had to resign, **0-1**

419 Mamedyurov – Kolev

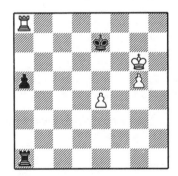

White conducted the endgame technically.

1 Kg7 a4 2 g6 a3 3 Kg8 a2 4 g7 Ke6 5 Ra5!

With this manoeuvre White prepares the transfer of the rook to the second rank.

5...♔d6 6 ♖d5+ ♔e7 7 ♖d2 ♖h1 8 ♖xa2 ♖h4 9 ♖a7+ ♔e8 10 ♖a5! ♔e7 11 ♖e5+ ♔d6 12 ♔f7, and Black resigned, **1-0**

420 Milov – Bacrot

White defends this endgame very beautifully.

1...h4+

Sooner or later he will have to play this.

2 ♔h2 ♘e6

The attempt 2...♘d3 is stopped by 3 ♗a5 ♔f4 4 ♗d2 ♔xf3 5 ♗xg5 e4 6 ♗xh4 e3 7 ♗f6 e2 8 ♗c3, with a draw.

3 ♗b6 ♔f4 4 ♔g2 ♘d4 5 ♔f2 ♘xf3 6 ♗e3+ ♔e4

7 ♗c1

By sacrificing a pawn, White places his opponent in zugzwang.

7...♘d4 8 ♗xg5 ♘f5 9 ♔e2 ♔d4 10 ♔f3 e4+ 11 ♔g4 ♔e5 12 ♗f4+ ♔e6 13 ♗c1, and he had to agree a draw ½-½

421 Zeidlek – Wagener

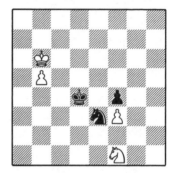

How can White not win this endgame?

1 ♔a7! ♘xf1

After 1...♘c4 2 b6 ♘xb6 3 ♔xb6 ♔d3 4 ♔c5 ♔e2 5 ♘h2 ♔f2 6 ♔d4 ♔g2 7 ♔e4 the white king is just in time.

2 b6 ♔e3 3 b7 ♔xf3 4 b8=♕ ♘e3

5 ♔b6?

In the first place he should 'latch on' to the passed pawn by 5 ♔a6, now the threat to take is illusory.

5...♔g2 6 ♕e8 ♘g4

Also possible was 6...f3.

7 ♕e6 ♔g3 8 ♔c5?

Correct was to slow down the pawn by 8 ♕d6!.

8...f3 9 ♕d6+ ♔g2 10 ♕f4 ♘h2 11 ♔d4 f2, and a draw! Fancy that...

422 Pavasović – McShane

The young English player finds a brilliant defensive manoeuvre in a difficult situation.

1...♘b8!! 2 f7

After 2 ♘xd4 ♘d7 the f6 pawn cannot be defended.

2...♘d7 3 b4 ♔e6 4 ♘g5+ ♔d5!

Clearly not 4...♔f6 5 ♔xd4 ♔xg5 6 ♔d5 ♔f6 7 ♔d6, and White wins.

5 ♔c2 ♘f8 6 ♔d3 ♘g6 7 ♘f3 ♘f4+ 8 ♔c2 ♘g6 9 ♘h4 ♘f8 10 ♔d3 ♔e6 11 ♔xd4 ♔xf7 12 ♔d5

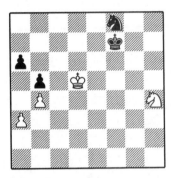

It seems that that White has real chances of victory, but Black hurries with his knight to c4.

12...♘d7 13 ♘f5 ♘b6 14 ♔c5 ♘a4+

Now 14...♘c4 is bad because of 15 a4.

15 ♔c6 ♘b2! 16 ♘d4 ♘c4 17 ♘c2 ♔e7 18 ♔b7 a5 19 ♘d4 axb4 20 axb4 ♘b2!, and as there is no possibility of winning after 21... ♘d3 – draw ½-½

Exercises

(21) **Fedorov – Dreev**
Samara 1998

Which is correct: 1 ♖d6+ or 1 ♖b5?

(22) **Tarrasch – Blümich**
Breslau 1925

How does White make a draw?

(23) **Minev** 1972

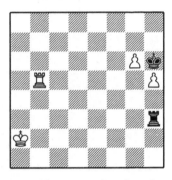

Minev: White wins; Smyslov: draw.
Which assessment is correct?

(24) **Yermolinsky – Miton**
USA 2000

Which is correct 1 ♔f2 or 1 ♔e2?

(25) **NN**

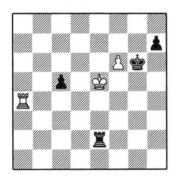

Which is correct 1 ♔d5 or 1 ♔d6?

(26) **Ruzele – Hübner**
Elista 1998

How can White defend?

(27) **Relange – Kouatly**
Meribel 1999

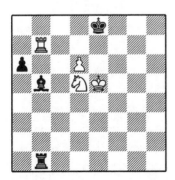

How does Black hold his position?

(28) **Fila** 1932

White wins

(29) **Tukmakov – Kakhiani**
Craus Montana 2000

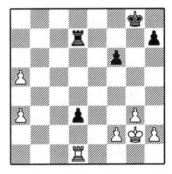

Which is correct 1...d2 or 1...♔g7?

(30) **Veselovsky – Firt**
Cesko 2000

What is the correct way?

(31) **Domingez – Pogorelov**
Ubeda 2001

What is White's most precise way?

(32) **Salov – Serper**
Irkutsk 1986

How does Black draw here?

(33) **Abken – Nogeiras**
Cuba 2001

Which is correct 1 ♔b7 or 1 ♔b5?

(34) **Reshevsky – Monticelli**
Syracuse 1934

Which is correct 1 ♖b4 or 1 ♖f6?

(35) **Albin – Von Bardeleben**
Germany 1892

Point out the right move for White

(36) **Naumkin – Shirov**
London 1989

How should White continue?

Solutions to Exercises

(1) Fries-Nielsen – Plachetka
Slovakia 1991

a) 1 ♔c6? (game) h5 2 ♔d5 h4 3 ♔e4 h3 4 ♔e3 ♔g3 5 ♖e1 h2, draw;
b) 1 ♖g2+! ♔f4 2 ♖h2! ♔g5 3 ♔c6 h5 4 ♔d5 h4 5 ♔e4 ♔g4 6 ♖g2+ winning.

(2) Kishnev – Nikolac
Germany 1991

a) 1...a1=♕? (game) 2 ♗xa1 ♖xa1 3 h7 ♖f1+ 4 ♔g4!, 1-0;
b) 1...♖f1+! 2 ♔g6 (2 ♔g4 ♖h1!) a1=♕ 3 ♗xa1 ♖xa1 4 h7 ♖h1 5 ♔g7 ♔e6 6 g6 ♔f5 7 ♔f7 ♖h6=;
c) 1...♔d6=.

(3) Skembris – Iotti
Italy 2000

a) 1 ♔d7? ♖e4!! 2 c5 ♖e7+ 3 ♔d6 ♖xc7 4 cxb6 ♖e7 5 ♔c6 ♔f6 6 b7 ♖e8 7 ♔c7 ♔f5 (game), 1-0;
b) 1 f5!! h5 2 h4 ♖g8 3 ♔d7 ♖g4 4 c5!!, and White wins.

(4) Dias – Dominguez
Cuba 1981

The correct way for White:
a) 1 ♔d6? f5 2 ♖e2+ ♔d4, draw, ½-½ (game);
b) 1 ♖e2+! ♔d5 (1...♔f3 2 ♖e1! f5 3 ♔d6 f4 4 ♔e5 ♔f2 5 ♖a1 f3 6 ♔d4 winning) 2 ♖f2! ♔e5 3 ♔d7 f5 4 ♔e7 f4 5 ♖f1! – Reti's manoeuvre – and White wins.

(5) Leal – Filguth
Mexico 1978

a) 1...♔xc4? 2 h6 ♔d5 3 ♔f5 ♖f1+ 4 ♔g6 ♔e6 5 ♔g7!, draw, ½-½ (game);
b) 1...♖h1 2 ♔g5 ♔d4 3 h6 ♔e5 4 ♔g6 ♔e6 5 h7 ♖g1+ 6 ♔h6 ♔f7 7 h8=♞+ ♔f6 winning.

(6) Dückstein – Keller
Germany 1963

a) 1 ♔b6? ♖f8 2 ♔a6 ♔b4 3 b6 ♔c5 4 ♔a7 ♔c6 5 b7 ♔c7, 0-1 (game);
b) 1 b6! ♔a5 2 b7 ♔a6 3 b8=♕! ♖xb8 4 ♔d6=.

(7) Lovegrove – Lasker
USA 1902

1...d4? 2 ♔xd6 d3 3 ♔e5 d2 4 ♖g8+ ♔h4 5 ♔f4 ♔h3 6 ♖d8 c3 7 ♔e3, 1-0

(8) Lein – Benko
Novi Sad 1972

a) 1...♔e2? 2 d4 exd4+ 3 ♔xd4, draw;
b) 1...♖d8! 2 b7 ♔e2 winning.

(9) Marshall – Duras
San Sebastian 1911

a) 1 ♔d2? h3 2 ♔e2 h2 3 ♖g5+ ♔h1!, draw;
b) 1 ♖g5+ ♔f3 2 ♖h5 ♔g3 3 ♔d2 h3 4 ♔e2 ♔g2 5 ♖g5+ winning.

(10) Adams – Kramnik
Moscow 1994

a) 1 bxa5?? bxa5 2 ♔xd5 ♔f4 3 ♖a3 g3, and he has to concede a draw (game);
b) 1 ♔xd5 ♔f4 2 ♖e1! axb4 (after 2....♔f3 3 b5 g3 4 ♔c6 ♔f2 5 ♖a1 g2 6 ♔xb6 a4 7 ♔a5! the win is quite simple) 3 ♔d4! ♔f3 (there is also a straightforward win after 3...g3 4 ♖f1+ ♔g4 5 ♔e3) 4 ♔d3! g3 (or 4...♔f2 5 ♖e2+! ♔f3 6 ♖e6 g3 7 ♖f6+ ♔g2 8 ♔e2, and everything is clear) 5 ♖f1+ ♔g2 6 ♔e2 ♔h2 7 ♖b1 g2 8 ♔f2, and Black has to give up all his pawns.

(11) Euwe – Pirc
Bled 1949

a) 1...a5? 2 g3 h5+ 3 ♔h4 ♔h6 4 g4 hxg4 5 ♔xg4 ♔g6 6 ♔f4 ♔f6 7 b3, (game), 1-0;
b) 1...a6! 2 b4 b5! 3 a5 ♔f6 4 ♔h5 ♔f5 5 ♔xh6 ♔f4 6 g3+! ♔f3 7 ♔h5 ♔e4 8 g4 ♔xd4 9 g5 ♔c3 10 g6 d4 11 g7 d3 12 g8=♕ d2=.

(12) Hamdouchi – Ibragimov
Germany 2000

a) 1...♔e4?? 2 ♔g4 f5+ (If 2...♔d5, then 3 f5 winning) 3 ♔g5 ♔e3 4 ♔xg6 ♔xf4 5 h5, (game),1-0
b) 1...♔e6=.

(13) Stangl – Schmittdiel
Germany 2000

a) 1 ♔d2? f3! (game), ½-½;
b) 1 f3! a4 2 ♔d1 a3 3 ♔c2 g5 4 hxg5 h4 5 g6 a2 6 ♔b2 a1=♕+ 7 ♔xa1 h3 8 g7 h2 9 g8=♕ h1=♕+ 10 ♔b2 ♕xf3 11 ♕f7+ winning.

(14) Vavra – Ftacnik
Czech Republic 1995

a) 1 ♔g7? g5 2 ♔xh7 ♔xa2 3 ♔h6 a5 4 ♔xg5 a4, and Black wins;
b) 1 h4! ♔xa2 2 g4 a5 3 h5 a4 4 ♔g7! gxh5 5 gxh5 a3 6 ♔xh7, (game), ½-½

(15) Janvarev – Scherbakov
Moscow 1995

a) 1...hxg4? 2 f4! ♔c3 3 h5 (game), 1-0;
b) 1...fxg4 2 fxg4 hxg4 3 h5 ♔e5 4 h6 ♔f6 5 ♔g3=

(16) Morozevich – Vyzhmanavin
New York 1995

a) 1 h4? b5 2 ♔d3 ♔d5 3 ♔e3 h6 4 ♔f4 ♔e6 5 g3 ♔f6 6 ♔e3 ♔e5 7 ♔d3 ♔d5 8 a4 bxa4 9 c4+ ♔c6 10 ♔d4 g5, (game), and Black wins;
b) 1 c4=.

(17) Kuif – Van der Wiel
Hilversum 1989

a) 1 ♔d4?? b5, (game), 0-1;
b) 1 ♔d2 ♔e5 2 h4=.

(18) Kamsky – Tukmakov

a) 1...e4? 2 f3! f5 3 g3! fxg3 4 hxg3 ♔e6 5 ♔e3 ♔e5? (better is 5...exf3+ 6 ♔xf3 ♔e5 with a draw) 6 fxe4 fxe4? (the last chance was 6...h5!! with a draw) 7 g4! ♔f6 8 ♔xe4 ♔g5 9 ♔f3 ♔g6 10 ♔f4 with a win (game);

b) 1...♔e6 2 ♔d3 ♔f5 3 f3 h5 with the idea of **h4, ♔e6, f5, e4, ♔d6-c6-b6, a5**, and Black wins.

(19) Poldauf – Prohl
Germany 2000

a) 1 ♔e3? ♔c5 2 f4 ♔b4 3 ♔d2 ♔b3! 4 ♔c1 ♔xa4 5 g4 ♔xb5 6 f5 gxf5 7 g5 f4 8 g6 f3 9 ♔d2 f2, (game), 0-1;

b) 1 ♔d2! ♔e4 2 ♔c3 ♔f3 3 ♔xc4 ♔xf2 4 ♔d5 g5 5 ♔c6 g4 6 ♔b7 ♔xg3 7 ♔xa7 ♔h4 8 ♔xb6! g3 9 ♔a6 g2 10 b6 g1=♕ 11 b7 ♕g3 12 a5 ♕c7 13 b8=♕!! – and a stalemate!

(20) Landa – Kozlov
Budapest 1991

a) 1...a5? 2 a4 ♔c5 3 ♔d3 ♔d5 4 ♔d2 ♔c4 5 ♔c2 ♔b4 6 ♔d3 ♔xa4 7 ♔c4!! d3 8 ♔c3! (game), draw;

b) 1...a6! 2 a3 d3! 3 ♔e3 ♔b3, and Black wins.

(21) Fedorov – Dreev
Samara 1998

a) 1 ♖d6+? ♔e3 2 ♔a3 e4 3 b4 ♖c3+ 4 ♔b2 axb4 5 a5 ♖a3 6 a6 ♔e2 7 ♖d4 e3 8 ♖d6 ♔e1 9 ♖f6 e2 10 ♖e6 ♔d2 11 ♖d6+ ♖d3, and White resigned, 0-1,(game) in view of the variation 12 ♖xd3+ ♔xd3 13

a7 e1=♕+ 14 a8=♕ ♕c3+ 15 ♔b1 ♕c2+ 16 ♔a1 ♕c1+ 17 ♔a2 b3+ 18 ♔xb3 ♕b1+;

b) 1 ♖b5! ♔d4 2 ♖xc5 ♔xc5 3 ♔c3

b1) 3...♔d5

b1a) 4 ♔d3 e4+ 5 ♔e3 ♔e5

b1a1) 6 b3 ♔d5 7 ♔e2 ♔d4 (7...♔c5 8 ♔e3 ♔b4 9 ♔xe4 ♔xb3 10 ♔d3 ♔xa4 11 ♔c2=) 8 ♔d2 e3+ 9 ♔e2 ♔e4 10 b4=;

b1a2) 6 b4? axb4 7 a5 b3 8 a6 b2 9 a7 b1=♕ 10 a8=♕ ♕e1 mate;

b1b) 4 b4 axb4 5 ♔xb4 ♔d4 6 a5 e4 7 a6 e3 8 a7 e2 9 a8=♕ e1=♕+ 10 ♔b5 ♕b1 11 ♔a6=;

b2) 3...e4 4 b3 ♔d5

b2a) 5 b4 axb4+ 6 ♔xb4 ♔d4 7 a5 (7 ♔b3 ♔d3 8 a5 e3 9 a6 e2 10 a7 e1=♕ 11 a8=♕ ♕b1+ and wins) 7...e3 8 a6 e2 9 a7 e1=♕+ wins;

b2b) 5 ♔c2 ♔d4 6 ♔d2 e3+ 7 ♔e2 ♔e4 8 b4 axb4 9 a5=.

(22) Tarrasch – Blümich
Breslau 1925

1 h6 ♖b6 2 ♖h5 a2 3 h7 ♖b8 4 ♖b5! ♖xb5 5 h8=♕+ =

(23) Minev 1972

1 ♖g5! ♔g7 2 ♔b2—zugzwang, 1-0

(24) Yermolinsky – Miton
USA 2000

a) 1 ♔f2? ♖a3 2 ♖h6 ♔g5 3 ♖b6 ♔f5 4 ♖d6 ♔g5 5 ♖c6? (5 ♔e2!) 5...♔f5 6 ♖b6 ♔g4! 7 ♔e2 ♔xg3, ½-½;

b) 1 ♔e2! ♖a3 2 ♔d2 ♔e5 3 ♖g6 ♔f5 4 ♖h6 ♖xg3 5 ♖h8! ♖a3 6 ♖a8 ♔g6 7 ♔c2 ♔g7 8 ♔b2 wins.

(25) NN

a) 1 ♔d5? ♖f2!! 2 ♔xc5 ♖f5+ 3 ♔d6 ♔xf6 4 ♖h4 h5 wins;
b) 1 ♔d6 ♔xf6 (1...♖f2 2 ♖g4+! ♔xf6 3 ♖h4 ♔g6 4 ♔xc5=) 2 ♔xc5 ♔g5 3 ♔d4, and a draw.

(26) Ruzele – Hübner
Elista 1998

a) After 1 ♖c4? not 1...♔b5? 2 a4+! ♘xa4 3 ♖g4= or 1...♘b5? 2 a4 ♘c3 3 ♖g4, ½-½ (game); but 1...a4! 2 ♖xb4+ (2 ♖xc3 bxc3 3 ♗xa4 ♖f1+; 2 ♗xa4 ♖xa2 mate) 2...♔a5 3 ♖c4 a3!! winning;
b) 1 ♗e6 b3 (1...a4 2 ♖xb4+ ♔a5 3 ♖h4 a3 4 ♖h1 ♖xg2=) 2 ♗xb3 a4 3 ♖xa4 ♘xa4 4 ♗xa4 ♖xg2=;
c) 1 ♗g8 ♔b5 2 ♖g5+ ♔a4?? 3 ♗b3+ ♔a3 4 ♖xa5 mate.

(27) Relange – Kouatly
Meribel 1999

a) 1...♔d8?? 2 ♖b8+ ♔d7 3 ♘f6+ ♔c6 4 d7 ♖e1+ 5 ♔f4 ♖f1+ 6 ♔e3, (game) 1-0;
b) 1...♖e1+ 2 ♔d4 ♖d1+ 3 ♔c5 ♖c1+ =.

(28) Fila 1932

1 ♖a1! ♖e8 2 ♔d6 ♖b8 3 ♖f1+ ♔g7 4 ♔c7 ♖a8 5 ♖a1!, 1-0

(29) Tukmakov – Kakhiani
Craus Montana 2000

a) 1...♔g7? 2 ♔f3 ♔g6 3 ♔e3 ♖a7 4 ♖xd3 ♖xa5 5 ♔d4 wins.

b) 1...d2! 2 a6 ♖d3 3 a4 ♖d4 4 a5 ♖d5 5 ♖a1 d1=♕ 6 a7 ♕d4! 7 a8=♕+ ♖d8 8 ♖a4 ♖xa8=;

(30) Veselovsky – Firt
Cesko 2000

a) 1...b4? 2 ♔b3! bxc3 3 ♔xc3=;
b) 1...♔c4 2 ♔c2 f5! 3 ♔d2 ♔b3 4 ♔d3 ♔a3! 5 ♔e2 ♔a2! 6 ♔d3 ♔b3 7 ♔d2 ♔b2 8 ♔d3 ♔c1 wins.

(31) Dominguez – Pogorelov
Ubeda 2001

In the game followed:
a) 1 ♔c2? ♔e5 2 f3 (2 ♔b2 ♔d5=) 2...♔f4? (2...♔d5! 3 g4 ♔e5!! 4 ♔b2 ♔f4 5 ♔a3 ♔xf3 6 ♔xa4 ♔xg4 7 c4 f5=) 3 ♔b2 ♔e3 4 ♔a3 ♔d3 5 ♔xa4 ♔c4 (5...♔xc3 6 ♔b5) 6 ♔a5 ♔xc3 7 ♔b5 ♔d4 8 ♔c6 ♔e3 9 ♔d6 ♔f2 10 f4 ♔g3 11 f5 ♔f4 12 f6, and the white pawn queens with check, and it's a theoretical draw, 1-0
But correct was:
b) 1 ♔d3! ♔e5 2 ♔c4 ♔e4 3 f3+!! ♔e3 4 ♔b4 ♔d3 5 ♔xa4 ♔xc3 6 ♔b5, and the same winning method as in the game.

(32) Salov – Serper
Irkutsk 1986

a) 1...♖c3? 2 ♖xb5 ♖xg3 3 ♖c5! ♖g6+ 4 ♔d7 ♖g7 5 b5 h5 6 b6 ♔g6+ 7 ♔c6 h4 8 b7 ♖g8 9 ♔c7 wins;
b) 1...♖c4! 2 ♖xb5 ♖g4 3 ♖b7+ ♔g6 4 ♖b8 ♔h5!!=.

(33) **Abken – Nogueiras**
Cuba 2001

a) 1 ♔b5? ♔h6? (1...♔g7=) 2
♔c5? (2 ♔b6! wins) 2...♔g6
(2...♔h7! or 2...♔g7!=) 3 ♔c6! ♔g7
4 ♔c7! ♔g8 5 ♔d6! ♔h7 6 ♔d7
♔h6 7 ♔e8, 1-0;
b) 1 ♔b7! ♔g8 2 ♔c8 ♔g7 3
♔c7! ♔g8 4 ♔d6! ♔f7 5 ♔d7 ♔g7
6 ♔e7 ♔g6 7 ♔e6 winning.

(34) **Reshevsky – Monticelli**
Syracuse 1934

a) 1 ♖b4? ♖xb4 2 axb4 ♔c6 3
♔c3 ♔b5 4 ♔d4 ♔xb4 5 ♔xe4
♔b3=;

b) 1 ♖f6! ♔d7 2 ♖f4! ♖c4+ 3
♔d2 ♔d6 4 f3 winning.

(35) **Albin-Bardeleben**
Germany 1892

a) 1 ♔h8!!=;
b) 1 ♔g8? ♔f6 2 f8=♕+ ♔g6, 0-1
(game).

(36) **Naumkin – Shirov**
London 1989

a) 1 ♔xb4?? ♖d1 2 ♔c5 h1=♕ 3
♖xh1 ♖xh1 4 b4 ♖c1+! 5 ♔d5 ♖b1
6 ♔c5 ♔g4 7 b5 ♔f5 8 b6 ♔e6 9
♔c6 ♖c1+ 10 ♔b7 ♔d7 0-1 (game);
b) 1 ♖g8+! ♔f2 2 ♖h8 ♔g1 3
♖g8+=.

Index of Players and Composers

(numbers refer to positions)